wair
13-93

KT-408-417

Deve loping Reflectiv

<71.102 LOU

For all of the time, help, support and encouragement, thank you to Dick Gunstone and especially to Airlie.

Developing Reflective Practice:
Learning about Teaching and Learning through Modelling

J. John Loughran

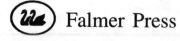 Falmer Press

(A member of the Taylor & Francis Group)
London • Washington, D.C.

UK   The Falmer Press, 1 Gunpowder Square, London, EC4A 3DE
USA   The Falmer Press, Taylor & Francis Inc., 1900 Frost Road, Suite 101,
      Bristol, PA 19007

First published in 1996

**A catalogue record for this book is available from the British
Library**

**Library of Congress Cataloging-in-Publication Data are available on
request**

ISBN 0 7507 0515 9 cased
ISBN 0 7507 0516 7 paper

Jacket design by Caroline Archer

Typeset in 10/12pt Times by
Graphicraft Typesetters Ltd., Hong Kong.

*Printed in Great Britain by Biddles Ltd., Guildford and King's Lynn on
paper which has a specified pH value on final paper manufacture of not
less than 7.5 and is therefore 'acid free'.*

Contents

List of Tables vii

List of Figures viii

PART 1: Conceptualizing Reflection 1

1 An Introduction to Thinking about Teaching 3
2 A Model for Learning about Reflection 13

PART 2: Learning through Modelling 23

3 Modelling Reflection 25
4 Perceptions of Actions: Student–teachers' Understanding of the Practice of Modelling Reflection 40

PART 3: Exploring Student–teachers' Thinking 55

5 Recognizing Reflection 57
6 Journals: An Insight into Students' Thinking 74
7 Understanding the Reflective Cycle 89

PART 4: Reflection 'in Practice' 105

8 Three Reflective Instances 107
9 Case-studies 120
10 Understanding Reflective Practice 152
11 Conclusion 189

Bibliography 194

Author Index 198

Subject Index 199

List of Tables

Table 3.1: Questionnaire results   38

Table 3.2: Themes from the open-ended responses on the questionnaire   38

Table 6.1: Number of coded journal entries per student for each   83

Table 6.2: Major topic groupings derived from all issues raised in attitude students' writings   85

Table 6.3: Number of student journal entries (from attitude coded segments) per issue   86

Table 6.4: Time frames for data analysis   86

Table 7.1: Number of coded journal entries per student per phase of the reflective cycle   90

Table 7.2: Number of journal entries (initiating reflection) per issue/concern   96

Table 7.3: Number of coded interview and journal segments of transcript for each phase of the reflective cycle per interview   98

Table 10.1: Number of coded segments for each of the reflective phases for anticipatory reflection from the interview-observation-interview cycle from the video-taped lessons   153

Table 10.2: Number of coded segments for each of the reflective phases for retrospective reflection from the post-teaching interviews   163

Table 10.3: Number of coded segments for each of the reflective phases for contemporaneous reflection from the interview-observation-interview cycle from the video-taped lessons   178

List of Figures

Figure 2.1: Conceptual framework 22

Figure 6.1: Concerns (determined by journal entries related to attitude) over time 87

Figure 7.1: Levels of use of the reflective phases 92

Figure 7.2: Reflective phases by group (interviewed/not interviewed) 92

Figure 7.3: Reflective phases over time using the three time-frames described in Table 6.4 95

Figure 7.4: Concerns/issues which initiated reflection (determined by the number of journal entries) over time 97

Part 1

Conceptualizing Reflection

Chapter 1

An Introduction to Thinking about Teaching

Teaching and learning about teaching are demanding tasks because they centre on complex, interrelated sets of thoughts and actions, all of which may be approached in a number of ways. This is true from the perspectives of both student–teachers and teacher educators. Therefore, in teaching, there is not necessarily one way of doing something. The more proficient one becomes in the skills of teaching, the more an understanding of the relationship between teaching and learning may influence practice, and the more deliberately a teacher considers his or her actions the more difficult it is to be sure that there is one right approach to teaching, or teaching about teaching.

Because of the complexities of teaching and learning about teaching, various approaches to pre-service teacher education have evolved over the years. However, one aspect of teacher education that continually receives attention in both curriculum and research is the way teachers think about their practice. Since at least the time of Dewey, such thinking about practice has been termed reflection and in teacher education courses there has been a focus on developing reflective practitioners. Programs designed to 'make' reflective practitioners have been vigorously pursued in pre-service and in-service education. One reason for this is the perceived common-sense link between reflection and learning, hence the value of its use in teaching and teacher education.

> Reflection is an important human activity in which people recapture their experience, think about it, mull it over and evaluate it. It is this working with experience that is important in learning. The capacity to reflect is developed to different stages in different people and it may be this ability which characterizes those who learn effectively from experience. (Boud, Keogh and Walker, 1985, p. 19)

But how might reflection be conceptualized and how might a teacher become a reflective practitioner?

In Dewey's (1933) revised edition of *How We Think* he clearly states what he defines as reflective thinking. In so doing, it becomes immediately obvious why reflection is so central to teaching and learning.

> *Reflective* thinking, in distinction from other operations to which we apply
> the name of thought, involves (1) a state of doubt, hesitation, perplexity,
> mental difficulty, in which thinking originates, and (2) an act of searching,
> hunting, inquiring, to find material that will resolve the doubt, settle and
> dispose of the perplexity. (Dewey, 1933, p. 12)

In illustrating the utility of reflection, he describes the relationship between reflection and some of the attributes of teaching and learning. In many ways his writings could equally be an appropriate preface to some modern day studies into the enhancement of teachers' professional knowledge and student learning (e.g., Project to Enhance Effective Learning (PEEL) project, Baird and Mitchell, 1986; Baird and Northfield, 1992). Dewey has much to say about searching for a balance between teaching that is transmissive as opposed to that which is solely student-centred, and how a reasoned approach to teaching by reflecting on that balance might impact on student learning.

Dewey writes in a manner which builds an argument from opposing view points in order to demonstrate both the strengths and the weaknesses of the contrary positions. He then introduces his views in terms of a balance between the two to show that the best value is gained by considering alternatives rather than dogmatically adhering to one view or another. He therefore illustrates well how dichotomous views in relation to teaching and learning are counterproductive and how the use of reflection for stimulating and directing thinking can bridge the dichotomy. Although the dichotomy is a wonderful rhetorical device designed to capture attention and to sharpen the lines of argument (Shulman, 1988), in reality, teaching and learning are not so readily separated into such distinct boxes. Reflection is a process that may be applied in puzzling situations to help the learner make better sense of the information at hand, and to enable the teacher to guide and direct learning in appropriate ways. The value of reflection in teaching and learning is that it encourages one to view problems from different perspectives.

Dewey sees reflection as a way of helping teachers to use their artful skills to help students learn in meaningful ways, thus leading to genuine understanding. Through this, the teacher is then able to 'supply the conditions that will arouse intellectual responses: a crucial test . . . of his art as a teacher' (1933, p. 260). To supply the appropriate conditions, the artful teacher needs to 'cultivate the attitudes that are favourable to the use of the best methods of inquiry and testing' (p. 29). By cultivating these attitudes, preparedness for, and use of reflection, might be enhanced. It is this view of reflection that I have adopted as the touchstone (Walker and Evers, 1984) for my teaching and learning and that of my student–teachers.

Dewey (1933) outlined three attitudes that he considered important in predisposing an individual to reflect. He continually demonstrates through his writing that it is not sufficient to 'know', there also needs to be an accompanying desire to 'apply'. The attitudes which he sees as important in securing the adoption and use of reflection are open-mindedness, whole-heartedness and responsibility.

Open-mindedness, as the term suggests, is the ability to consider problems in new and different ways, to be open to new ideas and thoughts that one may not have previously entertained. To be open-minded is to be ready to listen to more sides than one, to be an active listener, to be prepared and able to hear thinking that may be contrary to one's own, and to be able to admit that a previously held belief may in fact be wrong.

Whole-heartedness is displayed when one is thoroughly involved in a subject or cause. It is being enticed and engaged by thinking. It is associated with experiencing a flood of ideas and thoughts. Interest is maintained and ideas are sought in ways in which an enthusiasm and desire for knowing is enacted. 'A teacher who arouses such an enthusiasm in his pupils has done something that no amount of formalized method, no matter how correct, can accomplish' (Dewey, 1933, p. 32).

Responsibility is bound up in the need to consider the consequences of one's actions. It is the need to know why; to seek the meaning in what is being learnt. Intellectual responsibility underpins knowing why something is worth believing. Responsibility is often thought of as a moral trait, but it is equally important as an intellectual resource.

Possession of these attitudes is important if learning is to be embarked upon in a considered and thoughtful way. Therefore, cultivating these attitudes as essential constituents of a readiness for reflection is clearly valuable in pre-service teacher education.

Dewey characterized reflection as comprising five phases. The phases need not necessarily occur in any particular order but should fit together to form the process of reflective thinking. The five phases are suggestions, problem, hypothesis, reasoning and testing.

Suggestions are the ideas or possibilities which spring to mind when one is initially confronted by a puzzling situation. The more suggestions available, the greater the need to suspend judgment and to consider each in an appropriate manner. Therefore, suggestions are an impetus for further inquiry.

Problem or intellectualization is when the puzzle is seen as a whole rather than as small or discrete entities on their own. It is seeing 'the big picture' and recognizing the real cause for concern. It is understanding the perplexity of a situation more precisely so that courses of action may be more fully thought through and intellectualized.

Hypothesis formation is when a suggestion is reconsidered in terms of what can be done with it or how it can be used. Acting on a working hypothesis involves making more observations, considering more information and seeing how the hypothesis stands up to tentative testing. In so doing, 'the sense of the problem becomes more adequate and refined and the suggestion ceases to be a *mere* possibility, becoming a *tested* and, if possible, a *measured* probability' (*ibid*, p. 110).

Reasoning is when the linking of information, ideas and previous experiences allows one to expand on suggestions, hypotheses and tests, to extend the thinking about and knowledge of the subject. 'Even when reasoning out the bearings of a supposition does not lead to its rejection, it develops the idea into a form in which it is more apposite to the problem' (*ibid*, p. 112).

Testing is the phase in which the hypothesized end result may be tested. In so doing, the consequences of the testing can be used to corroborate (or negate) the conjectural idea. Overt testing is the opportunity to find out how well one has thought through the problem situation, yet results of the test need not always corroborate the thinking that preceded the actions. In reflection, failure is instructive. 'It either brings to light a new problem or helps to define and clarify the problem on which he has been engaged. Nothing shows the trained thinker better than the use he makes of his errors and mistakes' (*ibid*, p. 114). Testing may also occur as a covert action whereby a 'thought-experiment' is conducted to test an hypothesis.

In outlining his five phases of reflection, Dewey (1933) discusses ways in which the phases may overlap one another and how some phases might be expanded depending on the problem at hand. He places the phases of reflection in context by referencing the learning to both past and future actions and experiences; reflection is not only 'looking back' and it can persist for extended periods of time.

For me, reflection both is appealing and applicable in my work with preservice teacher education students, especially so if they are to master not only the technical skills of teaching but also to be thoughtful, purposeful and informed decision makers. Clearly this can only be achieved if student–teachers question their own actions, reconsider their knowledge and understanding in the light of experience, and use this to shape the way they approach helping their students to learn. Similarly, I believe, that they need to experience this as learners themselves in their preservice teacher education programs if they are to adopt this approach in their own professional practice.

Schön (1983) recognized this need in other fields of professional practice in which he described reflection in terms of the knowledge gained from a practitioner's own experience. Through his observations of professionals' thinking in action he drew a distinction between technical rationality and the knowledge of practice. Therefore, reflection was seen as an important vehicle for the acquisition of professional knowledge.

Schön (1983) described two forms of reflection; reflection-*on*-action and reflection-*in*-action. Reflection-on-action is the basis of much of the literature pertaining to reflective teaching and reflective teacher education, and is similar to Dewey's notion of reflection. This form of reflection is seen as 'the systematic and deliberate thinking back over one's actions . . . teachers who are thoughtful about their work' (Russell and Munby, 1992, p. 3). Reflection-in-action is understood through 'Phrases like thinking on your feet, keeping your wits about you, and learning by doing [and] suggest not only that we can think about doing but that we can think about doing something while doing it. Some of the most interesting examples of this process occur in the midst of a performance' (Schön, 1983, p. 54). Reflection-in-action comprises the reframing of unanticipated problem situations such that we come to see the experience differently.

The attention by Schön to reflection-on-action and reflection-in-action was the start of a new wave of research and learning about reflection. Books, papers, conferences and teacher education courses were forums for debate about what reflection is and how it might be developed. One way of describing and categorizing this literature was outlined by Grimmett and Erickson (1988) and MacKinnon (1989a) and encompassed three groupings. The first is a view of reflection as thoughtfulness about action, the second is reflection as deliberating among competing views of 'good teaching', and the third is reflection as reconstructing experience. Grimmett and Erickson (1988) describes Schön's work as being situated in this third grouping:

> His focus is on how practitioners generate professional knowledge in and appreciate problematic features of action settings. As such, Schön's contribution to reflection is distinctively important. He builds on and extends Dewey's foundational properties of reflection . . . The reflection that Schön focuses on takes place in the crucible of action. And it is his marked emphasis on the action setting that sets Schön's work apart. (p. 13)

Interestingly though, 'when Schön's Reflective Practitioner struck the consciousness of educationists in the mid-1980s, it was not always as a re-embracing of Dewey's notion, but as the discovery of a new concept' (Richardson, 1990, p. 3). But the impact was such that it caused many teacher educators to reconsider the structure and curriculum of their pre-service teacher education programs. Attempts to develop ways of encouraging student-teachers to develop as reflective practitioners have led to a variety of approaches and structures which have also played their part in shaping the pre-service program in which I teach.

Teacher Education: Structures to Promote Reflection

One structural feature is that of seminar group discussions. Goodman's (1983, 1984) research into the value of seminars in education generally concludes that such sessions can serve three important functions. They can counter the notion that there is one good way to teach through their *liberalizing role* which encourages unique and creative approaches to teaching. They can also serve a *utilitarian role* whereby student-teachers can reflect on the relationship between educational principles and practice, and they can serve an *analytic role*. In the analytic role there is an opportunity for student-teachers to raise specific educational issues or problems and jointly analyse the underlying principles and implications of the issue.

Goodman's work (1983) illustrates that although seminars are capable of fulfilling these roles, it does not necessarily follow that the desired outcomes will occur. He states that in order for these roles to be served it is fundamental that:

> . . . to help student teachers become more reflective about education, the atmosphere within seminars must be open and relaxed. It is difficult under the best of conditions for individuals to question their beliefs and to explore the implications of their actions. Challenging students to reflect upon their experiences and ideas must be done with sensitivity and respect for the individuals. If healthy dynamics are not established, challenging students to think may result in defensiveness, not insight. (pp. 44–48)

Therefore the role of the teacher educator in the seminar becomes very important if the purpose for the implementation of that particular structure is to be fully realized.

It is not enough to include structures to encourage reflection, teacher educators must embrace them in appropriate ways to insure that they do indeed serve the function for which they are intended.

Another tool for reflection is the use of journals. These are designed to encourage student-teachers to document their thinking about learning and teaching. It is anticipated that by writing about experiences, actions and events, student-teachers will reflect on and learn from those episodes. Approaches to journal writing in teacher education vary from the unstructured methodology of 'writing what one thinks about an experience' or a 'stream of consciousness' through semi-structured tasks which require a response to given 'prompts or cues', to highly structured formats which require the writer to adhere to prescribed criteria. For me, the purpose of journal writing is to help the writer look back on (or forward to) an event in the hope that it will be a catalyst for reflection.

The use of journals can be a powerful tool for reflection (Dobbins, 1990; Bean and Zulich, 1989; Rodderick, 1986) but, like seminars, requires the teacher educator's commitment to, and valuing of, the writing and thinking necessary in maintaining a journal. One way that I attempt to encourage this in my student-teachers is by maintaining a journal myself. This serves two important purposes in my teaching. One is that it models my approach to my thinking about teaching and learning. The second is that as I openly share my journal with my class, it becomes a public document and offers an opportunity for the 'unpacking' of my views of our shared experiences within the pre-service program. It therefore gives them access to my pedagogical reasoning.

Another tool used to aid reflective thinking in student-teachers is the use of video-tapes of particular teaching and learning situations. The use of video-tapes may be of oneself or of others and generally focuses on the teaching performance. Micro-teaching is one approach to the use of video-taped experiences of one's own teaching whilst the observation of someone else teaching is usually designed to give the observer a vicarious experience of a particular teaching approach or episode. In each case, observing the teaching on video-tape, coupled with discussion and debriefing after the event, is seen as a way of encouraging reflection.

A valuable extension to this form of 'guided reflection' is the observation of one's own teaching through video-taping teaching in action in the school setting. MacKinnon (1989a) spent a considerable amount of time with his student-teachers video-taping their teaching and their debriefing sessions with their school supervisors. Through this work, MacKinnon found that the video-tapes offered his student-teachers new ways of reliving and reviewing their experiences, and that with an appropriate working environment and supervisory support, reflection was not only encouraged but was also enhanced and valued.

MacKinnon's work hinted at a necessary and fundamental shift in focus for the development of reflective teachers through pre-service education. He started to look at the supervisor as a role-model for the student-teacher. As he explored Schön's (1987) three conceptions of modelling (Follow Me, Joint Experimentation, and Hall of Mirrors) in the practicum, he started to uncover the influence of modelling on student-teachers' learning about, and development of, reflection. It is not surprising that, as in the case of seminars, journal writing, supervisory meetings and teaching debriefings, the influence of the teacher/role-model is crucial if student-teachers are to develop their skills of reflection.

Richert (1987, 1990) also recognized the importance of teachers as role-models for their student-teachers' learning about and learning through reflection. However, even though research suggests there is implicit value in effectively modelling reflection, there is little to suggest that this explicitly occurs in teacher education programs. Gunstone *et al.* (1993) outlined the importance of modelling in pre-service education and linked this with the need for pre-service educators to reflect on their own practice in accord with their expectations of their students' thinking about learning. It may very well be obvious that this should be the case, but it is not uncommon to hear of teacher educators presenting cooperative learning, group work, problem solving or many of a number of other interactive learning approaches, by systematically detailing the approach via a monologue in a lecture, defeating the purpose of learning from and with others.

> Our ongoing student evaluations of the program point to the importance to them [student-teachers] of consistency between espoused pedagogical principles and actual behaviour by staff. This importance is shown by both positive comment on examples of consistency between espoused principle and actual practice, and negative comment, often detailed and perceptive, about examples of inconsistency. (Gunstone *et al.*, 1993, p. 54)

Valli (1989) also pointed to the need for university professors and cooperating teachers to 'practice what they preach'. In her study into the transfer of learning for novice teachers she described the lack of appropriate modelling as one of four factors which inhibited student-teachers' learning about teaching. Sadly, she found that it was difficult to alter this practice.

The research literature shows that there has been extensive incorporation of social and artifactual characteristics into teacher education programs. They have been taken up in teacher education programs because, when used in appropriate ways and under appropriate conditions, they are seen as positive ways of encouraging student-teachers to reflect. These social and artifactual characteristics, combined with teacher educators who genuinely model reflective processes in their pedagogy, could place student-teachers in a position whereby through the development of their skills in reflection, they could take more control of, and accept more responsibility for their learning about teaching. Under such conditions student-teachers might develop a greater understanding of what it means to be a reflective practitioner, and apply it in their own practice.

Clarke (1988) reminds us that research into teacher thinking highlights the value teachers place on reflection. Amongst a series of questions that he raises for teacher educators to consider, he asks whether teacher educators show that they value and use reflection in their own practice, and whether teacher preparation programs help to illustrate the 'intrinsic uncertainty' of teaching (which is the basis of reflection). But one of his most telling questions is:

Do teachers of teachers have the courage to think aloud as they themselves wrestle with troubling dilemmas such as striking a balance between depth and breadth of content studied, distribution of time and attention among individual students, making inferences about what students know and what grades they should be assigned, or with how to repair errors, teaching disasters, and the human mistakes that even experienced teacher educators make from time to time? (p. 10)

By combining the features of program structures designed to enhance reflection in student-teachers with the modelling of reflective practice, Clarke's question could well be considered as the next challenge for teacher educators who genuinely pursue the goal of developing reflective practitioners.

Through the use of a pre-service program's social tools (e.g., seminars, discussion groups, supervisory feedback, interviews) and artifactual tools (journal writing, video-tapes of student-teachers' own lessons), combined with my attempts to model reflective practice so that the intrinsic value of reflection on my own practice could made more explicit for my student-teachers, the influence of these on the way that my student-teachers develop and use reflection in their own practice can be explored.

The approach to reflection I employ draws on the deliberative, purposeful form of reflection described by Dewey (1933) and incorporates many of the pre-service education program structures developed, adapted and used by other teacher educators in the hope of producing more reflective teachers. In this book I will explore the link between my reflection and practice in my pre-service education teaching and the development of reflection in my student-teachers through the interplay of the experiences from the university-based coursework through to their school teaching experiences. In this environment student-teachers can be well nurtured through their struggle to learn about teaching and to start developing as reflective practitioners.

In order to discover how reflection by student-teachers might be developed and enhanced, I will explore and analyse student-teachers' thoughts and actions through their social and artifactual tools, combined with the effect of my modelling of reflective practice on one group of student-teachers from my Teaching and Learning (TAL) class in the pre-service secondary education program in which I teach.

The Context

The one year, post-degree Diploma in Education is an ungraded course (participants academic record shows pass or fail only) which has three periods of teaching practice, each of three full-time weeks, and coursework which is divided into two major areas: Methods and Practice of Teaching, and Foundation Studies. Students participate in two Methods and Practice of Teaching subjects, which are timetabled for two hours per week for the duration of the course. These subjects are designed to give students a grounding in the pedagogy of the subject and to familiarize them with subject content and curriculum at the school level.

A wide range of teaching subjects is offered in this course and the prerequisite for entry to these Methods Subjects is at least two consecutive years study of the subject during the student's first degree.

The Foundation Studies include Social Foundations of Schooling (SFS) and Teaching and Learning (TAL). The SFS subject examines contemporary schooling in its social and historical context. This focuses on the nature of teachers' work, what and how they teach, and how these are influenced by the way society and education are structured. The subject also investigates contemporary issues in education and how these have emerged over time. Social factors such as class and gender, and major issues such as the integration of students with disabilities, changes in teachers' work and pay, and the development of post-compulsory schooling are considered.

TAL is a subject that presents psychology and principles of teaching through a number of themes to do with knowing about oneself, students, planning and control, learning and teaching, and student progress. The purpose is to enable student-teachers to establish principles that will make their teaching a purposeful, rational and rewarding experience, both for themselves and their pupils. Within these themes, TAL covers topics such as theories of learning and their application in classrooms; physical, personality, and social development; knowledge and the curriculum; the nature of abilities; approaches to classroom control; questioning techniques and other teaching strategies; lesson structure; and the purposes and methods of assessment.

Students are allocated to a tutorial group at the start of the year and remain in the same group for the whole year for both TAL and SFS. Each subject is structured so that all students meet together for some lectures: once a week in SFS, perhaps once every two weeks in TAL, with the primary focus being on the tutorial groups which meet twice weekly for two hour sessions. Therefore, the same group of students is together for up to eight hours per week.

Selection of students for tutorial groups is organized so that there is as great a diversity of teaching methods as the timetable will allow. As students in a tutorial group spend so much time together, it does not take very long before the group is 'bonded'. This 'bonding' is also the focus of many early TAL activities. The relationship between the teacher educator (tutor) and students is important in encouraging them to speak openly and honestly about the topics under consideration. This is similarly enhanced through the use of student journals which are a component of the course.

Gathering Student-teachers' Views

Because of the complex nature of the thinking which needs to be accessed to explore the relationship between modelling and student-teachers' reflection on practice, I have used a diversity of approaches. The first involves journal writing which was designed to encourage students to reflect on their pre-service education experiences. The second was from nine members of my TAL class who volunteered to be interviewed throughout the year. These interviews were designed to probe their views of the course, their experiences and understanding of pre-service education, and to explore these in ways that might not have been possible through their journals or in class. Another was from four of the students who were interviewed who also volunteered to be video-taped teaching during their final school teaching experience. This was particularly designed to help gain insights into their thoughts and actions about their own teaching in action.

Exploring this relationship between the modelling of reflection and its concurrent development in student-teachers was initiated in response to a desire for pre-service teacher education programs (and teacher educators) to be able to help student-teachers develop an approach to teaching that might help them take more control of their own education, and to encourage them to be deliberative and thoughtful about their pedagogy. Not surprisingly it has also been a major factor in shaping my own pedagogy as my research and practice continually influence one another.

Chapter 2

A Model for Learning about Reflection

Introduction

The diversity of views on what reflection means, how it might be recognized and documented, and how it might be developed in student-teachers makes it difficult for researchers and teacher educators to agree on how (and in some cases if) pre-service teacher education programs can develop reflective practitioners. However, it is clear that the goal of preparing reflective practitioners is a worthwhile endeavour in teacher education. My involvement in teacher preparation has led me to believe that developing reflective practitioners in pre-service programs can be pursued, documented and analysed. Conceptualizing how this might be done begins with a need for teacher educators to use reflection to guide and inform their *own* practice and, in so doing, to explicitly model this for their students. Through this approach, the relationship between the modelling of reflective practice and its development in, and use by, student-teachers can be explored.

As I pursue this in my own teaching and research I consider it as a response to many of the calls in the literature to better link the theory of reflection to the practices used in teacher education. Dewey (1933) drew teacher educators' attention to this in *How We Think* and the calls have continued ever since. Goodman (1984) believed that a response to these calls needed to examine three areas: (1) the focus of reflection; (2) the process of reflective thinking; and (3) the attitudes necessary for reflective individuals. Ross and Hannay complemented these points by arguing that:

> . . . reflective inquiry has been promoted for many years as a progressive and effective method of teaching . . . its incorporation into classroom practice remains questionable . . . part of the blame [is due] to those interpreters of Dewey's inquiry model who advocate a procedural or technical rather than a dialectic approach to teaching. Teacher education practices also contribute to the lack of critical reflection existing in schools. Too frequently the rationale for reflective teaching is expounded through expository techniques and a technical inquiry approach . . . the university classroom must become not only the venue for transmitting traditional knowledge on teacher education but also a laboratory where such practices are modeled, experienced, and reflected upon. Such a truly reflective inquiry model needs to

be firmly grounded in critical theory by incorporating the application of principles, not procedures, in the investigation . . . (1986, p. 9)

As stated earlier, I define reflection as the deliberate and purposeful act of thinking which centres on ways of responding to problem situations in teaching and learning. Reflection can be seen as deliberate such that:

> . . . reflection involves not simply a sequence of ideas, but a *consequence*
> — a consecutive ordering in such a way that each determines the next as
> its proper outcome, while each outcome in turn leans back on, or refers to,
> its predecessors. The successive portions of reflective thought flow out
> of one another and support one another; they do not come and go in a
> medley. Each phase is a step from something to something — technically
> speaking, it is a term of thought. Each term leaves a deposit that is utilized
> in the next term. The stream or flow becomes a train or chain. There are
> in any reflective thought definite units that are linked together so that there
> is a sustained movement to a common end. (Dewey, 1933, pp. 4–5)

Reflection is, then, clearly purposeful because it aims at a conclusion. The purpose of reflecting is to untangle a problem, or to make more sense of a puzzling situation; reflection involves working toward a better understanding of the problem and ways of solving it. Reflection, then, can be seen as a number of steps in thinking which, when organized and linked, lead to a consequence in action. These steps are suggestions, problem, hypothesis, reasoning and testing. Although these phases need not follow in a particular order, the five phases combined comprise a reflective cycle. Also, even though reflection is aimed at resolving a problem, the results of testing in one reflective phase may well lead to further reflective action as the results of the test are reconsidered, evaluated and analysed. Just as the phases of reflection are linked, so reflective cycles may be linked. Because of the complex nature of teaching and learning, problem resolution is not absolute. It is context bound. Solutions from one context may guide thinking in another, but solutions are not necessarily universally appropriate or applicable. Reflection helps the individual to learn from experience because of the meaningful nature of the inquiry into that experience.

Learning about Reflection through Modelling

Student-teachers enter pre-service education with a wealth of experience as observers of teaching practice. But what they have generally been viewing and experiencing has been the end product of their teachers' thinking about how to teach particular content. They have most likely not been privy to the reasons why teaching strategies have (or have not) been employed, why a unit was taught in a particular sequence, or the influence of their learning on the teacher's approach to structuring future lessons.

Not surprisingly, then, many student-teachers enter pre-service education expecting to be 'told' how to teach. There is no doubt that there are teaching skills and strategies that aid in one's effectiveness as a teacher. However, teaching is far more complex than simply applying the *right* strategies or developing *the* skills necessary for content delivery.

Teaching is inextricably linked to learning. Teaching for understanding involves exploring the relationship between teaching and learning within the context of such things as: the content, and the teacher's understanding of the content; the nature of the students and their experiences; and the temporal and physical characteristics of the setting. The more these contextual issues are explored the greater the possibility that development beyond a purely technical approach to (and understanding of) teaching might occur. Hence there is a need for teachers to reflect on the relationship between the act of teaching and the experience of learning.

For student-teachers to understand reflection on practice the learning needs to encapsulate meaning within the experience. This is, as Schön (1987) pointed out, similar to being faced with the 'Meno paradox'.

[I]n the first instance, he can neither do it nor recognize it when he sees it. Hence, he is caught up in a self-contradiction: 'looking for something' implies a capacity to recognize the thing one looks for but the student lacks at first the capacity to recognize the object of his search. The instructor is caught up in the same paradox: he cannot tell the student what he needs to know, even if he has words for it, because the student would not at that point understand him. (p. 83)

Because unravelling this paradox of not knowing what needs to be known is difficult, many teacher educators attempt to simplify the problems associated with the 'uncertainty of practice' by reverting to a lecture on possible solutions. I suggest that a key to unlock the Meno paradox is found in the modelling of reflective practice for student-teachers as it helps them to see, experience, and construct an understanding of the nature of reflection from teaching and learning episodes in which they are active participants.

In order to gain that sense of competence, control, and confidence that characterizes professionals, students of professional practice must first give it up. As they act and reflect in situations of perplexing uncertainty, mystery and frustration, that which is given up for the sake of experimenting begins to emerge in their development. Out of the darkness of student unknowing comes the light of professional practical knowledge. (Grimmett and Erickson, 1988, p. 11)

If student-teachers see their teacher educators as reflective practitioners, if they experience the development of professional practical knowledge by being a part of that learning, then they might be helped to address the paradox in their own learning about practice. Modelling reflective practice must therefore involve much more than displaying the skills of an expert pedagogue (Berliner, 1986). It is not asking student-teachers to mimic the 'models' placed before them, it is showing that

> ... experimenting and the inevitable 'mistakes' and confusions that fol-low are encouraged, discussed, and viewed as departure points for growth ... a climate of trust, as well as the disposition to take learning seriously ... begin[s] with the supervisor's own capacity for reflection on teaching, together with his or her ability to make this evident to the student teacher. (MacKinnon, 1989b, p. 23)

Making reflection *evident* is a most important facet of modelling reflective practice for student-teachers. But how might this be adequately achieved?

Schön (1987) describes three forms of modelling that he proposes as ways that students learn from their supervisor's practice. The three models he proposes are the Hall of Mirrors, Joint Experimentation and Follow Me. Schön (1987) explains the three models as ways of 'coaching reflective practice' and sees them as import-ant ways for students to learn how to 'frame the problems of practice'. Therefore, for Schön, the three models are ways that students can learn to see how the practice setting appears through the eyes of an experienced practitioner.

The Follow Me model revolves around experienced practitioners being able to demonstrate and describe their pedagogical knowledge to their student-teachers. From these demonstrations and descriptions, the student-teacher attempts to develop and imitate the use of that pedagogical knowledge. With practice the student-teacher learns about the practice setting by *doing* in similar ways to the experienced practi-tioner. Discussing the actions from the experienced practitioner's and the student-teacher's perspective is important in learning about the practice setting.

The Joint Experimentation model involves the student-teacher being encour-aged to take the lead in reflective inquiry. The experienced practitioner then follows the student-teacher's line of inquiry, commenting, advising and offering alternatives as the need arises. In so doing, the student-teacher is able to question the problems of practice that occur in that setting.

The Hall of Mirrors model hinges on the need for the experienced practitioner's practice with the student-teacher to be an example of that which the student-teacher is attempting to understand and develop in his or her own practice. The import-ant facet of this model is that the student-teacher needs to experience what it means to be a learner in the practice situation. It is anticipated that this experience will then reflect the position of the student-teacher's learners when he/she is the teacher.

Although each of these three models is presented as a separate form of coach-ing reflective practice it is clear that there are important aspects of each which would be called upon at different times, under different circumstances and in dif-ferent situations, to help student-teachers learn about reflection. There is a need for consistency between a teacher educator's teaching practice and his or her supervis-ory practice. There must be an ability to be detached from one's feelings about action in order to focus on the action itself and the student-teacher needs to be able to conceptualize actions from both the teacher's and the student's perspective.

Beyond these underlying principles there is one other aspect which plays an important role in modelling; according to my conceptualization and practice. Because reflection resides in the mind of the individual it is difficult to directly observe. Therefore, if student-teachers are to have reflective practice truly modelled, if they are to be involved in experiencing and understanding the processes which shape the planning, implementation and reviewing of pedagogy, they need to hear what the teacher is thinking.

One way I use to respond to this need is through writing about the thinking that influences my teaching through a journal which I make accessible to student-teachers. Another is by literally 'thinking aloud' during teaching so that my student-teachers can access the processes, as they are occurring, that shape my pedagogy at that time. Both of these are integral components to the approach to modelling which I employ.

A difficulty created for student-teachers experiencing modelling of this nature is the need to continually juggle learning about learning and learning about teaching. Fundamentally they need to be able to juxtapose two perspectives on learning, the student's (i.e., their own position) and the teacher's, as they become involved in determining what it means to be a reflective practitioner. This is by no means a simple task and needs to be recognized and acknowledged by the teacher educator and the student-teachers. It is an element of learning that needs to be explicit and continually revisited.

Reflection in Perspective

If developing reflective practitioners is to be pursued in teacher education programs, and if modelling reflective practice is one method of doing this, then understanding stimuli for reflection is necessary. Reflection occurs in response to a puzzling situation. The problem, difficulty or concern needs to be apprehended and attended to. In so doing, reflection is an action which occurs in a context.

Reflection should not be taught as a process or algorithm ready and waiting to be applied at every possible opportunity. As Valli reminds us:

> . . . if program goals are to be realized, a potential danger resides in valuing, or over-valuing, process. A process focus could detract from more central questions of the purpose, content and quality of reflection. How to get students to reflect can take on a life of its own, can become *the* programmatic goal. What students reflect on can become immaterial. (1993, p. 19)

Therefore, if reflection is to be valued by student-teachers as a worthwhile attribute for their professional development, they must experience it as a logical consequence of learning to teach; not as a generalist process skill but as an appropriate tool for unpacking and learning from the uncertainties of practice.

There is a content to reflection, there must be something to reflect about. Therefore, as LaBoskey (1993) reminds us, Dewey's (1933) attitudes of open-mindedness, responsibility and whole-heartedness may be more critical to the reflective process than the specific steps of the process itself. Some student-teachers may not see a situation as puzzling while others might. Being attuned to 'seeing' is being open-minded, seeing the problem situation in different ways is being responsible, and wanting to respond, whilst accepting the consequences of action, is to display the attitude of whole-heartedness. Enhancing these attitudes in student-teachers is an important precursor to reflection and, just as the results of reflection differ with the context, content and purpose, so the preparedness for reflection will vary with each of the individuals entering a pre-service education program.

With this in mind, another important element of the conceptual framework which I employ relates to the value student-teachers place on reflection and the practice of modelling. If student-teachers are to value reflective practice it is important that they are educated about it not trained in it. This distinction is important, as Shulman points out, because seeking to know why is important if reflection is to be valued by student-teachers.

> Philosophers of education have distinguished between training and educating in part by pointing out the differences between teaching without reasons and teaching with explanations and understanding. To educate is to teach in a way that includes an account of why you do as you do . . . our obligation as teacher educators must be to make the tacit explicit. Teachers will become better educators when they can begin to have explicit answers to the questions, 'How do I know what I know? How do I know the reasons for what I do? Why do I ask my students to perform or think in particular ways?' The capacity to answer such questions not only lies at the heart of what we mean by becoming skilled as a teacher; it also requires a combining of reflection on practical experience and reflection on theoretical understanding. (1988, p. 33)

My conceptual framework is geared towards making the tacit explicit through modelling. But my intent is not that this be done by 'training' student-teachers in knowing and applying the phases of reflection, it is that this be done by probing, inquiring and challenging the student-teachers' attitudes and reflective processes (as well as mine, as their teacher) in the context of learning about teaching. This is based on the assumption that through the actions of modelling, reflection comes to be better understood, more meaningful and valuable to student-teachers, without explicitly stating the phases as they occur. Instead, this is done by illustrating the actions in the context of the learning at that time.

Difficulties in Learning about Reflection

The association between learning and reflection is an important focus for pre-service education programs that aim to develop reflective practitioners. Main (1985) stated that 'reflection comes slowly to some people because they have little sense of involvement in their own learning,' (p. 97) and it is this involvement in learning that is important in the development of one's use of reflection. However, there are difficulties associated with learning from reflection that need to be recognized. One of these is the time of reflection.

The 'when' of reflection (the time of reflection in relation to the pedagogical experience) influences the learning that might be drawn from that experience. Three time frames for reflection are discernible: before, during and after an experience. At each of these times one's thoughts and actions may be considerably different so that what one learns will be influenced accordingly. Hence, for student-teachers to learn through experience about these 'times' of reflection, the apparent and the real risks associated with learning from such experiences will also vary from individual to individual as they recognize and respond to the opportunities presented.

If these times of reflection impact on learning in different ways, then learning from experience also takes on new meaning as the content of reflection will also be influenced by when it occurs; changes in time lead to changes in context. Therefore *when* a student-teacher reflects on practice will influence the subsequent learning from that experience.

McIntyre (1993) believes that student-teachers need to consciously and deliberately plan almost every step of their teaching and he argues that they do not need to reflect in order to be conscious of what they are trying to do and know. Although it is indeed important for student-teachers to consciously and purposefully plan their teaching, I believe there to be a major difference between lesson planning (the mechanistic, structural and organizational aspects of a lesson) and reflection on possible pedagogical approaches to enhance student learning. For example, consider the student-teacher who has a 50-minute lesson in which to complete a science experiment with her class. In the first instance she will need to consciously and deliberately plan the lesson structure to ensure that the students know what they are expected to do, have the appropriate time to set-up and conduct their experiment, record their observations, hypothesize, test (and perhaps re-test), make inferences and draw conclusions, pack-up their equipment, conduct their work in accordance with safety procedures and so on. All of these actions occur with a sense of timing in order that the lesson is a cohesive, self-contained session. If the lesson is to be completed in 50 minutes, then an appreciation for the length of time necessary for each activity is important. For the student-teacher, all of these actions call for conscious and deliberate planning.

In another instance, a student-teacher might be considering how to conduct an experiment so that the students are actively engaged in the learning, rather than simply following the instructions in a recipe-style laboratory manual where thinking and understanding are not necessary for task completion. In this case, the student-teacher might apprehend a problem — for example, the students do not think about what they are doing and why — and wonder how this problem might be addressed. Suggestions spring to mind or ideas from others might be sought. The student-teacher might hypothesize that if the method for the experiment was not supplied then the students would *really* have to understand the aim of the experiment in order to conduct the exercise. Reasoning through this could lead the student-teacher to prepare a practical lesson where the aim and apparatus were supplied, while leaving the students to determine a method to meet the aim. Testing that approach might occur in the student-teacher's mind and be further refined before it was tested in the classroom.

Both of these instances are examples of conscious and deliberate acts. They may also be being performed by the same student-teacher. The first instance involves lesson planning, the second is reflection on action prior to the pedagogical experience occurring. The distinction is important if reflection for action (Shulman, 1993) is to be distinguished from planning. Reflection for action is a way of apprehending and attending to a situation in anticipation of the experience.

> Anticipatory reflection enables us to deliberate about possible alternatives, decide on courses of action, plan the kinds of things we need to do, and anticipate the experiences we and others may have as a result of expected events or of our planned actions. Anticipatory reflection helps us to approach situations and other people in an organized, decision-making, prepared way. (van Manen, 1991b, p. 101)

Anticipatory reflection is a means of accessing or framing a problem situation before it occurs. It is an opportunity to prepare; to consciously and carefully anticipate a course of action to be tested. Contextual factors which may influence reflection at this time (for example, content knowledge, the age of the students, previous experience with the same group of students, the degree of uncertainty in outcomes a teacher is prepared to risk, etc.) will vary, but, obviously, reflecting on the situation combined with the subsequent testing that occurs will shape what a student-teacher learns from that experience.

In a similar fashion, reflection on action after an experience will also influence what a student-teacher learns. Again, the context will also be important as it shapes what is apprehended and what is attended to. This looking back on experience, or retrospective reflection, offers opportunities to make better sense of past experiences and to develop a new or deeper understanding of that situation.

Consider the position of the student-teacher described earlier who decided to conduct her science class in a way that she hoped would lead to better student understanding of the experiment under consideration. Retrospective reflection allows her to question what happened during the class. Did the lesson work as planned? Was it a worthwhile experience for her students? How might that experience influence her approach to laboratory classes in future? Questions like these may well be the impetus for retrospective reflection which helps her to better understand her own pedagogical learning as well as the learning of her students. Finally, imagine what might be occurring during the lesson. How much of what is happening might she see? What type of problems lead her to reframe? In the complex environment of the classroom where management and learning issues are continually arising and subsiding, how does she find time to address any of the puzzling situations which she might identify?

Reflection on action during the pedagogical experience must also occur within contextual parameters. This contemporaneous reflection would seem to be most demanding as the time frame for possible action (if testing is to influence the experience at hand) is much less than is the case in either anticipatory or retrospective reflection. But, contemporaneous reflection may also be a most powerful and immediate experience of learning about pedagogy.

The conceptual framework (Figure 2.1) which I propose is constructed in the belief that if reflection is to be understood and valued by student-teachers then it cannot be presented as an isolated event or process. It needs to be an integral component in the curriculum. Reflection occurs at three distinct times in relation to pedagogical experience and within that experience it is highly context dependent. Therefore, these need to be evident in the modelling of reflection.

As already noted, I draw on Dewey's (1933) description of reflection. The appropriateness and applicability of his view of reflection offers distinct phases (suggestions, problem, hypothesis, reasoning and testing) which may be detected and described in a teacher's thinking about pedagogy. Dewey's phases offer opportunities for reliable and verifiable instances of reflection to be recognized and documented in ways which might be more discernible than the larger more complex groupings described by Schön (1983); one way of interpreting Schön's 'reframing' is that it involves suggestions, problem and hypothesis.

Summary

I consider reflection as the purposeful, deliberate act of inquiry into one's thoughts and actions through which a perceived problem is examined in order that a thoughtful, reasoned response might be tested out. This process involves the five phases outlined by Dewey (1933) of suggestions, problem, hypothesis, reasoning and testing, and, although they do not necessarily follow a particular order or sequence, the five combined comprise a reflective cycle. The results of the test from the reflective cycle may not satisfy the inquiring mind and may therefore lead to further reflection. Also, differences in context influence problem recognition and therefore influence the nature of reflection. Experience from one context may influence thoughts and actions in another, but the complex nature of teaching and learning means that each situation may effectively be a new situation.

In pre-service teacher education programs, some important social and artifactual tools (e.g., journals, seminars and discussions) may be employed to enhance student-teachers' use of reflection. However, these alone are not sufficient for genuine understanding of reflection on practice. Modelling of reflection within the context of the student-teachers' own teaching and learning experiences is important.

Although the term reflection on practice suggests a process of thinking after an activity, it does not mean that it is limited to this time. Reflection can occur before, during and after an experience, and in each case that which is recognized as a problem situation may vary, as will the reflective thinking and the subsequent

Figure 2.1:   Conceptual framework

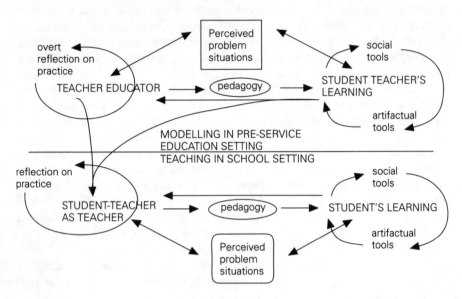

learning. In any case, modelling of reflection must also portray these differences if the process is to be understood, and valued by student-teachers.

Figure 2.1 represents the relationship between my modelling of reflection and my student-teacher's learning about reflection as problem situations are overtly apprehended and attended to through my pedagogy. As a result, both my student-teacher's learning and my modelling are influences on their developing pedagogy.

Part 2

Learning through Modelling

Chapter 3

Modelling Reflection

Introduction

I believe that teaching needs to be interactive and challenging as learning does not occur just by listening, it occurs by reconsidering one's understanding through deeds, thoughts and actions. Therefore, so that student-teachers' learning about teaching is meaningful, the teaching employed should challenge and motivate them to take steps to make new meaning from teaching and learning episodes. More so, attempting to understand the complex nature of teaching and learning must go beyond mere rhetoric such that, for me, teaching student-teachers revolves around the notion that I should 'practice what I preach'.

Clearly then, the philosophy that underpins my teaching is that students in my classes should be actively engaged in their learning so that their ideas and thinking are challenged in ways which provoke them to reconsider, and better articulate, their understanding of the subject matter. However, to encourage this, the following are important to continually keep in mind and work towards:

1. The teacher-learner relationship is built up over time primarily by demonstrating that withholding judgment is important in developing mutual trust and respect. As a teacher I need to illustrate that others' views are important, are actively sought, and are valued in the teaching learning environment. Meaningful learning is not encouraged if there is not a feeling of 'safety' for students to genuinely express their understanding of content/concepts. When learners are able to articulate their views publicly, reconsideration, construction of meaning and valuable learning are able to occur. Therefore there are important personal and social aspects to learning which need to be taken into account in guiding my teaching and my students' learning about teaching.

   I endeavour to develop 'trust' with my students by reinforcing good social behaviour within my classes. This means that all members of the class (students and myself as teacher) need to be supportive of one another because good learning involves risk-taking and this will not occur if individuals' ideas or thoughts are ridiculed by others. Therefore, recognizing that learners can be vulnerable is important. Above all else it is essential that the expectations I have of my students apply equally to myself. I consider that conveying a sense of trust is essential in creating a good learning atmosphere within my classes. This is the cornerstone of respect and is a respect of persons as learners not an expectation of respect because of 'position'.

2. Learning is complex and varies from person to person and from one context to another. This needs to be taken into account when teaching. The simple transmission of propositional knowledge may convey information, but to cater for a variety of learning styles it is not sufficient to adhere to one particular form of presentation. Good teaching requires reconsidering how one learns about the particular concept/content under consideration. The questions, scenarios, problems and concerns that impact on learning must shape the teaching. Therefore, it is important to me to highlight the different 'ways of knowing' that arise in teaching and learning situations. To do this, I try to help my students recognize what it is they need to know and why, then, how to apply their knowledge in different problem situations to further develop their understanding.

3. Teaching requires a working knowledge of a variety of procedures to enhance learning (e.g., cooperative group work, interpretive discussions, role-plays, Prediction-Observation-Explanation strategies, etc.). Applying particular teaching procedures in order to encourage appropriate learning outcomes allows me to better probe my students' understanding. Therefore, I need to have a number of strategies 'on hand' that will be appropriate for different situations and different students' needs. The use of appropriate procedures is important in planning for, and responding to, teaching situations. *But,* teaching procedures are not simply ways of breaking up the standard routine. There is a learning purpose related to their application. For example, I may use an interpretive discussion (Barnes, 1976) when I feel it is important to explore the range of views, explanations and opinions that students hold in relation to the topic/content being taught. This helps them to clarify their own views and to compare their thinking to the thinking of others and to understand the reasons behind different viewpoints. The major purpose for this approach is to encourage my students to reconsider their understanding through interaction with other members of the class.

   Interpretive discussions require a supportive atmosphere as they are high risk activities for learners, therefore everyone's comments and views need to be valued so that personal criticism does not creep into the discussion. It is designed to clarify thinking and understanding, not to see 'who's right and who's wrong.' For this reason, students need to learn and practice the acceptable behaviours involved in this process and, as the teacher, I am conscious of constantly reinforcing these behaviours in positive ways.

   I also use role-plays as a way of helping students better understand concepts. Role-plays encourage students to translate information from one form to another. In science classes I may use this strategy so that learning through translation of knowledge from one situation to another might create understanding which begins to extend beyond a solely theoretical view. For example, role-playing the gear ratios in machines or the movement of electrons in an electric circuit or the orbit of the moon around the earth, or changes of state from solid to liquid to gas are activities that broaden students' understanding of particular content knowledge.

One last example might be the use of Prediction-Observation-Explanation activities (POEs; White and Gunstone, 1992). The nature of these activities asks students to predict the outcome of an experiment, demonstration or problem, and to commit themselves to their prediction. After observing the demonstration in action, they then attempt to explain the 'how' of the demonstration so that they are either reshaping their understanding from an incorrect prediction, or clarifying their understanding for a correct prediction. I find POEs to be a very powerful teaching and learning tool and they can be a catalyst for an informative interpretive discussion. Again, real 'trust' is necessary in the class and the POE needs to challenge a student's understanding of a topic in the 'what if' domain. This encourages learning that is based on processing information, hypothesizing and reasoning.

The strategies described above are a small selection of those that I use in my teaching. It is important for me to have a good working knowledge of a variety of teaching strategies so that I can better align my teaching with the learning that I hope to encourage in my students. The teaching strategies I use are both content and context dependent. Also, being able to respond to changes in the teaching and learning environment is vital. Therefore, knowing how to use a strategy is one facet of my teaching, knowing why to use it is crucial, *but*, being able to adapt and change, to be responsive to the teaching and learning environment is fundamental to my pedagogy. If my teaching was constrained by 'sticking to what was planned' then no matter how useful a strategy might be, it would be compromised by inflexibility. I must be able to adapt to the changing needs of a pedagogical episode. I must be responsive to changes in student learning and be prepared to adapt, adjust and change my approach as necessary. Ultimately, knowing 'why' becomes crucial in knowing 'how' and I continually attempt to teach in ways that allow me to recognize students' learning needs and to respond in appropriate ways to enhance their learning.

4. As a teacher I am also a learner and should be challenged through the teaching and learning experiences in which I am involved. There is much to learn from both positive and not so positive teaching episodes. Reflection on practice encourages research on practice by shaping questions which explore the outcomes of particular strategies in particular situations. Reflection facilitates risk-taking in teaching. I must also be prepared to expose my vulnerability as a learner in ways similar to those which I encourage in my students, and to make this clear for them.

Through my teaching and learning, my skills are continually being challenged and extended. I am not 'untouched' by the experiences of teaching and learning because it is a two-way process. My teaching is designed to extend students' views of teaching and learning as I attempt to model approaches to teaching that encourage my students to reflect on both my teaching and their learning so that they might reconsider their actions when they are in similar situations when they are teaching. Consequently, as I work to help my students learn about teaching, I believe that they need to be able to access my thinking about pedagogy if they are to genuinely understand the complexities of teaching and learning, and to draw their own conclusions about how they might apply their learning from my modelling to their own practice. I therefore incorporate a 'thinking aloud' about my teaching so that my students are given an opportunity to understand the thinking which accompanies my practice.

Thinking Aloud

My thinking aloud about my pedagogy is an attempt to give students immediate access to the thoughts, ideas and concerns which shape my teaching. It would not be uncommon for me to preface my teaching at the start of a class with the reasons for the structure about to be employed. In so doing I would attempt to demonstrate my thinking about previous lessons, my intentions for the upcoming lesson, and what I anticipated for the following lessons, and that these are all linked in a holistic manner. Therefore, my reactions to what I perceived to be the learning as a result of a teaching experience is an important starting point for my thinking about the lesson to be taught. In essence, I would be giving my students access to the pedagogical reasoning which underpins my thinking as I attempt to develop the 'purpose' for, and approach to, a teaching and learning experience.

Inevitably then, the thinking associated with preparing for a session is linked to the outcomes from previous sessions, hence reconsidering past experiences is an important shaping factor in planning for future teaching and learning experiences. Consequently, my perception of how (or whether) the purpose of previous sessions is achieved is also an aspect of thinking about teaching that needs to be 'unpacked' for my students. This thinking back over experience could occur immediately after a lesson, or could extend over time and be revisited in a variety of different ways as I reconsider the experiences from that situation. In any case, how it occurs and its impact on my teaching needs to be made available to my students if they are to understand my perspective on my teaching and our learning.

Teaching and learning are interconnected through a dynamic system in which one continually influences the other. To appreciate this interplay 'in action' is difficult as the ideas, perceptions, reactions and recognition of anticipated and unanticipated learning outcomes ebb and flow in response to the stimuli which prompt the thinking. It is fundamental to my view of modelling that this thinking during teaching is overtly demonstrated for my students if they are to fully appreciate the complex nature of learning about teaching; even more so if they are to seriously consider their own practice in relation to my modelling.

Although I have described my thinking about teaching within three distinct periods (pre, post and during a pedagogical experience), clearly all three are linked and related in a complex web of thoughts and actions which are very much context dependent. There is not one route to learning about this thinking about teaching nor is there only one way of demonstrating it to others. The two approaches to learning about this thinking about pedagogy which I have employed in my teaching are journal writing and 'thinking aloud' (Loughran, 1995). The following sections demonstrate how I have used these to help my students better learn about teaching.

Journal Writing

As already noted in Chapter 1, in my pre-service Teaching and Learning class (TAL) I maintain a journal. I use my journal as a tool for reflection and write about my understanding of sessions, my pedagogy and our learning. This writing is then accessible to my students because my journal is passed around the class so that my views become public and so that students can question my thinking (which can lead to very interesting group learning opportunities) or write in my journal in response to my entries. In either case, the use of my journal is one way of allowing my students to better understand my views of our experiences and to use this to reconsider their understanding of those experiences.

I generally write in my journal about: 1) the way I have organized a session and why; 2) how I review a session after it has been taught; and 3) what and/or how I understand a session is going (when appropriate and possible) during a session, as the experience is unfolding. Writing at each of these times is again an attempt to give my students access to these three important times of thinking about teaching. The following examples from one of my journals demonstrates my use of journal writing at these times.

Before the first TAL session of the year:

Ah, here we go again. It's always difficult for me to start a new year because it means a new group of people and all the feelings that accompany that. I still have the strong memory of last year's group and it's hard to start again. How do I build that rapport and sense of openness and honesty with the class? Will it happen again? Even though I know these feelings will pass, it doesn't stop them from coming to the surface at the start of each new year, perhaps I'm just highlighting it now because I'm apprehensive too. What do I come over like to the class? Do they see the purpose in my approach? Does this help them to better understand how my feelings will also influence the class, it's not all them or me, it's made up of all of us. I hope that I can make people feel comfortable yet recognise that they'll be challenged to think carefully about their teaching and learning.

Before TAL session (4 weeks into the course):

Well it's been a little while since I've put pen to paper. Now that camp is over I've got a chance to slow down a little and think about what's been going on and what should be going on. Bill [visiting lecturer] was great last Monday, he is an excellent public speaker who can make a lecture an interesting learning experience (not all that common really is it?), he has a lot to offer. I now have to make sure that I follow up that session in a way that helps the class to capitalise on the learning.

What will I do? What should I do? It's important that I somehow reinforce the notion that as a student-teacher, planning a classroom management strategy is valuable. I'd like to try a few role plays but I know that this early in the course they're a bit risky both for you as learners and me as the teacher, but, I see the benefits of them for learning. Hmm! It'll be interesting to see what I do as I've still got the weekend to think about it . . . at this stage I'm thinking I'll try some discipline scenarios (using a video of critical incidents) and then try to give the class an opportunity to role play their responses. I've got to give them a chance to practice how they will respond, to get the tone and body language right, to feel comfortable practicing it here so that they have a chance of doing it on their first school teaching experience; because it's hard to do it if you haven't had practice and are not aware of how helpful it can be in establishing yourself with a class.

TAL session after the first school teaching experience:

Well it's good to see everyone back. Three weeks away is a long time [first school teaching experience has just been completed]. Anyway, we start learning theory now and I think it's the impetus for you to more actively pursue questioning your approach to teaching.

I'm a little worried about how to start this topic though because it is so important (in my mind) but I don't want my views to dominate, so I think I'd better use some group activities; it's interesting to see that even though I've taught this a number of times, each time it needs to be different in response to what I perceive to be appropriate for the class — you'll be the same (I hope) when you're teaching in school. Groupwork, hmm, that'll keep me quiet and optimize your chances to learn from one another. I want you to be aware of what others think, to know how and why they think they learn, not for me to 'tell' you about it. We'll see what happens.

11.35 a.m. (during the same session): Typical, I've launched into class and I haven't said anything about your tape analysis assignment [assessment task from the first school teaching experience]. Now I'm in trouble because I'll need to squeeze it in before we finish but it'll probably take the edge off this good learning as you refocus on administrivia. Should've remembered to do it first. The group work seems to be going well, it's as if you're involved and on task in ways that don't require my constant attention — good to see. I wonder if you all notice that and can see reasons for it? Is it because I left the task a little vague/open, and/or that you've accepted responsibility for the learning? I really enjoy the atmosphere of teaching in TAL, I hope your classes are like this for you when you're in school.

Before a TAL session second semester of the course; topic is assessment:

I've been worried about this assessment unit, we have allocated a lot of time to it but the structure is difficult. I never know what's right and what isn't. You all have different needs and concerns therefore trying to do a smooth and efficient run through is tough. Also, I'm going to use the essay/paper [that the students themselves had written] as our way into the real-side of marking etc. and that's a bit of a risk, however I want to do it because I think there will be more at stake and people will not view it as just 'another class with John' because it's their work. Also, it'll be more emotional and I'll need to be careful to manage that carefully.

I've got another idea for today's class to build on this too. I wonder how it will go? I'll think about putting it in if it's appropriate, we'll see how the class is going.

Following that session:

That session was really interesting. When they broke up into their groups to do the assessment of the papers, they all did it in different ways. I found it really hard to move from group to group and thought I was intruding each time, it's funny how that happens, I want to know what's going on but not to the detriment of the group's dynamics and their approach to the task; but see how when I as the teacher comes along everyone turns their attention to me? How come? Do you notice that with your classes?

The other thing that amazed me was the number who asked if I knew who had written which paper and if I would mark the papers too. Why does it seem that my approval (if that's the right word) is needed. Here's the dilemma for me as teacher. Some students openly (and I'm pleased they do) tell me that the hurdles [assessment tasks] in the course just have to be done and that they don't take some of it seriously, then in the same breath they want me to judge their efforts. It seems incongruous. What do you think? Anyway, there's a bit more to get through in this unit yet, we'll see how we progress hey?

Student responses:

Student A — Having tried to correct other people's work I found that I dislike this whole approach only because we did not set the 'essay' and therefore how can we assess it? Upon further consideration I also felt that we should have graded the papers only because it would make us justify the mark, not just/only with comments. However, the problems with 'emotions' involved could get out of hand!!

Student B — During the debate you should make sure people put their hands up please John, I was overlooked a couple of times when I had something to say as others butted in, it's not like you to miss me like that, keep an eye on it John, please!

Student C — I found it somewhat artificial — I did not set the task and that was a big problem for me. The fact that I was assessing work, done by peers, on work I *did not teach*, I do not think this is synonymous with my school experience. I would have preferred to be marking the work of another group. I think that would make it far easier to take on the teacher mantle, and assess the work. Within our group, we are all student-teachers at the same stage — I feel the 'student' part could have been highlighted better if the work had come from without our own TAL group.

These excerpts from my journal demonstrate the different thinking associated with my pedagogy in response to the learning within the class. Importantly for me, this is an aspect of learning about teaching that is not often obvious to student-teachers, yet common sense suggests that it should be if learners of teaching are to understand the teaching approaches of experienced practitioners. Therefore, being able to 'view' this thinking is one way of helping my students to better understand the reasons for the teaching approach adopted and to link this to their understanding of the learning which they experience, thus giving them a much better view of both sides of the experience; the teaching and the subsequent student learning.

Through my journal writing, accessing this thinking is useful for my students but it is in a delayed form. In order to give greater access to this thinking in a more immediate way, I also verbalise my thinking during teaching. The thinking aloud which I use in this form is designed to be similar to offering a commentary on my pedagogical reasoning as it is occurring. This then ties the thinking, the pedagogy and the student learning together in the 'action present'. It is difficult to describe how this occurs as it can be both spontaneous (as I respond to the changing learning conditions within the class) and premeditated (as I make changes to my pedagogy that I may have considered possible prior to the lesson). The following example is an attempt to demonstrate how this occurs during my classes. Whilst teaching in the unit on Learning, I may aim to present a particular theoretical perspective on learning, for example White's (1988) seven elements of memory.[1] In so doing, I would hope to help the students come to understand the value of knowing about these in order to reconsider the approach to learning they have been focusing on with their students through their approach to teaching. In many cases student-teachers have an understanding of these seven elements of memory but generally lack the vocabulary to discuss these. Therefore, developing their ability to distinguish between these seven elements in a meaningful way and to relate these to their own approach to classroom practice is important to me.

Before introducing these seven elements of memory, I may consider a number of pedagogical approaches for their introduction. It could be useful to compare students' existing understanding of each of these elements and then to relate these to the 'theoretical' terminology, *or* by using a jigsaw groupwork method allocate each 'expert group' an element or two to learn about and then teach their peers, *or* to attempt to create a situation whereby the students might need to know about the elements in order to complete an associated activity. Each of these possibilities, as well as many others, may be possible as I consider the conditions that might influence my choice; dependent of course on my perception of the problematic situation and how that might favour one approach in preference to another.

As I begin the introduction to the session, I might still be mulling over these options as I get a 'feel' for the needs of the class on that day. As I begin to decide on a particular pedagogical approach, influenced by the particular learning context, I would tell the class about these options, the decisions I make, the factors which influenced these decisions, and why I might have settled on a particular option. This offers my students an opportunity to understand not only how I approach my teaching, but why I might choose to teach content in a particular way at a particular time. However, in many instances, I may well teach in a way that is in accord with my pre-lesson planning. Therefore, my approach to thinking aloud about problematic situations as they arise 'in class', responding to unanticipated situations, takes this thinking aloud to another plane.

In these situations, my students are given immediate access to the thoughts that influence my understanding of my teaching and their learning as it is unfolding. This ranges from my reminders to myself about such things as the use of wait-time or allowing students to respond to issues/questions before I reply, to describing my feelings about the way an activity is influencing students' learning, to difficulties I perceive in the class from either a learning or pedagogical view and the changes I might make in response to this recognition.

Attempting to explain this in writing is difficult as it does not seem to me to really convey the meaning or the context of such events. Perhaps the following example of a vivid episode (in my mind) might help to make this easier to understand. An important aspect of my teaching is to encourage student involvement especially through discussion. On occasions, the topic under consideration might provoke group responses whereby everyone has something to say, but, as in any large group situation, everyone can not speak at once. I remember a session where we were discussing different views of student ability and some of the reasons that accompanied those views. As the discussion developed, I could see that more and more members of the class were frustrated at not being able to respond to others' statements, and that some members of the class had considerably more 'air time' than others. As I began to respond to this situation, I interrupted the discussion by saying that I was dissatisfied with the way the session was evolving, not because of the nature of the discussion but because of the structural or procedural constraints; I was pleased with the content of the debate, but I was not convinced that the format was conducive to good learning. Even though I was not sure what I would do about it, I was verbalizing the feelings that were influencing my thinking. I was able to describe the problem, reason through why it was a problem for me, and hypothesize about the likely outcomes if the discussion continued in the same way. Then, as I verbally sorted through some of the suggestions flashing through my mind which might address the situation, I introduced a different pedagogical approach which I explained as I introduced it and outlined why I was changing the teaching and what I hoped it would achieve. My response was to arrange the class in a circle and ask each member to take out one sheet of paper and to outline their position on the topic in about a paragraph. When this was completed, their sheet of paper was passed on to the person sitting next to them. As each student read and responded in writing to the views expressed on the sheets the whole class were able to voice their opinions, rebut arguments, develop their ideas and better see the cross-section of views of their peers, without having to compete to speak, or miss the opportunity to give their input at an appropriate time. Each class member also ended up with a record of responses to their views.

The introduction of this 'silent discussion' (which Filipa briefly refers to in a journal extract in Chapter 5) was a spontaneous shift in pedagogy in response to a problem situation. By talking aloud about the changes in my pedagogy and the influences on these as they were occurring, my students could see beyond the teaching itself to my reflection on practice which guided and directed the learning in which we were so intensely involved. This episode is one example of my thinking aloud about my teaching 'in action'.

To try and place this modelling in context with my approach to teaching I have included the following vignette. The vignette was constructed from an episode when an external observer, an experienced teacher in the pre-service program, attended my TAL class to ascertain the students' perceptions of my teaching. During the session, he noted a number of instances during the lesson which he thought were interesting examples of my pedagogical approach. The following session, he led the class in my absence and began to explore the students' views of my teaching. This session was audio-taped (from which the vignette is constructed) and the students also completed an open-ended questionnaire. In this follow-up session each of the instances from the previous lesson was individually introduced then discussed by the class. The vignette is designed to give an overview of the type of interaction that occurred in the session. All of the student-teachers' comments are taken from the actual transcript and insights into the observer's thoughts are taken from his notes of the session; he also edited the vignette.

Ascertaining the students' views

The class was unusually reserved. An air of uncertainty was apparent. Dick explained that he was simply trying to work out the class's understanding of John's approach to teaching. 'It's part of his self-study work', he said. 'It's got nothing to do with assessment of you or John.'

He turned on the overhead projector and placed the first transparency in position. It outlined an episode from the previous session. Much had been made of the gap between learning theory, which was the last unit before the school teaching experience, and the student-teachers' approaches to teaching. The transparency also had two questions. Why do you think John did/said this, and, do you actually learn anything from John's approaches?

The students gradually relaxed and opened up. They discussed the difference between knowing what a theory was and how it could be used to influence their teaching practice. Nigel said that he thought John was trying to hint that they needed to pay more attention to the concepts taught in class. Dorothy said that it showed how quickly students forget what they learn. Jack concluded that it highlighted the importance of learning for all of them. The discussion helped the class to loosen-up, they were warming to Dick and their early concerns began to subside.

Dorothy started to answer question one as Dick read it out. 'We are like the kids', she said, 'and he wants us to remember what it's like.' Anthony agreed saying, 'He'd had us all going through learning theory for several weeks and he didn't want us to just take it as something we were told. He feels that it's important and that we should see that it's important. I think he realizes and understands how it affects a student's learning, and he got the feeling that we didn't, so he was trying to get us to think about it again.'

Dick paraphrased the discussion to check that his understanding of the students' views was correct. 'So you're saying that John thinks this will help you teach better?' he said. Nick could barely stop himself from responding, 'What he's doing is telling us that it's not enough to know them, we need to know how to apply them,' he blurted. 'Yes, and it's actually that we couldn't do it, that's what he wanted us to see,' said Cleo.

Then Peggy made a statement which Dick latched on to. He'd been waiting for something that would give him a chance to explore John's purpose from the students' perspective. He couldn't believe his good fortune. Peggy said that John wanted them to think about the different ways of learning when planning a lesson. It triggered numerous responses throughout the group. Like a hunter stalking its prey he quizzed and probed skilfully as their understanding unravelled before him. Pearl spoke about the link between reflection and action and how her journal was important in easing the tension between the two. 'It helps you to look back and to think about what you did and why. There is no specific answer, but you have to keep trying', she said.

'Reflection and thinking all in one breath', he thought. 'This will be a good way to explore their understanding of the terms. And I didn't have to introduce it!' He asked for definitions of the terms. Nigel interjected with a line about self-evaluation, Jack said it had to do with asking yourself questions after, or perhaps even during, an event. Someone from the back of the class thought it had to do with suggesting alternative strategies. Then Perry posed a question that had been running through his mind for some time. 'So did John plan to highlight the problem that way or not?' he asked.

Dick explained how he and John had decided that the lesson after the school teaching experience would be a good one to observe but that he did not know how John had planned to teach the lesson. His opinion was that John wanted to show the importance of the links between a number of things from the course and the students' teaching but that he did not have in mind how he might specifically do it.

This opened up a major discussion on what the students thought John might or might not do when planning and running a session, how he might respond in different situations, and why he used various teaching strategies. Through this discussion Dick started to shape a scenario of his own.

'Well let's look at this next example,' he said placing another transparency on the overhead. 'When did John come up with that one?' Nigel, always quick to say his piece, said that it was spontaneous. Mitchell, while agreeing with Nigel, proposed a reason to support the spontaneous hypothesis. 'John wanted to link the two. He believed in those seven elements of learning [White, 1988] and he said early on that it's important and we'd be returning to them. I think his definition of a good teacher would be a thinking teacher. That's what he was doing. He saw an opening and he took it', he said.

Dick moved on saying, 'So does John force you to think or reflect?' The word force was of concern to all. Nadine thought that it was not so much a force as a suggestion or encouragement. Sabina suggested that challenge might be more appropriate than force. Jack was not so concerned with the term as the meaning. 'He tries to make us accept responsibility, to see the value', he said. The discussion continued for some time as Dick tried to give everyone an opportunity to speak, always hoping to involve the whole group. He decided to move on to his next question just as Marg said, 'He gives us tasks to do to make us think. After our school teaching experiences he gets us to write down things like, 'three things that I've learnt from this experience', and it's really difficult because during the school experience you don't really think about it, like he forces us to think when we come back here.' Dick seized the opportunity to make the transition between 'what' and 'why' as he carefully posed the next question.

'Do you have to do it? He might push you to, but he won't fail you if you don't do it. Will he?' he said with an inquiring tone. Stephen had not said anything in the session up 'til now so Dick was more than pleased when he picked up the non-verbal cue that Stephen had something to say. 'He doesn't force us, we force ourselves because we see him and the way he thinks so we should be able to learn from it too.' This was just what Dick was looking for. A chance to explore the reasons for their actions. He knew he was on the right track when Cleo said, 'The responses he puts in the journals are what make you want to do it. It's a relationship, it's not just the sort of teacher he is.'

Cleo's statement led to a great deal of discussion about the use of journals and the role that they played in making her think. But Dick had another issue to resolve. How could he determine whether or not what he was hearing was simply students defending their teacher, saying what they thought Dick wanted to hear. He needed to find a way of resolving this in his mind without making it obvious to the students what he was pursuing.

'I wonder', he started to say, 'how you see John's role in all of this? Why he's doing it?' The words came slowly as he searched through the sea of faces for signs that his question made sense; the wait-time increased.

Someone said something about learning but the point was lost as Perry spoke over her. He had volunteered to be interviewed throughout the course and was sure that John was trying to work out the effect of DipEd on their learning. 'It's also got something to do with how our perceptions change with time,' said Pearl. 'He hasn't really told us anything,' Peggy added. 'Actually, I'm one who he interviews too and I think he just wants to hear our responses to different things,' said Sabina. 'Why, is there a problem? Is this an issue?'

Dick was a little taken-a-back by how quickly the focus had come back to him so he felt obliged to explain. 'Well', he started slowly, 'it's a matter of validity.' The puzzled faces looking back at him gave him a sense of unease. 'You might write or say what John wants to hear.' Sabina closed the debate by saying that the interviews and their journals were dependent on the rapport that they had developed. It did not make any sense to say other than what they thought because it wouldn't serve any purpose. Anthony brought things back on an even keel by saying, 'Rather than giving you an answer he often asks you a question back. So you'd end up trying to answer things that you didn't believe anyway. You'd be going round and round in circles.' This brought a smile to most faces and a gentle wave a laughter wafted across the room.

Dick drew his breath and gently exhaled. He shuffled through some more of his papers and started to hand out a questionnaire which he spent some time explaining to the class. 'So, could you think about these, fill them in and I'll take them as you leave. If you've got any questions please don't hesitate to ask,' he said as he wandered around the room.

Perry, never one to miss an opportunity for a quick wisecrack, threw his hand up and quipped, 'So, will John pass?' Dick chuckled and said, 'Well we'll wait and see hey?' as the class started to work their way through the questionnaire.

The vignette is designed to demonstate the students' general perception of my teaching and is important for understanding the context and views that are expressed in Chapter 4. The questionnaire comprised three statements, each of which respondents were asked to rate by placing: a double tick next to the one which was most often the case, and a single tick for those that had occurred at sometime throughout the year. For each statement, an open-ended response was also sought. The numerical results associated with each of the three statements is outlined in Table 3.1.

Table 3.1: Questionnaire results

Statements	double tick	single tick	no tick
He makes me think and is confusing.	1	9	9
He makes me think and is helpful.	18	1	0
He does not make me think.	0	2	17

Table 3.2: Themes from the open-ended responses on the questionnaire

Statement	Reason suggested	Number of responses
He makes me think and is confusing, and/or, he makes me think and is helpful.	Thinking about myself	4
	Thinking about DipEd	2
	Confusion leads to reassessment of thinking	3
	Thinking about what/how I learn	9
	Thinking about how others learn	6
	Thinking about teaching or teaching strategies	15
	Thinking about students	2
	Thinking about the way John teaches	2
He does not make me think.	Does not challenge me enough about my students' reactions	1
	Does not make me think deeply enough	1

The open-ended responses to these questions demonstrate a wide range of reasons. Confusion (statement 1) is particularly interesting because it is seen as something positive. For many of the student-teachers who marked this statement, being confused was a precursor to sorting out the issue at hand. Therefore, confusion may encourage thinking, or be an outcome of it.

Tables 3.1 and 3.2 (Table 3.2 summarizes the themes from the open-ended responses proposed by the participants) both demonstrate that the student-teachers readily recognized the thinking and learning approaches I used in their TAL sessions. They appear to be adequately challenged by the pedagogical approaches used and were clearly thinking about their own teaching and learning. Interestingly, at this stage of the course (nearing the end of the first half of the academic year) only two respondents (Table 3.2) stated that my teaching caused them to think about the way I teach. The majority of responses are concerned with how they think, act, learn and teach.

Summary

This chapter has been written to demonstrate my approach to teaching as well as my modelling of the thinking which accompanies my teaching. So that my student-teachers better understand the thoughts which accompany my pedagogy, I actively pursue ways of demonstrating my reflection on practice through both journal writing and thinking aloud. This offers an opportunity for my students to draw their own conclusions about my teaching, but more importantly, about the factors which shape my teaching. From my perspective, I consider that this thinking aloud highlights for my students my use of reflection, while still allowing them to form their own views about its value to my practice. Therefore, they are able to make their own decisions about the extent to which they might actively develop reflection themselves, and how they might incorporate it into their own developing practice.

Note

1 White (1988) describes the seven elements of memory: propositions, strings, images, episodes, intellectual skills, motor skills, cognitive strategies. Each of these different elements of memory influence one's understanding by the nature of the knowledge developed through these, how they are, for example, accessed, synthesized and processed. The greater the cross-section of these employed in learning about 'content' the greater the likelihood that an understanding of the content will be able to be utilized in different contexts. Knowing the *what* of sublimation is very different from knowing *why* it occurs or *how* it is involved in phenomenon like that which occurs when dry ice is added to water.

Chapter 4

Perceptions of Actions: Student-teachers' Understanding of the Practice of Modelling Reflection

Introduction

My view of modelling was that through my teaching and my thinking about teaching I could demonstrate that I purposefully reflected on my own practice and that this would show, by example, something of the processes involved for me. Aside from my 'normal classroom behaviour', the student-teachers had the opportunity to 'see' my thinking through my journal. Also, after their first school teaching experience, I started to verbalize my thoughts about my pedagogy and my pedagogical reasoning in class in an attempt to give them greater (and more immediate) access to my thinking. This became an explicit act of modelling which was continued for the rest of the course. In essence, I was giving the student-teachers opportunities to hear the thoughts and ideas that influenced my actions as they occurred. When I had been reflecting about a session, I would introduce those thoughts to the class in the next session. Therefore, any of the suggestions, problems, hypotheses, reasoning or resultant testing I had been considering was open to public scrutiny; although I did not use those terms with my student-teachers. My reflection could be initiated by preparing for a session, during, or after a session. It was not uncommon for me to write in my journal during a session about what I thought was happening and why, how it matched my expectations and plans, and how it might influence my subsequent classes. More overtly, I commonly thought aloud about what I was doing, the decisions I was making and why. This was particularly so if I thought the session was not meeting the learning needs of the class. I felt that these actions would model my reflection on practice. This chapter is therefore designed to examine my student-teachers' perceptions of my modelling of reflection as well as their views of its purpose and value to them.

Modelling Reflection

Nine volunteers from my TAL class were interviewed during the year. The first interview was soon after the start of the course, the other three followed immediately after each of their school teaching experiences.

As stated earlier it was not until the session after the first school teaching experience (pre-interview 2) that I started to articulate my pedagogical thoughts and reasoning in class. Until then, I had imagined that my journal was the only observable link between my thoughts and actions. Therefore, the fact that six of the nine student-teachers interviewed spoke about modelling in their first interview is intriguing. However, this may in part be attributed to the considerable shift in teaching style in the pre-service program compared to the more formal lecture style of their undergraduate experiences.

Choosing an appropriate time to explain that I would be 'thinking out loud' and my purpose for doing so was important. I had to have a sense of trust in the class and they with me otherwise my behaviour could appear to be peculiar rather than purposeful. There was a danger that talking aloud about what I was or was not doing, and why, could be interpreted as lacking appropriate direction. This could be exacerbated by the fact that many beginning teachers enter the course believing they can be told how to teach. It could be a risk which might compromise my supposed 'expert' position as someone responsible for teaching teachers.

Oddly enough, as Andrea illustrates, the memory of the introduction and explanation of this practice was not particularly strong in the minds of some of the student-teachers.

Andrea:	*2nd interview*
Interviewer:	You've been watching me teach, do any ideas or thoughts pop into your head?
Andrea:	Well, you're self-explanatory.
Interviewer:	What do you mean?
Andrea:	Well, every second sentence is we're doing this because of such and such a reason, and do you understand why we're doing it, and if we don't you explain it. See, I think you think aloud a lot.
Interviewer:	What do you think of that?
Andrea:	I think you can do it because of the group we are, but I don't think you can do that in class. It's OK for you to do it in the sense that we should do this or we should do that but in a class it's up to the teacher, the person up front to decide where the class is leading to.
Interviewer:	So why do you think I do that?
Andrea:	I don't really know. I know you've explained it but it hasn't stuck.
Interviewer:	Have I always done it?
Andrea:	No. You started when we came back from the first round, and I think you even said from now on I'll be thinking aloud on what we should be doing.

Andrea shows that modelling reflection in this manner is not a problem to her. In fact, it has been assimilated into the teaching role and 'taken for granted' as acceptable in the context of TAL. However, she also signals that there is some confusion in her mind about my purpose. My actions are acceptable for demonstrating my thinking in class, but this is not something that she sees as possible to do in her own teaching. She is not really sure why I think aloud. At this stage Andrea has not fully grasped the difference between my efforts to model reflecting about learning to teach, and her efforts at teaching during her teaching experiences. Thinking aloud in her classes would be a major concern for her. Therefore, recognition of modelling is attained but understanding the purpose is not so simple. Over time, Andrea starts to re-structure her thinking about this modelling so that the purpose becomes clearer to her.

Andrea:	*3rd interview*

Interviewer:	What sorts of things pop into your head when I'm teaching?
Andrea:	I like your teaching, I always come back. I think it's entertaining and I think it's informative and it just makes me think about the way you teach. The way you present your points, and always give both sides even if you're biased.
Interviewer:	Do you think I think about my teaching?
Andrea:	Before [a class], you always come in with how you would like to teach, how you'd like the class to go but you always seem to change your mind. You're never sure of how to do it.
Interviewer:	What tells you that?
Andrea:	You do. You say I don't know how to do this or I'm in a bind I don't know what to do?
Interviewer:	What does that mean to you?
Andrea:	I just think that the material can be presented in many ways and you don't know which way we'd prefer.
Interviewer:	Does that worry you?
Andrea:	No. You do it because you explained it at the start of second term that you would always be saying out loud what you were thinking, just showing us how the class changes direction even though you've gone in one direction you change it, how your mind keeps working and how you see things and how you alter them to suit the class that day or whatever.

Andrea:	*4th interview*

Andrea:	You say things out loud when you're thinking all the time, through your journal, that's another way of seeing what you're thinking. Just the way your lesson goes, how you structure it. You always ask for our opinion and you just analyse how the class goes, you sit up the front and you say I've got this to do but I don't know which way I'm going

> to do it . . . maybe I'm [also] doing it sub-consciously, thinking to myself [about] how a class is going. I suppose it does [happen with me] because if I hadn't seen it done maybe I wouldn't think in my classes how is this class reacting, maybe I should change the pace of how this lesson is going.

The development of Andrea's understanding of the purpose of modelling demonstrates that time is a necessary and important component for it to be successfully established in her mind. She shows how the modelling process has slowly led her to think about reflection on her own practice. By the fourth interview (post third school teaching experience) she is starting to recognize that her own actions are being influenced by her reflection on practice. It has taken until almost the end of the course for her to come to understand my purpose for the modelling process.

How each member of the class understood this process of modelling varied throughout the year. For some, modelling was initially seen as demonstrating some of the technical aspects of teaching (similar to van Manen's, 1977, first level of reflectivity) such as wait-time, questioning techniques or withholding judgment. Those who held this view cited examples of modelling in terms of remembering 'handy tips'.

Miranda: *2nd interview*

Interviewer: So you've been watching me teach. What sorts of questions or ideas pop into your head when you're watching me teach?

Miranda: I wonder sometimes, if you'd actually teach a Year 9 science class the way you teach us. Your style is very easy going and I don't know how a younger class would cope with that. I think it's good now that you tell us your processes of thinking. Like we're in a discussion and you say things like bad wait time John, and that's good because it helps to make us conscious of them. I wasn't very good at it on teaching rounds, and I noticed it on the tape [tape-analysis of a lesson*], even though we'd been over it in class, but by you doing it, I'm much more conscious of it and you must say it twice a lesson now, not that I'm counting; that's one example. So I'm much more conscious of these things now and I hope that next time on rounds I'm better at it.

   (*The tape analysis is a TAL assignment task where students audio-tape a lesson during their teaching round and analyse their use of language, questioning skills, etc.)

In a similar vein, modelling also helped to build confidence. It demonstrated that teaching is a complex task and that actions and outcomes do not always reflect that which was intended. So, for some it showed that teachers at all levels face similar problems and that things did not always go 'smoothly' or 'according to plan'. In this case it modelled the reality of not just thinking about teaching but also the teaching itself.

Sarah: *3rd interview*

Sarah: I don't know [pause] your expression changes, or something in your mannerism but there's something that comes across that you're rethinking what you're doing like perhaps your expression might change for a minute or so but you're concentrating on something else and I take it for granted then [that] when you're concentrating on something else you're revising your game plan so to speak.

Interviewer: If I do those sorts of things then what does it mean for you, for your teaching?

Sarah: ... sometimes I think that you're changing tack and I think aha, he's our tutor but he's got the same struggles that we have, he's not infallible so we don't have to be either. So when I'm in a school and I see things not going so well, I have every right to change tack, it doesn't make me a better person or something it's just that it'll be good for the students, they'll learn as much if not more, it's just a confidence boost for me.

For others, understanding involved recognition that reflection on practice was an important element in learning and thinking about teaching. Modelling reflective practice was a way of offering opportunities for others to reflect on this learning process. But, as Jack states, it is only an opportunity, and as such is an invitation, not a directive.

Jack: *3rd interview*

Jack: Well when you talk in class about what you're thinking it helps to demonstrate to us that you're reflective.

Interviewer: Why do I bother to go about it the way I do?

Jack: Because it's something we have to discover for ourselves and see for ourselves, it's not something that you can just give us. You can help us but you can't just tell us you have to reflect, you have to do it in more subtle ways.

For Pearl, modelling highlighted ways of revisiting her own practice. It gave her the chance to reconsider her actions, to reconceptualize her problems and to think about different ways of testing her hypotheses.

Pearl: *3rd interview*

Pearl: With my year 11s I was particularly disappointed, they relied on me, they looked to me all the time so I was interested, when I came back from the last round, to see how you coped with it with us. I think [what you do] is sometimes there's a lot more [that] could come up but it would be in conflict [with what we're doing] and I think you make judgments about those things and close them down, also to stop us getting too sidetracked. Also, with some of the personalities you do it to stop things going too far, that's not a bad thing, but you think about it. It's good that we get beyond the surface things and that doesn't happen much outside, maybe only one or two people do it. It's good that you point out all of the different things that are happening, I still find that very useful . . .

Modelling for Perry was a way of looking into the relationship between reflection and action from the teacher's perspective. It highlighted for him the need to carefully consider the alternative approaches (suggestions) possible in a pedagogical experience, and how they might offer different routes of accessibility to the learner.

Perry: *4th interview*

Perry: . . . you reflect constantly and put diligent work into it.
Interviewer: What tells you that?
Perry: The fact that you sit down and prepare for class and worry about it, and it's structured and there are a lot of hidden things woven into the fabric of the lesson, you've got lots of escape hatches and doors and things to move onto, yet there's still the flexibility there that if something's working well, then we'll use more of the lesson. Also, you show that there is a sense of purpose, you say let's move on now and the subtle message is we're moving in a direction [for a reason].

Finally, Sabina intimates that modelling reflection does not necessarily present her with 'answers' to her questions. Rather, it empowers her to explore and question matters more fully than may have otherwise been the case. Hence, in her own way she is suggesting that there is a reflective cycle and that resolving a problem is part of a process, not just an end in itself.

Sabina: *4th interview*

Sabina: TAL's taught me to reflect on different aspects of teaching that I might not perhaps have reflected on on such a level, I don't think it's taught me any answers. Which I don't think is a bad thing. Sometimes I just feel a little bit bamboozled, just not being able to accept anything as valid but to question everything and I think that's really hard . . . a concrete example of the way you've tried to show us that you're reflective is by the way you write your journal and distribute it around. It's not the most important part of the way you show us that you reflect, I think the most important way for me is the way you prompt us in the class to question our thinking, the way you speak out aloud about your thinking which shows us that you are reflecting on what you do. But now having just said that, now remembering how we do read your journal in class we can see how what you say out loud you go on further to develop in your journal. And some of the activities, I suppose, forces us to think. It's quite interesting watching you in class sometimes like I noticed from the beginning of the year to the end of the year now, sometimes you just sit back and let the class run itself and you gauge whether you need to be there [involved in the discussion] and when the class needs your input.

The quotations above demonstrate how it became 'taken for granted' that modelling reflection was part of my teaching practice. Although there was some initial confusion about my purpose, I believe that by the end of the course all of my student-teachers had a good understanding of why I was talking aloud about my teaching and of my approach to journal writing. However, how this modelling influenced their thinking about learning to teach varied. This could be attributed to the fact that 'telling' does not in itself lead to learning and this dictum influenced my approach to modelling such that I rarely (if ever) admonished the class to 'reflect'. Instead I chose to model its use through my practice. By adopting this approach my student-teachers were given the opportunity to accept or reject the use of reflection in their own practice, and to incorporate its use in ways which they saw as appropriate. Inevitably then, individuals drew their own conclusions about the process in their own time.

By the end of the year, it was clear that my TAL class recognized that my modelling of reflection was designed to highlight an often hidden and somewhat implicit aspect of teaching. But the path to understanding was constructed differently by each individual. This is not meant to imply that the participants were unable to reflect on their practice without it being modelled. Rather it highlighted the processes for them and subtly challenged their understanding of the use of reflection on practice.

Stephen: *4th interview*

Interviewer: Do you think you'd have considered reflection in this way if you were in a different class?

Stephen: No I don't think I would've identified it. I guess the fact that you've said this is reflection and you've been through it now I think hey I've been doing that but it's just been sort of done without putting much effort into it, now I do and I recognize it as reflection time and developing it rather than it just being something you can do.

Modelling reflection on practice gave the student-teachers an opportunity to see how it may be used to shape learning about teaching, and teaching practice.

Valuing Reflection

For many of my student-teachers, making sense of what they were experiencing (overt modelling) raised a number of questions. Is reflection a personal characteristic found in some people but not others? Do these personal characteristics therefore govern the use of reflection? Does reflection on practice make for a 'better' teacher? How much does experience influence the ability to reflect on practice? Questions such as these were raised by them in their interviews. Their answers influenced their understanding of the value they placed on reflection. Also, as in the case of modelling, it was difficult for some to disentangle the actions from the individual. I was both their tutor and the researcher and, in one sense, this made it difficult to determine that which was being valued. Although this was not always apparent, it did sometimes seem as though the distinction between me as a person and me as a reflective practitioner was blurred. Although it was widely accepted that I was a reflective practitioner, for some it was more a matter of that being my style of teaching rather than as something that could be applied to teaching generally. This point is demonstrated by Andrea.

Andrea:	*2nd interview*
Andrea:	This is a different field for me, because in my Degree and even in HSC [final year of high school] my classes have been on the board with a lecture, you're given the theory or a prac. sheet and then you do it. Whereas these classes [TAL] are all new to me. I've never been in class discussions where opinions and views are thrown around so I really can't compare it, it's new. It's something I haven't done for years.
Interviewer:	Is that the same in all of your classes?
Andrea:	Don't ask me to compare you to [another teaching method lecturer]. I can't compare it. In TAL I can see the purpose of it, in [the other teaching method] I think they're wasting my time.
Interviewer:	What makes it that way?
Andrea:	Well it is presented in the lecture form, you hear it, you

> see it, it's up to you to apply it. You don't see it applied or
> used. It's really hard to compare to TAL, they're just two
> different things.

Understanding that teaching is purposeful and goes beyond conveying information can, as in Andrea's case, be in conflict with prior experiences. Therefore, the
consequent value placed on the learning outcomes may be interpreted as a result
of the teaching style, not the reflective underpinnings to the practice. Hence, for
Andrea, she initially found this quite difficult. In fact, this led her to compare
individuals and their teaching style rather than the possible reasons for it. The
transcript demonstrates that (at this early stage in the course) she values what is
being done but does not recognize why it is occurring.

On the other hand, Jack readily acknowledges and recognizes the value of
having reflection modelled. He quite clearly sees a purpose for the exercise and
how it applies to learning about teaching. His understanding of the value of reflection is different to Andrea's. Even at this early stage (2nd interview) Jack is capable
of abstracting from learning and thinking about teaching to teaching itself. He has
no difficulty in differentiating between the reflective processes and me as a person.
He views the modelling of reflection as a way of understanding pedagogy and dis-
tinguishes this from personal attributes.

Jack: 2nd interview

Jack: You tend to forget that you need to do that [reflect] as a teacher,
        so it [modelling] highlights it a bit more, the decisions and what
        you're doing. It'll get us thinking about the decisions that you have
        to make in front of the class so it's maybe not as new to us when
        that situation comes on us when we're teaching. You are always
        stressing the fact that you do have to be thinking when you're a
        teacher as well, that's one of the things you're stressing, you have
        to always be analysing, deciding, making judgments . . . I can see
        you looking around, thinking into space, it's hard to see that with
        other people. You're more aware of those sort of things, you let us
        know you're more aware. I think it's a valuable thing. Also, by you
        opening up and telling us what you're thinking, it helps our rela-
        tionship with you it makes us feel more comfortable because we
        know that you're opening up to us so we can as well, that's one
        part of it apart from the fact that it emphasizes that you should be
        thinking.

The value Jack placed on reflection continued to develop throughout the course.
He incorporated reflection into both his teaching and his learning. He genuinely
believed that if he reflected on his teaching it could lead to better learning outcomes
for his students.

Jack: 3rd interview

Jack: . . . it means my teaching will be better for it [reflection] because you're more in tune with what's happening, what your kids are learning. It's not easy during a lesson because there's so much to think about. You've got to make time to reflect and not to have the pressure on you all the time as the focus.

He also believed that the use of reflection could enhance the quality of his own learning.

Jack: *4th interview*

Jack: There are so many different ways to learn, you learn by listening to people and by looking at things, you learn by doing it in a manual sort of way, often you learn when something just sort of hits you but it's not a conscious effort like something stimulates you like the light bulb flashes. I think I do tend, once it's happened initially, I do try to reflect on it, it usually happens, whether that's a case of reading over my notes, sometimes it's by asking some questions or doing some reading, I think I've done that a bit it reinforces it I often reflect on it a couple of times on some things, to help reinforce it, particularly if it's something difficult. I quite like to read too, and I often try to read if I don't understand something because I like to learn it in my own time. I think I've made more of an effort to try and analyse things more at the time this year probably through your coaching it's happened to an extent but I'm still working on that.

Interviewer: What sorts of things have prompted you to do that?

Jack: Your encouragement and your comments in my journal and things like that, and through that my recognition that that is probably a better way to optimise my learning, because then you have two exposures to it so you can analyse your reflections more than once. I do ask myself lots of questions and I've come to recognize that this year.

Jack's incorporation of reflection into his practice is an explicit example of valuing reflection. He demonstrates a fine understanding of the value of having reflection modelled, and how that influences his teaching and learning.

Reflection was most commonly valued as a learning about teaching tool. All spoke about the relationship between modelling and its value for demonstrating how they could apply it to their own practice. They felt that this was important because it helped them to focus more on some of the mechanics of teaching. This seemed to be reinforced by my thinking out loud. Many saw this as a 'self-correcting' process and something that was a teaching skill that they could use.

Miranda: *4th interview*

Miranda: ... after you've done something you might consider that you could've done it differently and you tell us. I think it's important because we have to kind of be into the process of thinking that way ourselves, we probably won't say that to a class, but I think you have ... I think it, whether we're conscious of it or not, we, oh well I have, started to do the same thing. I mean I've sat there in class and asked a question and thought oh no I shouldn't have done that and I find myself looking back on things that I've done at school or on the last teaching round or a week ago or something and thinking about how things worked then, if they did or didn't work and how I could change them. Just going back and reflecting on what I've done in the past.

Pearl: *2nd interview*

Pearl: ... it [modelling] has a lot of impact on how I think I should teach, whether you can actually see that in my teaching I'm not sure. Yeah it has an impact, it makes me think about how I should change my stuff, but that actually doing it is different. But it's given more examples or possibilities about how to do something so I've got more practical examples of saying well perhaps I could use this or. ...

Sarah: *3rd interview*

Sarah: Well for one thing I had a class that wasn't going well, I had split them up into groups and it wasn't going well, and I thought to myself well it doesn't really matter if I change my plan because it's probably better for them to work on their own anyway so just the fact that I'd think back to perhaps you changing your tack or whatever, and you've said a few times that this hasn't gone the way I've wanted it to go, but I've seen that by doing that it hasn't hurt the class at all but I haven't been put off by thinking no this isn't working I'll change it, I mean it hasn't fazed me in a way that I've thought oh no, the rest of my class is going to be awful.

The value of reflection for these student-teachers is that it gives them the confidence to test their hypotheses about their teaching and their students' learning. They are able to think about what they are doing and why, and reason through their problems so that their pedagogy is more appropriate to the given situation.

This practical application of reflection is interesting and is a common and concrete form of valuing reflection, particularly when confronted by something new. The need to understand the mechanics of the situation precedes an under-standing, and valuing, of some of the more abstract principles. An interesting aspect of this though is raised by Nigel's perspective. He was a part-time student who was in my TAL class as an 'additional extra'. As a part-time student, he was not involved in school teaching experience because that part of the program fol-lowed in the second year of the course, hence his understanding was associated with a major lack of classroom experience. Therefore, he generally spoke about what might be possible rather than what he would do, and again underpinned the importance of classroom teaching experience as a crucial aspect of learning to teach, and said how important it is that such experience is a concurrent component within the teacher education program.

To be able to value reflection most likely requires teaching experiences that challenge the individual beyond just coping with classroom management or control. There needs to be a focus on the pedagogy which transcends the transmission of factual information. This was demonstrated at two levels. First, with the exception of Nigel, all of the student-teachers felt that they were beyond simply surviving in the classroom. Therefore, their concerns shifted (see Figure 6.1, p. 87) from con-cerns about self to concerns about the task of teaching. Because they had some teaching experience they valued new ways of viewing their work. This was how they saw reflection, as a tool to analyse their teaching.

Perry: 2nd interview

Perry: Well in TAL you encourage us to question and reflect on your teaching so that when we go out and we get out of that survival mode type of thing that we try and improve on some aspect of our teaching ... that's what I believe you're on about, I don't know if it's verbal, but that's what I believe it's on about.

The second level of this approach is linked to the breadth of experience necessary to act on the problems recognized through reflection. Having had some teaching experience and being concerned with how they were 'performing' poses a dilemma due to the limited range of suggestions possible from their own experience. They are not 'experienced' teachers with an array of ways to teach particular content, therefore their suggestions are limited and this affects their ability to test their hypotheses.

Sabina: 3rd interview

Sabina: I know that I'd like to be a flexible teacher and that's what it [value of reflection] is. But I think it's something that's going to take a little while to achieve, I have to be comfortable with the curriculum, I think it would depend on the school and lots of other things.

By the same token though, the exploration of appropriate pedagogy in context (i.e., type of school, students, content, etc.) is not linear. It is not a search for an end-point, more so a search for understanding. The value of reflection is something greater than the ability to devise and conduct a good lesson. Sabina attempts to articulate this point during her third interview.

Sabina: *3rd interview*

Sabina: I've seen teachers in lots of different areas, I think you reflect on your teaching. I don't think that — I don't want to name names — in some other subject areas that people reflect because if the strategies haven't had any affect they haven't been altered. Yet, other lecturers here are so secure in the way they teach something to DipEd students that they think they have the teaching experience so they know what they're on about so I don't think they can reflect very much or that if they do it doesn't show in their teaching . . . in schools I think quite a few teachers do reflect on their teaching, they might not have a great deal of time to sit down and analyse in depth but they reflect on the success or failure of what they were doing in their classroom and I think that will reflect on how they teach future units, even if it's just to do with the curriculum. Like if it's English and it's a book and it gets a poor reaction then there's no way that you'd set it again, you'd look for an alternative, if the kids don't engage in the text then it's pointless just hashing it to pieces. I think some teachers remember the things that were successful in the classroom, they do try to use them again. Then I had one example of a teacher who said come and watch this whiz-bang lesson and it was, it was a great lesson getting Year 7 into poetry. But I thought he's got that really set in his mind how to teach that, it works for him and it works really well and the kids gain a lot from it but I think he probably teaches that to the Year 7s year in year out, that's his one good lesson. You just wonder how much reflection's gone into that . . . [then musing to herself] is it necessary to reflect on everything. If it's successful, why change it?

One possible difficulty related to how the student-teachers understood reflection and thus valued it, is that I never outlined any of the fundamental or philosophical underpinnings to my view of reflection. I did not ever give a formal definition of the term, nor did I outline any of the major theoretical conceptions of a reflect-ive cycle, e.g., Dewey (1933) or Schön (1983). Rather, I left the development of understanding to the individual and attempted to rely on modelling as the most important form of teaching about reflection. Any form of valuing that was implicit in my student-teachers' conception of reflection was interwoven with their under-standing of reflection itself. For me, this ensured that I was genuinely learning about how my student-teachers learnt from my modelling of reflective practice. They did not have an explicit and well-defined research protocol to follow that might encourage them to tell me what they thought I might like to hear. Consequently, Perry's statement during his fourth interview is a fitting way of demonstrating that reflection and the modelling of reflection was indeed valued by the participants in this group.

Perry:	*4th interview*
Perry:	... I like to watch you in TAL you're more interesting than what's going on, just watching you thinking what am I going to do here, which area am I going to go on with now, how long will we spend on this task, how many people have finished, people are getting fidgety, others are still reading, this is working, this isn't working, where to from here. All of those are sort of obvious, but then when you're doing your own teaching you've got to sort of go back and say well what worked here and what didn't? How much time should I spend on this, am I going down the right track, is there a better way I can present it etc. So they happen, and I guess that's the reason that I reflect is that I can see the value in it.
Interviewer:	Where do you see the value in it?
Perry:	By improving and by learning about teaching, and teaching about learning. So the reason I reflect is for personal growth plus professional development. They're the two areas that I see as reflection, because once something's over if you can gain something from what went before then there has to be an advantage I suppose, that's where I see reflection.

Summary

This chapter was designed to understand my student-teachers' perspectives on modelling and valuing reflection. The transcripts demonstrate that modelling of reflection is an appropriate and valuable way of highlighting this aspect of teaching and that it can be successfully incorporated into learning about teaching. They also show that the value of both the modelling and the act of reflection are closely linked to a student-teacher's school-teaching experiences and again reinforces the view that quality learning occurs through reflection on one's own experiences.

Part 3

Exploring Student-teachers' Thinking

Chapter 5

Recognizing Reflection

Background

Schön (1983) and Yinger (1990) recognized the 'reflective conversation' — the responsive interchange between thinking and acting — as an insight into reflective practice. This reflective conversation can be regarded as an entrée to the data of reflective practice. But how might this reflective conversation be documented, and how might such thoughts be recorded? In this case, I have attempted to document the conversation of reflective practice by using:

- my student-teachers' journals
- my journal
- transcripts from individual interviews with student-teachers
- transcripts from an interview-video-interview cycle of my student-teachers teaching, then jointly reviewing the process with them.

The basis for the analysis of the reflective conversation documented throughout this book is therefore derived from these sources as supplied by the student-teacher participants as they progressed through their one year pre-service education course. In order to understand the substance of my students' 'reflective conversation' I have focused on four major topics:

1. what the student-teachers wrote about, the concerns or issues which prompted them to reflect
2. Dewey's (1933) attitudes of open-mindedness, responsibility and whole-heartedness
3. Dewey's (1933) elements of reflection: suggestions, problem, hypothesis, reasoning and testing
4. when reflection occurred in relation to the episode which initiated it.

Consequently, the reflective conversations documented here illustrate the presence in context (the topics that prompted the writing) of the three attitudes and instances of the reflective cycle from the student-teachers' thoughts and actions.

What the Students Wrote About

The total number of topics discussed by the students in their journals was twenty-seven. The topics have been collapsed and grouped so that similar issues could be listed together. These common groupings are categorized in the following manner:

1. issues initiated as a result of considering specific topics in the course
2. issues initiated by concerns about self
3. issues initiated by concerns about classroom teaching
4. issues initiated by concerns about learning.

Adopting this structure offers opportunities to view trends or relationships so that such documentation over the extended period of the pre-service course (one full academic year) highlights the shifts in the student-teachers' concerns (in a manner similar to Fuller, 1969; Gunstone and Mackay, 1975; Fuller and Bown, 1975), as well as changes in their writing emphasis such as from the empirical (Kemmis and McTaggart, 1988) to the phenomenological (Oberg, 1990). It also allows the possibility to explore relationships between topics and student-teachers' attitudes and/or reflective processes.

In order to see how my student-teachers' reflective skills were developing throughout the course, I decided to apply Dewey's (1933) framework to their reflective conversations in an attempt to consistently identify (and quantify) their approach to, and practice of, reflection. Therefore, being able to recognize the three attitudes and the five phases of reflection was important to both validate my conclusions about their thinking and to allow me to genuinely map their development over time using the same common principles for 'seeing' their reflection in action. The following sections demonstrate how I was able to recognize these attitudes and phases across different contexts and at different times and is intended to give the reader a good grasp of the principles which underpin my view of their development.

The Search for Three Attitudes

Open-mindedness, as the term suggests, is characterized by a willingness to consider new problems and new ideas. This includes 'an active desire to listen to more sides than one; to give heed to facts from whatever source they come; to give full attention to alternative possibilities; to recognize the possibility of error even in the beliefs that are dearest to us' (Dewey, 1933, p. 30). The following journal excerpts are examples of open-mindedness.

Peggy
Context: Writing about a unit of work in TAL

The unit we did on learning made me view teaching very differently than before, and now the unit we have done on assessment has changed it all again. You can't talk teaching without talking learning, and you can't talk teaching without talking assessment. But as you plan what you are going to teach, you must think how students learn, and you must think how they are going to be assessed, so if students all learn differently, they must also be assessed differently . . .

Peggy illustrates an open-mindedness to ideas concerned with teaching, learning and assessment. Having worked through some of the issues, she now recognizes the complexities and difficulties associated with the topics. Her open-minded approach has allowed her to link units of work rather than to view them as discrete entities. She has benefited from her ability to heed different points of view, to listen to more than one side.

Nigel
Context: Writing about the variation of teaching approaches used in TAL

We are constantly exposed to experiences which help to shape to some extent the way we think, behave, react, etc. The important thing is that great diversity of characteristics will always occur in a classroom and it is the aim of the course to point these facts out to us.

In this quote Nigel is starting to open his mind to the experiences placed before him in the course. He has started to think about the purpose of different activities and to see that his learning is influenced by those around him in the myriad of experiences associated with the course. This indicates a willingness to pay attention to facts from varying sources.

Filipa
Context: Writing about one of the teaching approaches used in TAL

It seems to me that it is easy to teach the way you have been taught and I notice John pulling us up and asking us to stop, consider different positions, and find the answer to that. Also, that a successful learning method to us becomes the only way to teach something to them [students] — this is a trap for us as teachers.

In this instance, Filipa considers alternative possibilities for actions. By recognizing it in others she demonstrates that possessing the attitude of open-mindedness encourages her to draw appropriate conclusions, and also to note them for her own actions.

Sharon
Context: Writing about a unit of work in TAL

I seem to spend most of this year changing my opinions and beliefs. Having come up through a system of A–E grading and assessment I thought this was the best way to assess. However, I'm not so sure anymore. Too often assessment is done only as a means of ranking students or making a comment i.e. end of tem reports etc.

By considering an appropriate approach to assessment, Sharon is confronted by her own beliefs. By musing over the purposes of assessment from a teacher's perspective, her previous (student) perspective is challenged. She notices that her prior views may be incongruous with her emerging understanding of the issue.

As the examples above illustrate, open-mindedness is an attribute distinguished by the ability to consider other points of view and other approaches to problems in light of one's own ideas. Open-mindedness is an attitude which encourages the individual to grapple with new ideas; it whets the appetite for productive, active thought.

Responsibility is an attitude that is necessary to extend and unravel the thoughts taken up by an open mind. It is the ability to consider the consequences of actions and to be able to accept such consequences following action taken. Intellectual responsibility is highlighted by the ability to carry something through to its conclusion, to be aware of 'the reasons that make things worthy of belief' (Dewey, 1933, p. 33). The following journal excerpts are examples of the attitude of responsibility.

Jack
Context: Writing about a school teaching experience

As a school I think it [the school] does well in teaching kids new to this country . . . it helps the kids to adjust to a new way of life, and integrate into our society. I really think this is great for these kids. If there is a problem, then it is that a 'casual' sort of atmosphere pervades the school, through both teachers and kids, and I think that the kids who don't have the language problems, and all that is associated with that, are not really pushed or extended as much as they could be. These 'normal' kids sit in classes with the new kids and for whatever reasons, don't feel compelled to achieve anymore than the new kids. This is a complex issue and I don't like making hasty judgements, or over-generalizing, but I think this is what I saw during my brief stay there.

Marg
Context: Writing about groupwork after it had been used in TAL where the DipEd students were the learners

PS. Group work does have its disadvantages. Within my group I felt as if I had little to contribute even through I was thinking about a lot of different things. Because there were other students who were increasingly more dominant and confident than me. I believe this adversely affected my own contribution.

In these quotes, both Jack and Marg demonstrate intellectual responsibility in their consideration of the consequences of action. They have an attitude that encourages them to see beyond the initial episode to some of the possible implications.

Anthony
Context: Writing about a session in TAL

Getting back to the reasons behind why we did these exercises, they are really good ways of getting students to understand about what is happening, but better still, they make the person think about what's going on, which is a victory in itself, and also allows them to get through the process of forming explanations about what has happened.

Pearl
Context: Writing about teaching during a teaching round

After two lessons there are problems in my approach and I think what I need to do is do some Venn Diagrams, Concept Pyramids and maps myself. Because it's so blooming abstract. Imaginary lines on the earth. Determined by angles from centre to surface of earth . . . Agh! Looks so simple. [When you] jump into it [it] is very complicated. If I can sort it out first and get a clear idea of where and how the whole unit is going it will be better. Yes — I should have done this before. That's the point. I thought I had it clear — it's only in the midst (well, once I've started) of it I realize I haven't.

Anthony and Pearl both reconsider their teaching in light of the consequences which follow. In so doing, they show a preparedness to accept the outcomes resulting from the positions already taken. By being intellectually responsible, one searches for meaning in what is being learnt. There is an acceptance of responsibility for thoughts and activities which make a difference to future beliefs and actions.

Whole-heartedness is an attitude whereby the individual is enthralled in the subject in such a way that it urges one to think. This leads to an enthusiasm, a desire for learning, in which the individual is absorbed in the subject matter. As Dewey (1933) explains, 'When a person is absorbed, the subject carries him on. Questions occur to him spontaneously; a flood of suggestions pour in on him; further inquiries and readings are indicated and followed; instead of having to use his energy to hold his mind to the subject, the material holds and buoys his mind up and gives an onward impetus to thinking' (p. 31).

To be absorbed by the subject and flooded with questions and suggestions is illustrated clearly by Perry in the following extract. In this instance he is reviewing a teaching episode he had conducted in a TAL session.

Perry
Context: Writing about teaching his peers in a TAL session

Well, an interesting class today. P.O.E. [prediction, observation and explanation] ... Wow! John! Did I perhaps push myself out of the *comfort zone*. Yuck, I still hate that expression. I also threw in a few of the comments that came to my mind whilst I was conducting the class. Can you reflect during a class? What is that called? I always feel that reflection is looking back ... To go with the flow, did you notice what I considered to be an excellent use of wait-time as I asked people for their predictions of what would happen if we gave the poor [people] money that the government simply printed? I was conscious of not expressing opinion or body language, just looking at the respondent, thereby encouraging them to reconsider their answer. But rather than respond, I moved on to another student. That's what I felt like I was doing anyway. I only had a loose plan of where I was going. I was a little more on edge than if I had prepared more thoroughly but I think that contributed to the learning experience for me. I think it challenged me.

It took longer than I expected, but as long as that was alright with you, I was prepared to let it continue as I felt people were getting value from the exercise. The biggest BUZZ of all though was when Miranda came up to me later and said she was glad I had done that topic as it was something she had never understood properly. [Miranda is a BEc graduate.]

People did get involved with the task. Next time I would have a student auctioneer whom I thought could handle the job (perhaps I could choose one whom I thought couldn't).

I think these P.O.E.s can be a useful tool/method for teaching, perhaps their use needs to be drawn out more.

In this example, Perry is indeed buoyed by the subject — his teaching episode. He reconsiders what has happened, how he conducted the lesson, what he might do differently in future, and the value of the P.O.E. strategy as a means of encouraging students to think. The experience has been an impetus to thinking. He demonstrates an attitude of whole-heartedness.

Another example of whole-heartedness is when Pearl is considering her approach to classroom management. Having attended a session on this topic she begins to think about her teaching rounds and attempts to match her teaching behaviour to her philosophy. She demonstrates her conviction to resolve in her own mind the difference between what is possible and what is acceptable for her practice. She is whole-heartedly engaged in her enquiry.

Pearl
Context: Writing about approaches to classroom management after a TAL session on the topic

Okay, now I am much happier. [I've] been sweating over the issue of manipulation and whether that's what I've been basing my teaching on, whether that is what the course has in effect been teaching us; or whether that is how it has generally been interpreted . . . a few essential points.

1) *Discipline* can lead/guide/direct/encourage/remind a child to own their own behaviour and to respect the fact that *other people have rights*; without damaging self-esteem. This is nice because although you can interpret the first part as being a hidden means of manipulation — the fact that you want students to own their behaviour cancels it out, can only achieve that through honesty — it's for their own benefit so there's no point in manipulating.

No. [have not been basing teaching on manipulation] Because if you deny people a part in the process, of if they don't reach an understanding of their behaviour/decisions themselves — at the difficult moment they will recant. It also puts discipline firmly in its place as a means to make learning possible not an end in itself.

2) It was interesting to hear Bill [visiting lecturer] talk about the importance of a 'conscious repertoire'. It would seem to fulfil a variety of purposes. It takes seriously the need for preparation or rather 'prepared thinking' — that there is a continuation between different activities . . . what I like most is that it circumnavigates the emotional response, the way it steps out of conquer or be vanquished mode. The differentiation between the primary and secondary behaviour is a useful distinction . . . surely that's why Bill's model of assertiveness works, it's about keeping things on track. (This will require an assessment of our own power relations at some point.)

3) Non-confrontation. Yep I reckon.

It's interesting going back to school [from a teaching round] and how difficult I found that. I hated the idea of confrontation . . . one of my supervisors operated solely in terms of threat-response, the other did not but advocated Canter as an approach. She had good reasons but it left me feeling like jelly . . . Cyril Halley's comment re: dynamics still makes sense.

4) You can only control your behaviour.

Only is a misleading term. I would think that if each person managed to control their own behaviour we'd be doing quite well. It comes back to the concept of teachers following through, not having expectations of students which they don't meet themselves.

What I really liked about this session was that it suggested I can get together a coherent picture/strategy that includes much of what we've been learning this year. The fact that I haven't done it yet doesn't mean it won't happen if I keep working at it. Yes — conscious inefficiency — but there are strategies to move on.

In both cases, these student-teachers are thoroughly involved in examining the topic. Their thoughts are not merely superficial attention to the issue but illustrate a whole-hearted approach to developing a better understanding. Perry and Pearl display an enthusiasm which is a driving force in their intellectual development. It is a desire to resolve the difference between philosophy and practice, to achieve harmony of deed and purpose.

Overview

The quotes presented above give an insight into student-teachers' thinking. They demonstrate the diversity of responses and ideas articulated as a result of their pre-service education experiences. They also illustrate the range of thoughts that comprise the three attitudes of open-mindedness, responsibility and whole-heartedness.

The search for examples of these three attitudes in the nineteen student-teachers' journals can be viewed as a search for their personal disposition toward these attitudes. These are the attitudes which are favourable to the development and use of the best methods of inquiry and testing. They are the attitudes that predispose an individual to reflect. An important feature of the examples cited demonstrate that as each of the three attitudes can indeed be identified in pre-service teacher education students, then under appropriate conditions, they can also be enhanced and developed.

Recognizing Reflection

Dewey (1933) described reflection in terms of a sequence of five phases (suggestions, problem, hypothesis, reasoning and testing). In a similar fashion to recognizing his three attitudes, so these elements of reflection in the thoughts of the student-teachers can be discerned. Although the five phases need not occur in a set order, the five together are what Dewey considers to be a reflective sequence and are the 'indispensable traits of reflective thinking' (p. 116). The writings cited for each of the following phases are indicative of these phases.

Teachers often do things without stopping to consider why they do them. However, when a situation arises which causes one to stop and think, options for action begin to spring to mind. When pondering two or more ideas, direct action is inhibited. These suggestions need to be examined so that the most appropriate course of action may be followed. In teaching, such situations may be commonplace. To momentarily halt one's actions to consider these suggestions is important if a course of action is to be carefully considered. These suggestions are one phase in Dewey's reflective sequence. In the following example, Anthony is thinking about how he can restructure his use of classroom activities. In so doing, suggestions occur to him.

Anthony
Context: Writing about teaching during a teaching round

I think I'm structuring my lessons by teaching the content, and then using other activities as a medium to reinforce the content. I should also be using activities to: introduce topics, find out what the kids know/don't know, use them more as an initial learning method rather than a follow up, reinforcing the learning method . . .

In a similar vein, Sharon is confronted by a situation which causes her to reconsider her options. She lists her suggestions.

Sharon
Context: Writing about teaching during a teaching round

Year 10 I am teaching Japanese history — an area I'm hardly familiar with. I am trying to learn this subject quickly, but there are limited hours in a day. Therefore, I fear these lessons are becoming somewhat boring as I need to get the kids doing all the work. They resent this and are normally lazy anyway. How can I make the lesson interesting?

> perhaps shorter activities
> more variety in activities
> videos
> group work
> role play?

Despite being a private school, many of these students are unruly and undisciplined.

These examples illustrate the flow of suggestions and possibilities that may occur when thinking about particular experiences. An interesting extension of this is presented by Andrea when she considers the same situation at two different times.

Andrea
Context: Writing about teaching during a teaching round

Yesterday, my supervisor commented that my voice sounded very antagonistic and sarcastic towards the students and that some students may find this off putting. I realized sometimes that I was putting them down too much but, after trying to be polite and nice to them and them not taking any notice of what I was saying I believed that it was time to 'put them in their place' and not let them walk all over me. Anyway, this didn't go down well with my supervisor. So, today I decided to be more gentle and less antagonistic. What a waste of time! My supervisor thought I handled the class better, but I think that's not true. The class did no work, and walked all over me. Trying to not get angry stressed me out. At least when I was 'more stern' with them I managed to end the class with my nerves intact. Thank God I've only got them once more. Maybe I do expect a bit more from the class because I got used to no discipline problems [at previous school] but nobody should have to put up with a class like that. I know I'm also having these problems because I'm only a student teacher.

Andrea
Context: Writing about a TAL session on classroom management

The lecture today by Bill Rogers made me really think of my teaching round. This is the 2nd time I got to hear Bill talk and he inspired, or rather, he made me think a lot about the way I treat students. During my 3rd round I had some problems with the way I presented myself to the class. I found I was sarcastic and antagonistic which led to resentment from the students. But when I did some of the 'discipline' that Bill Rogers presented I found that students don't really always do as you ask. It sounded great and easy when Bill was role playing but I found it difficult. But thinking back now I'm thinking to myself that maybe I was 'begging and pleading' with students rather than leaving options for the students. I know that I spoke down to them a lot which I'm sorry for now. I've always admired teachers who were respectful and treated me as an adult at school and I'm mad at myself for not doing that.

In reviewing her manner with the class she perceives her actions in a different light. Suggestions that she enacted initially — at the behest of her supervisor — she later rejects. Suggestions — from Bill Rogers, a visiting lecturer — which she did not document but must have considered on the first occasion, she thinks about again. By adopting this approach to possible options she reframes (Schön, 1983; 1987) the situation and considers her suggestions once more.

Andrea also demonstrates that in some cases suggestions may only be possible when there has been sufficient experience from which to derive alternative options. (Similarly, suggestions may not be laid out as a distinct and easily recognizable sub-set of the reflective cycle waiting to be documented by others.)

In a setting where action ceases due to a perplexing or worrisome situation, the position may at first be viewed as a difficulty. This may lead one to re-inspect the conditions which have led to the occurrence of the situation. When this happens, the situation becomes further defined and intellectualized so that it is viewed as a problem.

In the context of a reflective sequence, Dewey (1933) notes '. . . there is a process of *intellectualizing* what at first is merely an *emotional* quality of the whole situation. This conversion is effected by noting more definitely the conditions that constitute the trouble and cause the stoppage of action' (p. 109).

In the following example, recognition of the problem becomes clear as the conditions which caused the stoppage are considered.

Peggy
Context: Writing about teaching experiences after a teaching round

Up until now I haven't mentioned the Year 10 USA history classes I took. That is because I would rather forget them. They just didn't work. I am very disappointed that they didn't work out because when I found I was going to teach U.S. history I was pleased because it is so interesting. I think there are several reasons why they didn't work. Firstly I could only observe 2 classes before I had to teach, and both of these consisted of the teacher just talking to the students about the topic being studied. There were no note-taking or written exercises. Yet they were very interesting lessons. I used these lessons as the model for the ones I took. I had to take 2, and the teacher gave me the material to use, handouts, etc. So my lessons didn't work because of both these things. I couldn't talk to the students and ask the right questions in the interesting and informative manner that the regular teacher did. I also wasn't sure what to do with the handouts she gave me. The information the students needed was condensed in point form in the handouts and all I could think of to do with it was get the students to read it out and ask some questions along the way. I suppose you have to have lessons that aren't successful in order to learn more. Unfortunately it's not nice when you're standing in front of a class, and it's not working, and at this stage I don't have enough experience to be able to change my methods midway through a lesson.

Initially, Peggy is disappointed that her lessons did not 'work' when she was teaching a topic in which she was interested. As she considers more carefully the context of the situation, as she intellectualizes the problem, she begins to recognize some of the conditions which led to her inability to make the lessons more interesting for the students. Her lack of experience in adapting her teaching methods inhibited the development of student interest in the lessons.

Recognizing the problem may also be triggered by a similar experience in a different context. The intellectualizing of one contextual dilemma leads to the appreciation of a problem setting in another. Perry, who worked part-time in the Army Reserve, had such an experience.

Perry
Context: Writing about experiences outside DipEd that related to teaching

I was rather disturbed the other night after cadets whilst I was collating the answers to a survey I had taken . . . one question asked who cadets would prefer to conduct the lessons. Currently cadets (aged 14–18) take most lessons. Perhaps egotistically I felt that cadets may prefer adults to take the lessons. To me cadets' lessons (whilst they try hard) seem ill prepared, less entertaining and their presentation of factual content makes me cringe. They said that they like a mixture. Fair enough. But later I followed this up with some of the more senior cadets whom I thought would answer more honestly. Their response was that cadets like to be taught by cadets because they can relate to them better. 'They're on the same wavelength.'

Think about that. Perhaps schooling is all wrong. Perhaps we should rely on students helping, assisting, teaching each other more. I remember at school often it would be the student next to me or someone else in the class that would explain something to me. It makes some sense.

- more compatible vocab. level
- less intimidation (in more timid students this may play a vital role)
- more time for one to one interaction
- one student has just learnt it, so the way he learnt to understand it is fresh in his mind, unrefined and unviolated.

Perry had been writing about his school teaching experiences and was musing over the links between teaching and learning. His coursework in TAL had concentrated on learning theory. In this instance he identifies a problem in one setting which initiates a corresponding recognition of a quandary he had been concerned with in his teaching.

He had been concerned about teaching strategies he should adopt to enhance his students' learning. As he considers the conditions that perplex him, a tide of suggestions pour forth. In this situation, comprehending the problem is the key to its resolution. Until the problem has been intellectualized, knowing what may be as vague and tentative as knowing how.

A suggestion may be just an idea if it is not acted upon. It is in acting upon a suggestion — the controlled use of what is done — that introduces the intellectual element to the situation. By being able to define the problem, conception of a possible solution is more likely.

In a scientific sense, the data that is brought to bear on the problem helps to modify, adjust and develop the suggestion so that it begins to take shape as a hypothesis. In a real sense what was once a possibility becomes something that may genuinely be tested, validated or negated.

A good example of hypothesis generation comes through in the following excerpt from Ralph. In this case he is struggling with classroom management issues. He has been disillusioned by the lack of control his supervising teacher exerts on her class. When he becomes their teacher he is confronted by a similar problem. He links the students' apparent inability to apply themselves to a task to their behaviour. He hypothesizes that if there is no class control there is no meaningful learning.

Ralph
Context: Writing about teaching during a teaching round

This class is like 10E, very noisy. I refuse to talk over anybody. For 5 minutes I stood in front of the class and did not say a word. The class simply got louder. I finally raised my voice to shut them up. This is not right, I should not have had to raise my voice. These kids haven't been trained. I was constantly stopping the lesson to get quiet. We got through very little. Barbara [supervising teacher] remarked that I should work them harder. I disagree — there's no point in pushing on if there is no progress. Until this class is under control there will be no learning for anyone. At the present I am at a loss as to what to do about Year 10s. Discipline is a real problem.

Classroom management is a major concern for pre-service teachers as they struggle to make the transition from student to teacher. For Joshua, this took longer than most. During his third (and final) school teaching experience he was eventually able to hypothesize why it was that he had struggled to discipline his students.

Joshua
Context: Writing about teaching during a teaching round

Again on this round as I found on the others I want to work on separating myself form the students and not fall into the trap of being 'one of the kids'. That definitely is my greatest weakness I feel because by nature I'm not a very serious person and I don't like disciplining kids because it wasn't long ago that I was a student. Also it's difficult for those memories of my school days to be wiped out of my mind. I see a lot of myself in some of the kids.

Being attached to the kids I would imagine would be a natural progression if you taught for the whole year.

Hypothesis formation becomes an important phase in the reflective process. It enables one to transform suggestions by shaping and moulding these ideas into tenable suppositions. Hypothesizing is therefore a precursor to the controlled testing of a solution.

Pre-service teachers spend a large proportion of their time during school teaching experience observing experienced teachers in action. Pre-empting this structured and purposeful observation, though, has been years of observation as a student. This is important as *reasoning* draws on the observations and experiences that are used to build an individual's store of knowledge. Reasoning through a situation leads to the linking of ideas and these links are enhanced by the store of knowledge able to be drawn upon.

The extent to which an individual may reason through an idea will be evident in the supply of intermediate links brought to bear on the whole. 'Acceptance of a suggestion in its first form is prevented by looking into it more thoroughly. Conjectures that seem plausible at first sight are often found unfit or even absurd when their full consequences are traced out. Even when reasoning out the bearings of a supposition does not lead to its rejection, it develops the idea into a form which it is more apposite to the problem' (Dewey, 1933, p. 112).

Developing an idea so that it is more 'in line' with the problem is illustrated by Nadine as she carefully reasons through her ideas about critical incidents.

Nadine
Context: Writing about a TAL session

Looking at these critical incidents made me aware of how important it is to question the student personally before implementing disciplinary measures as the problem may be solved with discussion and this is desirable as: 1) strict discipline may be unfair in some cases; 2) the child deserves a say; and 3) I may be able to arrive at a better understanding of the child which will obviously increase my chances of getting through to him/her. The session also posed the question of how important is the immediacy of discipline and, where I was first inclined to say very important and that it should be enforced immediately, after listening to Monica I could see that it would depend on the situation and that most of the time it is best not to disrupt the lesson, but to discuss the matter with the offending student after the class instead. However the instances in which I feel discipline should be implemented immediately are when a child swears directly at myself — in this case I would send the child from the classroom to be reprimanded by the person in charge of that area and take it up with the student myself afterwards. This way the lesson would not be greatly disrupted and the other students would be aware of the severity of the disciplinary measure for such behaviour. I think this action is appropriate especially from the point of view of the other students as to ignore the behaviour or simply say, 'I'll talk to you later', makes the behaviour appear less severe . . . Thus I think the immediacy of discipline is largely dependent upon the situation and the severity of the misbehaviour in most cases if I only wanted to reprimand the offending student it is not worth disrupting the rest of the class' learning, and I would discipline the child at a later time in private.

In this case, Nadine is reasoning through her ideas of how to respond to inappropriate classroom behaviour. She concludes that her initial notion of acting immediately may be acceptable in some instances but not all. By reasoning through her ideas what follows becomes more 'apt and fruitful'.

Reasoning may also be a method used to reinforce or better articulate a belief. This may be by comparing one's views to their observations and experiences. An example of this is when Mitchell is considering his approach to classroom management.

Mitchell
Context: Writing about a session in TAL on classroom management

I thought that Bill Rogers' lecture was one of the most interesting things I've attended all year.

He has done a lot of thinking about the dynamics between people. He gave examples of how incorrect responses to behaviour can lead to an escalation of problems. He also pointed out where/how a different response can quickly defuse the situation. What I found most interesting was that I could recall/identify instances from my own teaching experience which relates to both kinds of responses.

For me, Bill Rogers gave a coherent and logical framework which I could hang some of my experiences on. Previously, through trial and error, I'd developed my own haphazard rules for classroom management that seemed to do the job.

I had already decided that fairness and consistency was important. I had seen one or two teachers, during my rounds, behaving in an unfair way towards students. The students in turn clearly didn't have much respect for their teachers, even though the teachers were very strict. The students could clearly see inconsistencies when a particular teacher tried to cover his mistake. I had also discovered that avoiding the argument with a student greatly reduced the scope of a student towards disruption. However, this technique didn't always sit neatly with being fair.

Reasoning is a way of expanding upon an initial idea or supposition so that it leads to the linking of experiences and observations into a consistent whole.

The final phase is that of testing which may be either overt or imaginative action dependent on the situation at hand. Reasoning leads to an understanding of the natural consequences which might follow an action. Hence, it is left to direct observation or experimental testing to corroborate the hypothesis.

In testing, it may be that the consequences do not always lead to confirmation of the hypothesis being tested. It is through testing that is not successful that the value of reflective thought may be highlighted '. . . possession of the habit of reflective activity is that failure is not mere failure. It is instructive. The person who really links learns quite as much from his failures as from his successes. For a failure indicates to the person whose thinking has been involved in it, and who has not come to it by mere blind chance, what further observations should be made' (Dewey, 1933, p. 114).

Imaginative testing occurs at different times and as a result of different stimuli. For student-teachers, imaginative testing probably occurs when considering how to adapt, adjust or change a teaching strategy from one subject area to another. On one occasion, Filipa thought through a test of a teaching strategy in her journal, hence demonstrating the use of imaginative testing.

Filipa
Context: Writing about a teaching strategy used in TAL

I enjoyed the first exercise of writing a sentence and passing it on. I think this could be used in my own classes. Have a bar of music, one composer writes a bar of music and passes it on. Obviously when time is short, then the group size needs to be limited so that the work is finished. A very useful exercise when you want peace and quiet! This gave us all something to read about our classmates' reactions to our initial statement. We were not asked, at the end, to comment on what was written, but rather on the mechanics of the task itself and whether we liked it or not.

The purpose, that of giving everyone a say, was good and in a large class you need some means of getting everyone to have a go.

If we had had enough time I think we would have all dug pretty deep into our ideas. This would work well with music.

In this example, Filipa demonstrates the ability to take an idea from one context and translate it to another. She then performs a test of imaginative action by considering the observations and experiences associated with it.

The more concrete form of testing is that of overt testing. In the following example, Pearl demonstrates overt testing of an approach to classroom management, though the result of the test is not one of overwhelming success.

Pearl
Context: Writing about teaching during a teaching round

For the good of my soul I've had 9B again. Had long discussions with Robyn [a teacher supervisor] re: discipline measures — particularly Canter theory.

It's a horrible way to run a class. *But* it works. The kids worked. Bit of a crisis throwing safety out but it had to happen. 'Follow through with the threat' etc. Once I started on that path it wasn't that difficult but it's all that concentration on management.

Theoretically I knew it was the option I had to take. But I didn't like it. The difference between supervisors is interesting.

Sia [another teacher supervisor] uses that model everyday — her lessons are tight, controlled and boring. Robyn recognizes the method as a way of setting parameters which you can then work within.

Uses them as a tool — not as an end. And Robyn's classes are good. And she works *hard*.

I suppose it's a good thing to learn these different approaches and then pick and choose from them — it's hard to try and mould yourself to other people's requirements, but forces me to evaluate.

Sia's method could become attractive — dictate, talk, maintain low noise, terrify kids. But Robyn's is the harder and I think better way. After 15 years she knows kids and has worked out how to make them give.

Pearl uses her test to experience an approach so that she might better understand the complexities of managing students in her classes. As she has recognized a problem, considered suggestions — which are not yet all her own — reasoned and tested she begins to reconsider her hypothesis. The test is instructive as it leads her to reconsider her own stance and actions.

As Dewey points out, these five phases of the reflective sequence need not occur in a set order. Some phases may be expanded upon, depending on the situation being confronted. The importance of each step is that genuine thinking is educative. In essence 'Each improvement in the idea leads to new observations that yield new facts or data and help the mind judge more accurately the relevancy of facts already at hand. The elaboration of the hypothesis does not wait until the problem has been defined and adequate hypothesis has been arrived at; it may come in at any intermediate time . . . any particular overt test need not be final; it may be introductory to new observations and new suggestions, according to what happens in consequence of it' (Dewey, 1933, p. 115).

Just as the three attitudes can be recognized, understood and developed in student-teachers, so the components of the reflective sequence can be identified. This clearly then has important ramifications for helping develop reflective practitioners through their pre-service education programs as each can be highlighted (and modelled) in teacher educators' and student-teachers' thinking and actions in relation to their teaching practice. In my mind, this is a most important aspect of helping student-teachers learn about teaching.

Concluding Remarks

Drawing on the work of Lakatos (1970), Walker and Evers (1984) outline touchstone theory. The value of touchstone theory is that it 'consists of the overlap between competing theories, such as common theoretical claims and methodologies — "evidence" (p. 27). This chapter has been written as the touchstone from which the elaboration and discussion in the following chapters may be viewed as valid evidence for the interpretations and conclusions I draw from my work with my pre-service education students. It is anticipated that the extensive descriptions and explanations of attitudes and elements of reflection offered in this chapter will free the reader to engage in the subsequent chapters with a good working knowledge of the framework which underpins my view of reflection and its identification in my student-teachers' thoughts and actions.

Chapter 6

Journals: An Insight into Students' Thinking

Background to Journal Writing

Dialogue journal writing has been defined as 'written conversation between two persons on a functional, continued basis, about topics of individual (and even mutual) interest' (Staton, 1988, p. 312). Recent research (Rodderick, 1986; Bean and Zulich, 1989; Richert, 1990; Ferro and Lenz, 1992) illustrates the value of the data derived from journal writing with respect to students' thinking about teaching.

By incorporating the use of journal writing in a pre-service teacher education course, teachers and students are able to explore topics of interest in ways that may not be possible within the time frame of a class, and an additional avenue of communication beyond the verbal is offered. Also, the 'non-public' nature of journal writing provides opportunity and encouragement to reflect on experiences in varied ways through writing.

Polanyi (1962) states that all knowledge has a tacit dimension through which understanding is possible, but experience alone does not lead to knowledge. Rational reflection upon, and examination of, an experience is necessary to develop one's understanding. Polanyi calls this 'personal knowledge'. In order to help student-teachers learn through reflection on their experiences there is a need to help them make the tacit explicit. In so doing, they might be able to re-examine their experiences and learn from them in new ways which may not have been initially apparent. Through deliberately and purposefully reconsidering their experiences and by reviewing their thoughts and actions in light of this type of rational reflection, they might gain a deeper understanding of the teaching and learning episodes they experience. In my Teaching and Learning class (TAL) I attempt to foster this reflection and examination through the use of journal writing. It is an integral component of the course and students are encouraged to maintain a journal throughout the year. Their course outline has regular reminders, questions and prompts to foster this, and individual tutors also adopt their own strategies. However, it could be argued that many structured journal tasks are simply an assessment tool, hence student-teachers may write what they think the teacher educator wants to read. They may also resent the imposition of journal writing and grudgingly consider it as an obligation rather than as a useful focus for their own learning (Krogh and Crews, 1989). I therefore use a number of approaches with my TAL classes to minimize the likelihood of student-teachers' writing in ways similar to that described by Krogh and Crews (1989). These approaches are derived from my own previous experience with, and practice of, journal writing as a TAL tutor and include:

1. Although the TAL course outline includes prompts, reminders and questions to encourage student-teachers to write, my class are continually reminded that they should not view these as either limiting or compulsory. Other issues should influence what they wish to write about at any given time.

   My first few TAL sessions conclude with reminders that the day's classroom activities provide opportunities for participants to think about their own learning, and that they should try to write about this in their journal. Some of the focus questions I use to encourage this are:

   What did I learn?
   How would I have conducted the session if I were the teacher?
   What caused me to be interested/disinterested in the session?
   How did this session influence my views on teaching and learning?

2. Student-teachers are encouraged to write honestly and openly about the teaching and learning episodes that they experience through my classes. By the very nature of the task, they are being asked to take risks in expressing their views on topics, content, my teaching and 'our' learning. Therefore, the degree of risk taken by each individual is influenced by the sense of trust apparent between myself as the reader, and the individual student-teacher as the writer. This is something that can only be established over time and needs to be recognized and addressed by both participants. As the journal is an ungraded task and its contents are confidential, external constraints on content and 'right or wrong' views are minimized.

3. In an attempt to illustrate that I value their journal writing, I read their journals at regular intervals. I ask for volunteers to leave their journal with me at the end of a session, to be returned by the start of the next session. The comments and questions that I write in their journals are an attempt to probe their understanding of the teaching and learning episodes and to challenge their thinking. This personal and private form of dialogue between teacher and student is often a catalyst for developing and refining their attitude and approach to journal writing.

4. Journal writing is not mandatory. Other options are available to those who feel unable to meet the demands of the task. However, such options are not commonly taken up by members of my TAL class.

5. Except for sporadic reminders, maintenance of the journal is the student-teacher's responsibility. Little, if any, personal pressure is placed on them to conform to any notions of quantity or quality in their writing.

6. By keeping a journal myself I attempt to model its use and purpose. At the start of each lesson my journal is circulated amongst the members of the class who are encouraged to read it and comment in it and/or their own

journals. By using my journal this way the thinking, planning and reactions that I relate to my own teaching and learning, and to the learning of the class, are illustrated. It becomes an important tool for demonstrating my attitude towards reflection. It also helps to reinforce the approach in point 2 above through the role reversal of 'writer' and 'reader'.

7. To stimulate class discussion and illustrate relevant points with regard to teaching and learning, reference could be made to any of the entries in my journal by any member of the class; my journal is passed around the class at the start of each session. This is designed to encourage open and honest dialogue about the thoughts and actions associated with the teaching and learning processes in the class. But, student-teachers' entries in their own journals are confidential and remain that way unless individuals introduce them to the class of their own accord.

8. Student-teachers are encouraged to re-read their own journal so that they can appreciate changes that they may have made in their approach and attitude to teaching and learning. This also gives them an additional opportunity to respond to the comments and reactions I have written in their journals.

Student-teachers' journals develop in varying ways through the interactions conveyed in them and as a result of the communication between myself as their teacher and them as a student. As a consequence, each journal portrays in different ways and at different times, the complexity of factors associated with learning about teaching.

The prospect of journal writing elicits varying student responses. Initially there is some trepidation as to what it should contain, how it should be written, who will read it and for what purpose. However, the value of journal writing often becomes more apparent to the writer as the experience continues (Dobbins, 1990). This is not to suggest that some students do not find it to be routine, but, for most, the keeping of a journal helps them to become more aware of their own learning. It also helps them to articulate and explore their own assumptions and beliefs. It can be used as a tool to aid reflection.

The use of journals to encourage reflective practice is prevalent in many pre-service teacher education courses. Bean and Zulich consider the benefits of journal writing to be that

> it helps students generate their own questions in a course, explore hunches and hypotheses, and begin to perceive the multiplicity of views inherent in human experience. Most importantly, journals provide professors with windows of their students' hidden thoughts that would otherwise go unnoticed. Dialogue journals afford a regular opportunity for students to share something about themselves as learners and future teachers. (1989, p. 36)

Capitalizing on such benefits is important if pre-service teachers are to be encouraged to reflect on their experiences. Richert (1990) employed journal writing as one of four conditions in a study that explored ways of encouraging reflection in the practice of novice teachers. She concluded that it was useful in structuring opportunities for students to reflect, that it gave students the time and safety to reflect in ways that were helpful in understanding their classroom experiences.

Many of the benefits of journal writing centre on student outcomes. Mikkelsen (1985) found them to be a useful tool for discovering how students made links between theory and practice. But in researching the modelling of reflective practice, the inherent benefits go beyond this student-centred view. They also offer opportunities for teachers to reflect on their own ideas and practices.

Roderick's use of journal writing highlighted the benefits of such an exercise for the teacher educator.

> I see myself trying to do the following: find ways to learn more about myself and my students; develop meaningful experiences in which students, colleagues, and I can participate *with* each other; identify or create new lenses for viewing my interactions with others, and finally, deal comfortably and creatively with the inconsistencies within myself and between me and the many contexts I inhabit. (1986, p. 314)

Journal writing, through the mutual conversations it encourages, can therefore be seen as liberating. As Shor and Freire (1987) point out, this liberation is through teachers' learning with and from their students. If this learning with and from students is to be fully realized, then modelling my own practice of journal writing is important in encouraging students to write themselves. My journal becomes a document that allows students to see beyond my classroom actions and practice and into my thinking. Thus what I ask them to do through their journals, I also attempt to do through mine. As I gain insights into their thinking through reading their journals, they have the opportunity to do the same through mine.

Students' Views of Dialogue Journal Writing

Many students wrote, unprompted, about the value of journal writing as they considered different issues and topics. The stimulus for noting this point was varied but was most commonly linked to considering one's own learning and how it had been influenced by writing about it.

Pearl
Context: Writing about her approach to journal writing

Dear John, this journal's got out of control. In no way feel obliged to wade through it all — I just like to use it as a record/sounding board for thoughts.

Pearl
Context: Writing about her thinking after a TAL session

John — now I'm embarrassed. I don't quite know how I got onto this — or that it makes any sense [previous paragraphs]. It was your question [in class] about forcing people to think my way. But it is from this view that I am developing my ideas on teaching and learning — and maybe it is only from this perspective that they make any sense.

Nadine
Context: Writing about the value of journal writing

This indicates for myself the value of getting the students [in school] to keep a 'general' journal about all the work that they do in a subject — in order to stimulate reflective thought — about their learning and as a 'manageable' means for the teacher to collect and comment on the student's self-evaluative progress. Keeping a journal for DipEd has certainly sold me on this anyway.

Sarah
Context: Writing about her concerns before the second teaching round

John, there are so many doubts going through my mind. Can I keep the kids entertained? Will they like me? Will my supervisors be OK? Will I cope? . . . I suppose 3 weeks [school teaching experience] isn't really a very long time but I'm scared just the same.

Writing this down helps me to analyse how I'm feeling and why I feel this way.

These examples portray an image of student-teachers using their journals to think about their own learning. In so doing they recognize that their journals are a conduit between their actions and their thoughts. The journals serve as a purposeful tool that encourages their thinking. But, even recognizing this does not necessarily mean that all will embrace the notion so heartily.

Although all of my student-teachers keep a journal, there are those who struggle with the task. Being asked to communicate in a written form can be a restriction for some. Even though the purpose may be clear, it does not guarantee that appropriate action will follow easily. Comments related to this point are interesting as some students recognize and overcome the difficulties as they get into the 'habit' of journal writing. Others struggle to write regularly.

Ralph
Context: Writing about his own journal writing

If anyone else should read this journal don't expect to find a great piece of literature. I usually spend many hours thinking about what I want to write before I actually put it down on paper.

Miranda
Context: Writing about her attitude to journal writing

Speaking to students with other TAL leaders, we appear to do things very differently to other groups and we treat our journals very differently.

I admit that at the start of the year I thought that the idea of keeping a journal to record our thoughts was strange and a bit pointless. Even now I often think 'what is the use?' However, having just sat down and read over what I have written in the past, I found it amusing and think that it is probably a good idea to actually write down what we want to and what we think, and be forced to put them to paper, rather than just store these ideas in our heads. I'm glad you've adopted the attitude that we are free to write what we want to; rather than rely on certain questions. If the latter was the case, I would really be thinking that this is a pointless exercise.

Stephen
Context: Writing about his attitude to journal writing

I will now point out to those who may be reading this other than myself, that I do *not* write everything. In fact, I do find writing almost a chore . . . Okay John?

Stephen
Context: Writing about his attitude to journal writing

Who am I kidding? Definitely not you John! Must be me. The reason I write in the journal is so I get some credit for something in TAL . . . I find writing a chore if it's something I don't particularly enjoy writing about. I wish it wasn't so but I have been trained to write wonderfully insightful essays for a mark not a bloody 'S' [satisfactory, an ungraded pass]. If I was graded on this journal I would write regularly and in depth (and probably legibly as well!) . . . I think you have tried hard to get me (and others) to view the journal as worthwhile but it is only a medium by which you and I communicate. I doubt that I will employ a journal next year or in the future. I write very little in it I must admit. I am not overly skilled with written words. I guess I prefer talking.

Sabina
Context: Writing about her use of the journal

Dear John, this is a note to say that I have been incredibly slack and disorganised. I haven't written up journal entries for ages and my note-keeping technique at best has been erratic. So anything I write from now on is based on my memory being jogged by my notes — and they are lucky if they've been dated correctly.

I'm not super sure why I stopped writing in my journal. It is not because I've lost interest in TAL, rather because I find I have to leave enough time to make the journal entry. I try not to just make trite and facile comments i.e., I have to think that I have something worthwhile to say. This usually involves concentrating quite closely and seeking to ana-lyse the lesson in detail. All of which takes time. And sometimes I ques-tion whether what I write is worthless. I mean, it is very wanky to observe and read into a lesson something which may not even be there. Sort of like trying to go beneath the literal meaning in a book.

I know I've survived a University Degree and should be outrageously self-disciplined. However, when it comes to my journal self discipline has waned. This will sound very juvenile, but it might help (as might you becoming very nasty and heavy) if you were able to do slightly more regular journal checks. You might not find this an option for solution to my slackness.

I'm confident that if I start afresh with diligence and you will excuse my ineptitude then I will continue to make regular journal entries, no matter how trite and facile!

If you think that I need extra assignments in addition to my journal, let me know. Basically sometimes I find self analysis too mentally draining.

I hope you don't think that my disinterestedness in writing up my journal reflects on any lack of your innovation in the classroom. It doesn't, so I hope you don't view my journal entry lapses as a personal failure.

Basically once I'd left one journal entry, they all piled up so that I knew that I was facing writing for increasing lengths of time. The prospect just became too daunting.

Now this must make for one of the longest 'I haven't done my home-work because' excuses, but I felt that you deserved an attempted explanation.

It is intriguing to note that in these examples, the very act of writing about the difficulties of keeping a journal has helped the author to unravel his or her own thoughts. Stephen, in particular, demonstrates how his attitude to writing influences what he records in his journal. In this case it is clear that writing skills make a difference to the content that is communicated. Therefore, much may be reflected upon without being shared in a journal, so journal writing is really only a guide to the individual's thoughts, not a total picture.

Throughout the TAL course, the emphasis on journals is encouraged by my personal use of journal writing and by regularly reading the students' journals and commenting in them. This has benefits in different ways for different students. For Stephen and Sabina, it helped them to persevere with their writing and to discuss issues that they may not have otherwise broached. For many others it encourages them to reconsider their thoughts and actions.

Sabina
Context: Responding to comments I wrote in her journal

Goodness this takes time [journal writing]. Two last points. 1) a reminder to slow down my speech for the benefit of others' comprehension and 2) briefly read John's journal and noted how conscious he was of having miscalculated last lesson by placing a single boy, Perry, in an all girl group.

Well 'Dear John', I've just re-read your comments in my journal and responded to some of the questions you raised alongside your response. Guess what. I'd previously found writing my journal a bit of a chore, but having re-read it, and analysed what was written in the light of your comments, I really enjoyed the experience.

Time having lapsed b/w the earlier written entries and now, I was able to re-live a lot of my DipEd learning experiences. In fact, I was able to realise that by keeping a journal it focuses my learning on aspects of my learning which I may not have acknowledged as learning; let alone remembered, had I not written it down.

Peggy
Context: Responding to a question posed in a TAL session

John has asked how I felt about not getting a grade for my essay. As I said before, a grade, if it is a good one, always makes anyone feel good, myself included. However, with this essay the positive and constructive comments pleased me very much, because they were there, and because John's feelings about my essay were quite clear.

Marg
Context: Re-reading her own journal

Looking back over my journal demonstrates to me a clear development in my teaching and personality. I feel confident and know that I can effectively teach. Even though I have a long way to go and much more to see.

Sharon
Context: Responding to a question raised in a TAL session

How does your approach help me to learn? Comments in my journal certainly help by forcing me to try to think deeper and by directing my attention in other directions.

The ideas expressed in these quotes provide a glimpse of their impressions and approaches to journal writing and is designed to help reinforce the view that the journal writing is valuable. There is an honesty about the writing that illustrates the individual's perspective. This gives credence to the belief that they are writing for their own purposes rather than to meet any perceived expectations of the teacher educator. Hence, I think it is reasonable to propose, that my approach to journals appears to be valuable in gaining insights into my students' thinking and in allowing them to control — and be responsible for — the issues and views expressed. Recognizing this is important in securing an understanding of student-teachers' readiness for, or attitude towards reflection.

Because of the importance of attitudes, ability to train thought is not achieved merely by knowledge of the best forms of thought. Possession of this information is no guarantee for ability to think well . . . there is such a thing as readiness to consider in a thoughtful way the subjects that do come within the range of experience — a *readiness* that contrasts strongly with the disposition to pass judgment on the basis of mere custom, tradition, prejudice, etc., and thus shun the task of thinking. The personal attitudes [open-mindedness, responsibility and whole-heartedness] are essential constituents of this general readiness. (Dewey, 1933, pp. 29, 34)

Consequently, the journals present an opportunity to explore students' attitudes or *readiness* for reflection.

In considering the determinants of reflectivity in student-teachers, Krogh and Crews (1989) attempted to identify whether the three attitudes described by Dewey (1933) were present in their subjects by analysing their journals. They stated that '. . . these three attitudes can make the difference between thinking that is self-oriented, short sighted and flat and thinking that is productively reflective' (1989, p. 7). Thus, determining whether or not these attitudes are present in student-teachers is important because, 'We only need to bear in mind that, with respect to the aims of education, no separation can be made between impersonal, abstract principles of logic and moral qualities of character. What is needed is to weave them into unity' (Dewey, 1933, p. 34). The moral qualities to which Dewey refers are the three attitudes of open-mindedness, responsibility and whole-heartedness.

Through journals I try to encourage and cultivate the use of these attitudes by the probing and questioning I employ in communicating with my students. As these attitudes are intertwined with the individual's way of thinking, it is important that their attitudes are able to be challenged in order to foster the development of reflective practice.

Attitudes: What Trends are Apparent?

Table 6.1 shows the number of coded journal entries per student-teacher for each of Dewey's (1933) three attitudes. The order has been arbitrarily determined by the frequency of journal entries based on the sum of entries for open-mindedness and the grouping (Int/No Int) identifies those individuals who were interviewed during the year and those who were not interviewed.

This overview is for the course as a whole and, as such, displays a general pattern. This pattern is characterized by a decrease in the number of coded journal entries from open-mindedness (most frequently displayed), to responsibility, to whole-heartedness. Generally, a student displays open-mindedness more often than responsibility, and displays responsibility more often than whole-heartedness.

It is interesting to speculate on the trends apparent in Table 6.1. Open-mindedness is the most common attitude amongst these student-teachers and it is reasonable to suggest that this *should* be the case as they need to be ready to listen

Table 6.1: Number of coded journal entries per student for each attitude

Pseudonym	Attitude 1 (Open-mindedness)	Attitude 2 (Responsibility)	Attitude 3 (Whole-heartedness)	Group
Pearl	43	30	18	Int.
Jack	41	32	19	Int.
Miranda	41	37	17	Int.
Perry	37	23	8	Int.
Sabina	35	26	11	Int.
Nigel	35	15	3	Int.
Stephen	28	20	8	Int.
Filipa	27	15	6	No Int.
Marg	26	2	0	No Int.
Trixie	25	12	8	No Int.
Sarah	24	21	7	Int.
Peggy	24	11	3	No Int.
Nadine	19	12	3	No Int.
Sharon	19	6	2	No Int.
Mitchell	18	10	2	No Int.
Joshua	16	3	1	No Int.
Ralph	15	4	0	No Int.
Anthony	13	6	0	No Int.
Andrea	13	4	0	Int.

to others if they are to learn new skills. This would surely be foremost in the mind of anyone embarking on learning something new. Responsibility takes the listening a step further. It requires more from an individual than simply adding a teaching strategy to one's repertoire. It may include exploring the meaning or philosophy that underpins a point of view, as well as attempting to understand the pedagogical reasoning which accompanies decisions on how to teach specific content in a particular context or what Shulman (1986) describes as pedagogical content knowledge. This involves questioning; to genuinely desire to ask 'Why?'. Therefore, displaying an attitude of responsibility can be regarded as requiring more effort and commitment than is necessary for open-mindedness, hence the lower frequency of coded journal entries for this attitude.

Open-mindedness and responsibility can be viewed as precursors to whole-heartedness. To be engrossed in learning, to be thoroughly interested in a subject, requires a disposition toward open-mindedness and responsibility so that the act of learning generates spontaneous questioning and suggestions for possibilities and actions. It is difficult to imagine how an individual could genuinely be whole-heartedly engaged in an activity if such attitudes were not present to encourage the questioning, and to act as an impetus to thinking. It is unlikely that a student-teacher would be whole-heartedly involved in every subject or topic in a course. Thus the number of instances where this attitude is displayed would be expected to be less than for open-mindedness and responsibility.

Frequently displaying open-mindedness should lead a person to be challenged more often by different or conflicting points of view. If due consideration is given to these points of view, a yearning for better understanding could be expected to follow. To better understand an issue or topic, there is an implicit need for questioning.

If the subject is of particular interest to the individual, the result may be a whole-hearted approach to learning and understanding. Consequently, it is plausible to postulate that an individual who exhibits a high degree of open-mindedness will be more inclined toward displaying responsibility and whole-heartedness than an individual who is less open-minded. As these attitudes are essential constituents of a readiness to consider matters in a thoughtful way, the results illustrated in Table 6.1 may be seen as a guide to the *readiness* for reflection.

Given this conclusion, then, the results illustrated in Table 6.1 could be interpreted as displaying the relative disposition of each individual towards reflection. Table 6.1 also demonstrates that those student-teachers who were interviewed are generally more likely to be pre-disposed to reflect than those who were not. This may be the result of being interviewed — a separate intervention into their thinking that the whole class did not receive — but may also reflect the tendencies which led them to volunteering to be interviewed. Perhaps this is linked to the interviewed student-teachers displaying their thoughts in their journals more than those who were not interviewed. The very nature of the overt intrusion into their thinking through interviews may well be being reflected through their journal writing. The interviews heightened their awareness of their own thinking and reasoning, hence highlighting the importance of interpersonal communication between teacher educators and student-teachers beyond the mere contact during class time.

In a similar vein, it is also noticeable that not being interviewed did not preclude individuals from displaying a readiness to reflect. Their lower tallies are perhaps indicative of not being regularly asked to consider, for someone other than themselves, their thoughts and actions in light of their experiences.

Varying issues were associated with the many notations related to each of the three attitudes in students' journals. Therefore, an understanding of the topics which prompted students to write is important. As students' concerns change through their pre-service training (Fuller, 1969; Gunstone and Mackay, 1975; Fuller and Bown, 1975), it is important to recognize these and to consider how they might relate to their journal entries.

What the Students Wrote About

Individual instances of an attitude were recorded with reference to the topic with which it was associated. The aggregate topic list totalled twenty-seven. This was then condensed to form four major groupings, as illustrated in Table 6.2.

Table 6.3 demonstrates that the issues in rank order (from highest to lowest) which prompted students to write in their journals were concerns related to teaching, the course structure/requirements, learning and self. This overall pattern was demonstrated by the interviewed group and is very similar to that for the non-interviewed group, suggesting that the overview is a reasonable generalization for both groups. The generalization is not equally applicable to all individuals of

Table 6.2: Major topic groupings derived from all issues raised in students' writings

---

1. **Issues initiated as a result of considering specific topics in the course.**
   Course structure, format or requirements
   Micro-teaching
   Journal writing
   This research project
   Communication
   Modelling
   * Camp week
   Teaching and Learning (the course)
   Triangulation — involvement of an observer in TAL tutorials
   Schools; their role and function
   University lecturers/supervisors

* Student-teachers enrolled in the teaching methods of English or Science (Physics, Chemistry, Biology and General Science) attend camps in week 4 where they work towards teaching a small group of students prior to their first three week teaching experience.

2. **Issues initiated by concerns about self.**
   Classroom management and discipline
   Personality traits, concerns or perceived weaknesses
   Ability to praise students
   Prospects of teaching as a career
3. **Issues initiated by concerns about classroom teaching.**
   Teaching round experiences
   Assessing students' work
   Teaching experiences other than on teaching rounds
   Student motivation
   Other teachers; pedagogy, actions or views
   Teaching as an occupation
4. **Issues initiated by concerns about learning.**
   Learning; self and others
   Role of society as a shaping force in students' learning
   Students' rights and responsibilities
   Student learning

---

each group but is a reasonable indication of the likely importance of particular issues.

Fuller (1969) describes two studies which explored student-teachers' concerns during pre-service education. These illustrated a shift in concerns from themselves early in the course to their pupils later in the course. Fuller notes that the self–other dichotomy proposed is only one way of explaining all of the observations made. But, with this in mind, it is worth considering how student-teachers' concerns could impact on their journal writing, which could also influence the extent to which attitudes might be displayed.

To explore this point further, the issues have also been analysed in relation to three time-frames during the pre-service program. Each time-frame consists of approximately equal periods of time and each corresponds to a mixture of university coursework and a three week school teaching experience. This has been done to help focus on trends over time for the whole group as well as for particular individuals. It is also intended to illuminate any possible links between concerns and the writing topics.

Table 6.3: Number of student journal entries (from attitude coded segments) per issue

Interviewed	1. Course	2. Self	3. Teaching	4. Learning
Jack	42	5	19	23
Perry	7	7	40	22
Nigel	23	5	17	16
Pearl	20	16	40	15
Sabina	29	11	18	14
Stephen	28	0	29	9
Miranda	37	16	35	8
Andrea	3	5	8	2
Sarah	15	8	28	0
Sub-total	**204**	**73**	**234**	**109**

No Interview				
Filipa	17	6	9	14
Peggy	12	5	9	12
Trixie	7	10	18	10
Nadine	16	1	8	9
Sharon	7	4	7	9
Mitchell	3	4	18	5
Joshua	8	1	8	5
Ralph	7	3	5	4
Anthony	7	4	4	4
Marg	13	4	10	1
Sub-total	**97**	**42**	**96**	**73**
Total	**301**	**115**	**330**	**182**

Table 6.4: Time frames for data analysis

Block A	February 11th–April 19th.	Five weeks of coursework and a school teaching experience.
Block B	April 22nd–July 19th.	Six weeks of coursework and a school teaching experience.
Block C	July 22nd–October 25th.	Seven weeks of coursework and a school teaching experience.

The three time-frames, in context with the university coursework and the school teaching experiences, are illustrated in Table 6.4.

Figure 6.1 illustrates how student-teachers' concerns, as a group, shifted throughout the course. In this case, the sum of coded journal entries for all participants in each of the three blocks of time has been used to construct the line graph. The graph demonstrates the increase in concern with both teaching and learning in the second time-frame. It also shows the degree to which these two concerns tend to overshadow concerns about self and the course. The emphasis on these two concerns may well be a guide to the degree to which these student-teachers are reflecting on their developing teaching skills. Such a shift in concern toward one's own teaching and teacher/pupil learning is worthy of note as recognition of this can be used as a way of concurrently influencing the nature of the pre-service curriculum,

Figure 6.1: Concerns (determined by journal entries related to attitude) over time

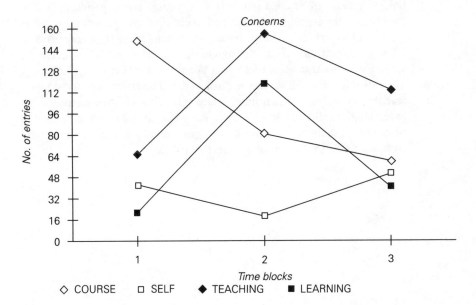

so that the emphasis of the course can better match the perceived needs and concerns of the student-teachers.

Summary

Journal writing is one window into student-teachers' thinking. This chapter has portrayed individuals' attitudes and concerns throughout their pre-service education program. The purpose of this has been to establish a reasonable base from which the exploration of these student-teachers' reflective processes might be pursued.

It is important to remember that journals are only one tool for exploring students' thinking and that the nature of the tool may of course inhibit some individuals more than others. It is to be expected that the results of this analysis may not fully credit the thoughts of some of the student-teachers as their attitude to journal writing also impacts on that which is documented. Nonetheless, I believe that there is sufficient evidence to support the following propositions:

1. There is a marked variation in the extent to which these student-teachers display the attitudes of open-mindedness, responsibility and whole-heartedness. This may be influenced by the degree of 'extra' involvement i.e., being interviewed.
2. Open-mindedness is most commonly displayed by student-teachers, followed by responsibility and whole-heartedness. This trend is a guide to

the readiness of student-teachers to reflect as it may be less difficult to with-hold judgment (to be open-minded) to new ideas and experiences, but to then reason through the purposes and likely outcomes of actions requires more than superficial inquiry. Finally, to whole-heartedly engage in following thoughts and actions through to their conclusion, and to accept the subsequent consequences, requires a genuine commitment to thinking.

3. The extent to which an attitude is displayed will be affected by the student-teacher's concerns. Shifts from concerns related to self to concerns related to learning, parallel the development of a preparedness to reflect. This will be examined in more detail in Chapter 7 as I attempt to uncover how these attitudes relate to the use of a reflective cycle.

Understanding the Reflective Cycle

Introduction

Journals, as a window into students' thoughts, have demonstrated how the attitudes of open-mindedness, responsibility and whole-heartedness can be detected and understood. In a similar vein, journal entries that illustrate any of the five phases of reflection (suggestions, problem, hypothesis, reasoning and testing) can also be uncovered in students' writing. As a consequence, journal entries allow one to identify and view these phases and are one way of determining the presence of reflection and how it is developed and used over time.

The sequence of the five phases is not fixed. The relationship of one phase to another may vary depending on a number of factors, such as the context of the situation, the experience of the individual or the complexity of the problem. As the framework for writing in the journals was not fixed or rigid, the extent to which these phases might be noted could also vary accordingly. One individual may focus more on the apparent *problem* in a situation, another might be concerned with offering *suggestions* to solve the problem whilst another might be more involved in considering how to *test* a hypothesis. Regardless of the particular emphasis of each student-teacher's thoughts, if these phases can be detected through their journals then it is reasonable to conclude that reflection is being employed as an active process in learning about teaching. This chapter is designed to give a broad view of the emerging reflective processes of my student-teachers.

Detecting Reflection

Each journal was coded for the five phases of the reflective cycle. As a result of coding for reflection in this manner, it was immediately obvious that students did not use all five phases in every situation. In fact, it may be that the number of phases employed and their variation over time is an indication of the development of an individual's reflective processes.

Table 7.1 gives an overview of the number of coded journal entries for each phase of the reflective cycle for each member of the TAL class (N=19). The rank order has been arbitrarily determined simply from the number of suggestions. However, it is interesting to note that a similar ranking would also apply if testing was used as the determinant of rank. Once again the participants who were

Table 7.1: Number of coded journal entries per student per phase of the reflective cycle

Name	Group	Suggestions	Problem	Hypothesis	Reasoning	Testing
Pearl	Int.	35	40	35	26	17
Miranda	Int.	29	28	28	24	19
Jack	Int.	20	24	24	19	9
Nadine	No Int.	17	20	19	10	3
Perry	Int.	16	17	17	16	14
Sarah	Int.	16	15	12	9	4
Sabina	Int.	13	16	15	12	5
Stephen	Int.	13	13	13	9	5
Ralph	No Int.	13	21	9	0	3
Sharon	No Int.	11	13	14	7	7
Filipa	No Int.	9	14	14	4	5
Mitchell	No Int.	9	16	10	3	2
Peggy	No Int.	8	16	18	12	4
Marg	No Int.	8	15	9	2	0
Nigel	Int.	8	11	11	7	0
Andrea	Int.	6	10	6	2	0
Anthony	No Int.	5	9	7	2	3
Joshua	No Int.	5	5	3	0	0
Trixie	No Int.	3	8	5	4	1
Total		**244**	**311**	**269**	**168**	**101**

interviewed generally displayed a higher ranking than those who were not inter-viewed. Pearl, Miranda, Jack and Perry particularly stand out as they have overall totals for each of the five phases of reflection which consistently and dramatically outstrip those of the remainder of the cohort. Marg, Nigel, Andrea and Joshua are at the other end of the spectrum; they did not record any instances of testing in their journal writing.

Table 7.1 also gives an overview of the total number of coded journal entries for each phase of reflection. From this it can be seen that in the reflective cycle the phase most frequently written about was the *problem*, followed by *hypothesis* gen-eration, then *suggestions*, *reasoning* and finally *testing*. This overall trend is similar to that for most of the individual scores.

Reflection clearly appears to be initiated through recognition of a problem situation. In identifying the problem (or being confronted by a puzzling situation), the student is prompted to form a hypothesis to guide further observation about the problem. At the same time this prompts suggestions about possible solutions; the impetus for reflection is ignited.

In the majority of cases, the coded entries for each of the phases of the reflective cycle recorded in Table 7.1 are not sub-sets of complete reflective cycles. Whether the 'missing phases' were occurring in the student-teachers' minds but were not written in the journals is not known; the coding of the journals did not occur until after the participants had completed their pre-service program, and therefore they were not able to be quizzed about it. Also, as they were not aware of the coding procedure or the approach to analysis (and were writing as a course requirement not a research project), there was no way of their knowing how to con-struct their writing to 'fit' any coding procedure.

One way of interpreting these results is that, as the number of coded journal entries for the first three phases was noticeably higher than for the final two phases, it may be that the grouping of these three phases is an indication of an initial (or naive) level of reflection. The frequency of coded journal entries for reasoning and testing shows that these two phases are less frequently used during reflection. If the first three phases together are one stage in reflective thinking, then the incorporation of reasoning followed by testing may be an indication of an increased degree of sophistication in the use of reflection.

Reasoning requires a purposeful approach to working through the hypothesis and considering it from different perspectives. This is not a subconscious act. Reasoning through a situation is a purposeful act which requires more deliberation and thought than suggestions where the ideas more readily appear to 'spring' to mind. The reduction in the number of coded journal entries recorded for reasoning may be a sign that this more active and conscious thinking is occurring.

Table 7.1 also demonstrates a decrease in the number of coded journal entries from reasoning to testing. Again, this may be indicative of a further refinement of the use of reflection. Individuals who display the ability to test their solution to a problem (whether it be by overt or imaginative action) are demonstrating a commitment to resolving the issue which initiated their thinking. The decreased number of entries for testing may well indicate that this is the most difficult phase of the reflective cycle. This final step is the most demanding and least spontaneous, demonstrating that reflection is a considered and active process of thinking.

The reflective cycle might therefore be viewed as comprising five phases or elements with varying levels of use. An initial level of use may include the first three phases as (from this study) they are most frequently employed. The next level of use might follow when reasoning through a situation becomes a more conscious and active process in reflection. Finally, there might be a third level of use in which testing the hypothesis actually occurs in an attempt to resolve the problem situation. The use of the third level may illustrate the most sophisticated form of reflection as the 'building blocks' of thought have been used as a foundation to purposeful pedagogical action. Testing could lead to resolution or to reconsidering the problem, dependent on the outcome of the test. The proposition that the five phases or elements of reflection might correspond to three different levels of use is schematically represented in Figure 7.1.

Figure 7.2 shows that the pattern of use of the five phases in both the interviewed and non-interviewed groups is similar and that problem, hypothesis and suggestions occur more frequently than do reasoning and testing. The relative proportion of journal entries for these three phases (suggestions, problem, hypothesis) are similar while the distinction between these three phases and reasoning is marked, as might be expected from the schemata proposed in Figure 7.1. The quantitative difference between reasoning and hypothesis is greater than that for hypothesis and suggestions, and problem and suggestions. The number of journal entries could therefore be a sign of a differentiation between the first and second level of use. The number of entries for the third level of use (testing) is also noticeably different from that of the preceding level.

Figure 7.1:   Levels of use of the reflective phases

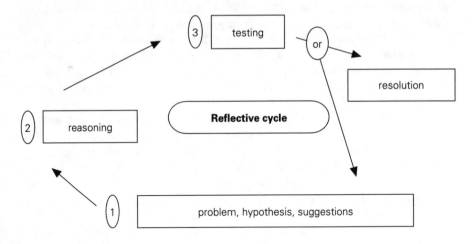

Figure 7.2:   Reflective phases by group (interviewed/not interviewed)

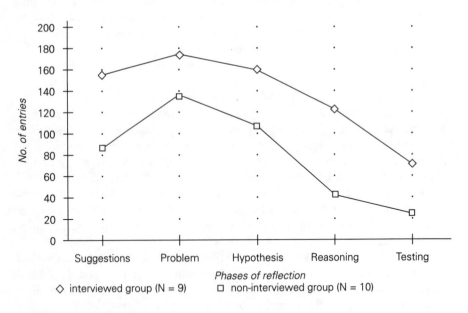

The non-interviewed group, as shown in Figure 7.2, demonstrates a greater difference between the hypothesized first level of use and the second than that which is illustrated by the interviewed group. It is a most noticeable distinction and again supports the idea that reasoning is a deliberate phase which may be quite separate from the first three phases. Recognition of a problem, suggestions springing to mind and the formation of a hypothesis may occur, but being able to reason through the situation calls for a more considered and purposeful process, something which does not always naturally follow on from the first three phases. The non-interviewed group also shows a difference between the second and third level of use but it is less than it is for the interviewed group. The levels could then relate to an increase in the need for conscious deliberation resulting in an increase in the degree of difficulty associated with so doing, thus suggesting that the more adept one becomes at deliberating through reasoning and testing, the more developed one's reflective actions become.

The movement from level one to level two is more apparent in the non-interviewed group while the movement from level two to level three is not as distinct for this group. However, the total number of journal entries is also much lower for the non-interviewed group than the interviewed group. Hence the change is initially accentuated (as in the difference from level one to level two), then not as noticeable (as in the difference between level two and level three) as the overall number of journal entries approaches its baseline.

If the use of the reflective cycle is something that is developed and refined over time, then perhaps what these students' journal writing demonstrates is their *learning* about reflection. There may be an increase in the use of these levels of reflection over time as student-teachers become more aware of, and more skilled in, their use. Using the three time-frames described in Table 6.4 (p. 86), Figure 7.3 demonstrates that there is a marked increase in the number of coded journal entries for each of the five phases from the first to the second time-frame, particularly so in relation to reasoning and testing. Even though there is a decline between the second and third time-frames, the number of coded journal entries for the third time-frame is generally still greater than that of the first time-frame. It is likely that the decrease in the number of journal entries in the third time-frame is related to the inevitable winding down at the end of the course. Although the third time-frame still had a school teaching experience, it was followed by five weeks of coursework and electives which received less attention in the student-teachers' journals than did the third school teaching experience and the previous time-frames. In fact, the results of the third time-frame also illustrate how important it is for student-teachers to have school teaching experience as an immediate and personal impetus for reflection.

This decline in the number of coded journal entries in the third time-frame is understandable as much of the student-teachers' energy is directed toward learning about and refining their teaching skills. In their minds, the major focus of their studies is to prepare for their school teaching experiences, therefore after the third (and final) school teaching experience there is a winding down as the focus shifts from their immediate teaching needs. The impetus for reflection consequently decreases.

Despite this, the number of coded journal entries for each phase of reflection, and consequently each of the hypothesized levels of use, is still greater in the third time-frame than in the first. Therefore, it does appear likely that the student-teachers have become more adept at using reflection and that their increased teaching experience has led them to be more capable of reasoning and testing. Over time, the increase in the number of coded journal entries suggests that their experiences have aided their ability to more deliberately consider and plan their thinking about action. Their use of the reflective cycle has increased over time.

Figure 7.3 strongly supports this view. The testing column in Figure 7.3 shows how dramatic the increase is from the first time-frame to the second. Also, considering the fact that the third school teaching experience was very early in the third time-frame, the high frequency of testing at this time is again evidence of the close link between teaching practice and increased use of reflection. The general trend of higher values in the second time-frame (for all phases of reflection) could be due to student-teachers reconsidering their second school teaching experience and casting their mind forward to their upcoming third (and final) school teaching experience. Therefore, in the second time-frame they may well be at their optimum level of need as they can readily think back over experiences and anticipate their future experiences.

An important point that accompanies this notion of increasing levels of use is that this argument is being applied to student-teachers' *learning* about, through the *use* of, reflection. This means that as they develop their reflective skills they do so through a progression that leads them to move through problem recognition, to better understanding the problematic nature of the situation, to devising a way of testing a possible resolution to the problem. When this progression leads to testing the reconsidered or reformulated pedagogical action then the elements of reflection become a whole reflective cycle and, just as Dewey (1933) suggested, so the elements become a consequence of events which do not necessarily follow a set order. Rather, they occur in concert, each initiating another element as the mind purposefully reconsiders action. It is this difference between learning about reflection as a student-teacher as opposed to being an experienced reflective practitioner which needs to be recognized. Once the learning leads to fruitful results, then the use of a reflective cycle may well become an event which no longer draws on these individual levels in the same form as it did in the initial stages of learning.

Attitudes and Reflection

Problem recognition is most frequently employed by all of the student-teachers and it is most likely the catalyst for reflection. As the number of entries for problem increases, so does the number of entries for hypothesis and suggestions. This suggests that the ability to recognize a problem influences the number of suggestions and hypotheses proposed, but the ability to reason and test is not so well developed.

It is most noticeable that in all five phases of the reflective cycle that the interviewed group's aggregate of journal entries was much greater than the non-interviewed group's totals. This could further support the rankings (suggested in Table 6.1, p. 83) where attitudes were seen as a guide to preparedness for reflection. As the first seven rankings from Table 6.1 were from the interviewed group, it is logical to expect that they would also register a higher number of entries for the reflective cycle. The greater the number of coded journal entries for attitude, the greater the number of entries present for each of the five phases of reflection. Therefore, attitudes are a substantial indicator of preparedness for reflection.

Figure 7.3: *Reflective phases over time using the three time-frames described in Table 6.4*

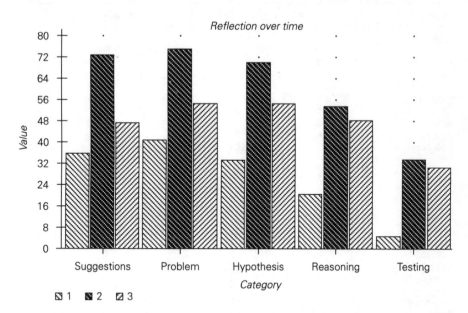

Whole-heartedness seems to be the major indicator of the extent to which the reflective *cycle* is used. If open-mindedness is an indicator of preparedness for reflection, then whole-heartedness is an indicator of the use of the three levels of reflection, or of the complete use of the reflective cycle rather than individual phases. The greater the number of entries for whole-heartedness, the greater the overall use of the reflective cycle.

The proposition that there are levels of use of the reflective cycle therefore takes on further significance as the use of the reflective cycle and attitudes appear to be very closely linked. If there are levels of use, open-mindedness may be an indicator of initial use of reflection at level one, responsibility may suggest a development of greater deliberation and use of reflection incorporating level two, and whole-heartedness may indicate the full use of a reflective cycle and correspond to the incorporation of use at level three. The importance of this for teacher educators is that — as is demonstrated in this case — it is indeed possible to observe the use of reflection by student-teachers and to recognize probable determinants of its use. Therefore, the ability to foster the development of reflective thinking becomes a reality through enhancing the attitudes of open-mindedness, responsibility and whole-heartedness in student-teachers. Thus teacher educators should actively pursue this through their teaching and interaction with their teacher education students.

Initiating Reflection

Table 7.2 demonstrates that for both the interviewed and non-interviewed groups, teaching is by far the most common issue that causes student-teachers to reflect.

Table 7.2: Number of journal entries (initiating reflection) per issue/concern

Interviewed	1. Course	2. Self	3. Teaching	4. Learning
Jack	22	16	33	25
Perry	3	9	45	20
Nigel	7	0	17	6
Pearl	28	12	80	33
Sabina	12	10	9	27
Stephen	8	5	35	5
Miranda	11	20	67	32
Andrea	0	17	4	3
Sarah	6	12	38	0
Sub-total	**97**	**101**	**328**	**151**
No interview				
Filipa	0	2	39	5
Peggy	0	14	21	23
Trixie	0	0	21	0
Nadine	9	31	21	8
Sharon	2	22	25	6
Mitchell	0	7	27	6
Joshua	0	2	6	6
Ralph	3	15	26	2
Anthony	1	4	11	2
Marg	2	15	15	2
Sub-total	**17**	**112**	**212**	**60**
Total	**114**	**213**	**540**	**211**

The higher number of entries for the interviewed group again supports the rankings suggested in Table 6.1. This could also be due to the additional probing of this topic in the individual interviews, thus maintaining a more persistent awareness of teaching issues with these student-teachers throughout the year. It also supports the view that interaction with student-teachers in forms which extend beyond 'normal classroom teaching' are beneficial for their pedagogical thinking and development.

An important difference between the interviewed and non-interviewed groups is the number of journal entries for topic 4: Learning. Learning is ranked second for the interviewed group and third for the non-interviewed group. Further to this, the number of journal entries for this topic is 2.5 times greater for the interviewed group than for the non-interviewed group. This is in stark contrast to the non-interviewed group where, with only one exception, concerns for self are greater initiators of reflection than their concern for learning. Again, this may be indicative of the extra interaction related to being interviewed throughout the year helping those individuals to focus attention on issues which extend beyond those related to self.

Issues initiated as a result of considering specific topics in the course were, for both groups, the least cause of reflection. Yet the marked difference in the number of journal entries between the two groups for course related issues is interesting. The interviewed group's number of entries is almost six times greater than the non-interviewed group's number of entries, and over half the non-interviewed group's entries for this issue came from one student-teacher (Nadine). Again, the interviewed

Figure 7.4:   Concerns/issues which initiated reflection (determined by the number of journal entries) over time

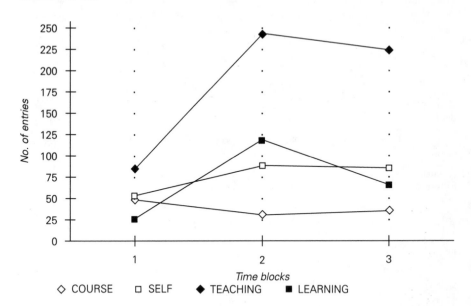

group appear to be more prone to reflect on issues and this may be indicative of a greater propensity to identify and link issues across contexts and content; again, perhaps also related to the extra probing in the individual interviews.

Finally, Figure 7.4 shows how the issues that caused these student-teachers to reflect varied over time. In a similar fashion to that demonstrated in Figure 6.1, concerns related to teaching and learning peaked during the second time-frame. As this was at one of the most intense periods for the student-teachers (in terms of both the course and teaching practice), it is heartening to see that their thoughts were primarily focused on their actions more so than on themselves. It is also interesting to see how reflection about teaching so dramatically overrides all other concerns for two-thirds of the year.

During the interviews, participants were questioned and probed about their views and were given more explicit foci for their dialogue than was the case for their journal writing. As a result, the number of coded segments of the reflective cycle for each participant is markedly higher than in Table 7.1 (the interviewed student-teachers' data from Table 7.1 have been added to Table 7.3 for ease of comparison).

The most dramatic increase is in the area of suggestions, so much so that it becomes the most predominant phase of the reflective cycle for all participants. This is in contrast to Table 7.1 in which problems recorded the highest number of coded segments. The change in communication from written to verbal is no doubt responsible for this shift as most of the interview questions were designed to probe the range of suggestions able to be proposed in different situations. Also, in an

Table 7.3: Number of coded interview and journal segments of transcript for each phase of the reflective cycle per interview

Pseudonym	Interview time	Suggestions	Problem	Hypothesis	Reasoning	Testing
Andrea	1	27	11	4	6	0
	2	24	9	5	4	3
	3	25	5	5	5	2
	4	28	7	2	8	4
Total		104	32	16	23	9
Journal*		6	10	6	2	0
Jack	1	40	11	8	6	2
	2	47	10	16	9	2
	3	49	8	8	8	1
	4	73	15	14	22	8
Total		209	44	46	45	13
Journal		20	24	24	19	9
Miranda	1	39	4	7	7	2
	2	43	6	10	9	5
	3	46	2	4	10	3
	4	52	5	12	17	6
Total		180	17	33	43	16
Journal		29	28	28	24	19
Nigel	1	29	7	8	8	5
	2	42	12	19	13	6
	3	33	8	10	14	5
	4	24	6	12	9	6
Total		128	33	49	44	22
Journal		8	11	11	7	0
Pearl	1	44	12	15	16	3
	2	35	15	9	7	6
	3	26	12	9	14	4
	4	36	17	10	17	5
Total		141	56	43	54	18
Journal		35	40	35	26	17
Perry	1	64	10	11	14	7
	2	51	19	18	25	11
	3	31	17	13	14	5
	4	43	20	17	26	11
Total		189	66	59	79	34
Journal		16	17	17	16	14
Sabina	1	37	7	6	6	1
	2	32	11	11	8	4
	3	42	6	5	7	3
	4	25	8	6	10	4
Total		136	32	28	31	12
Journal		13	16	15	12	5
Sarah	1	39	6	9	9	3
	2	29	9	10	11	8
	3	32	8	5	13	4
	4	25	8	7	12	4
Total		125	31	31	45	19
Journal		16	15	12	9	4
Stephen	1	40	6	7	9	2
	2	32	20	16	13	8
	3	36	7	9	12	7
	4	26	11	6	12	6
Total		134	44	38	46	23
Journal		13	13	13	9	5

* Journal: figures taken from Table 7.1, number of coded journal segments from student-teachers' journals

interview where the participant is being probed for further information the flow of suggestions is more easily recorded than in the case of journal writing where conscious decisions about what to write could override the documenting of a number of suggestions that spring to mind. Clearly, the ease of suggesting ideas verbally, or being questioned about possible alternatives to those initially suggested would lead to a greater response from interviewees.

Another reason for the differences between Table 7.3 and 7.1 is that the interview structure was designed to place the interviewees in a position which challenged them to reflect. Therefore, they were being encouraged to talk about how they would think in a given situation and why and how this could impact on their actions. Although the questions were not individually of that form, the sequence of questions created that scenario. So it is only reasonable to expect an increase in responses for each phase of the reflective cycle. Also, the interviews gave the opportunity to probe the participants' use of the reflective cycle as a whole thus increasing the understanding of how an individual actually approaches reflection. Miranda's second interview is a good example of this point. It demonstrates the complex nature of reflection and how the linking of episodes creates opportunities for enhanced understanding and learning. (Elements of the reflective cycle are included in the transcript for ease of identification: S = suggestions, P = problem etc.)

Miranda:	*2nd interview*
Interviewer:	If you had to teach a topic that you were unfamiliar with, how would you do it?
Miranda:	I wouldn't teach it until I felt comfortable with it. To do that I'd find out as much as I could about the topic [S 1]. I don't really think that I could go into a classroom not knowing much about the topic and carrying it off successfully, because I think I'd lack the confidence [P]. I feel that if I knew the subject matter and was confident with it I'd be willing to try different methods and strategies in the class room [H]. On the teaching round I found myself teaching the topic of insurance to Business Education and most of the stuff I did with them was chalk and talk, whereas I compare that to my Year 10 criminal law class that I knew a lot about and I felt really comfortable with the topic and I did heaps of stuff with them, role-plays, videos, because I felt comfortable with the topic [S 1 and R]. I really understood it so I was more willing to take risks and do things that were a bit out of the ordinary rather than just chalk and talk [T].
Interviewer:	Did you recognize in your Business Education class that you were more boring?
Miranda:	Yeah.

Interviewer: When did it occur to you?

Miranda: Probably after I had taught about two lessons of it. I wasn't happy, I was trying to do things differently, I did a few worksheets for them, I found this video that they seemed to like but because I wasn't as familiar with the topic [S 1]. I tended to stick to my structured notes and didn't really deviate from them [P]. But my Criminal Law class I hardly looked at my notes, the kids would ask me questions and that was fine, I could answer them straight off.

Interviewer: You said in Criminal Law you would take more risks. What do you mean by that?

Miranda: Just to do something out of the ordinary with the students.

Interviewer: Why would you do that?

Miranda: Because I thought it would help their learning more. Like I did a role-play with them, which I think given the same opportunity if I didn't understand what was going on I wouldn't have. The kids loved it and I used it in the next lesson after that and after that to draw it back, you know to say: What did Hugh do when he was Clerk of the Courts? [R]

Interviewer: If you think of those two classes, how does your planning for the two different classes vary?

Miranda: When I was planning Business Education I was more concerned with me, whether I would understand it. Criminal Law I was more concerned with the students, how they'd be taking it. I was fine so I was more receptive to how they'd understand. [R]

Interviewer: And when you walked out of the classes, what sort of thoughts did you have?

Miranda: After Business Education, I thought Thank God, it's over. After Crim., really good. In fact most of the time after Crim. I had lunch and the kids would stay in and ask me questions, they found it fascinating, so I always felt really happy, like I'd achieved something. The kids would come in next lesson and they'd seem more eager.

Interviewer: Did you notice any difference in the way you thought or questioned during the two lessons?

Miranda: Yes, my Crim. classes I was more prepared to have a less structured lesson, like I was more prepared to have students ask me questions and I was pretty quick with the answers, there was more class discussion. I did tape one of these lessons and it was more of half me and half them, but in Business Education, I did most of the talking, I directed it. I had a few times when they asked me questions and I didn't understand the content and I just tried to bluff my way through it [T 2].

Interviewer:	So you recognized those differences when you were teaching?
Miranda:	Yes, and after the round I thought I could've been better prepared [S 2]. Like what [another TAL staff member] was saying sticks in my mind saying about being able to teach anything at all as long as you stay a lesson ahead of the kids [P 2]. Some people might be able to, but not me and that's what I've been thinking lately, I feel much more comfortable teaching things that I know about [H 2]. I don't agree with [the other TAL staff member] it might be fine for some people, but I would question how much the students are getting out of it. They would sense that you didn't know much more [R 2].
Interviewer:	So that statement of [other TAL staff member] from about four months ago, you re-visit?
Miranda:	Constantly.

This transcript shows how Miranda is reflecting on a teaching experience and then linking the learning from that to a statement made by a lecturer at the beginning of the year. The two reflective cycles combined demonstrate how a problem from one situation can be revisited through another. This conversation illustrates the point that the sequences of the reflective cycle are not fixed but may occur in any order. It also supports the notion that testing does not have to lead to the immediate resolution of a problem. So the reflective cycle as demonstrated in Figure 7.2 can occur over an extended period of time with testing leading back into the cycle again. The context of one scenario influences the reflective processes of another.

The difference between the thinking demonstrated in journals and interviews is interesting. The interviews encouraged the participants to think and allowed them to demonstrate their reflection more fully. In the journals, individuals did not have to respond to the prompting and probing of others unless they chose to; the very nature of interviews makes it difficult not to respond. These two sources serve different purposes and each are important in their own right for showing that these student-teachers do indeed reflect on their practice. However, Miranda's data is considerably different to all the others in Table 7.3. She is the only participant whose number of coded entries is greater for the journal data (problem and testing) than for her interview data. Miranda may well be illustrating that her thinking about teaching is not as markedly influenced through the interviews as the rest of the cohort and that her writing more fully demonstrates her reflection. She may be the type of developing reflective practitioner who questions all aspects of her reflective cycles as she works toward the ideas that she wishes to test. In fact, reviewing her categorization for attitudes (see Table 6.1, p. 83), she displays the highest number of coded journal entries for responsibility for the whole TAL class. Likewise, she is also ranked second (see Table 7.1) for the number of coded journal entries for each phase of the reflective cycle. Miranda's writing is a good indication of her reflective thoughts.

Table 7.3 also demonstrates that testing is still the least employed phase of the reflective cycle and therefore perhaps the most difficult, or the most sophisticated level of use (refer to Figure 7.1). Testing requires one to try an alternative approach to a problem situation. Throughout the interviews the distinction between what might be possible to test as opposed to what an individual would do or had done in a given situation was apparent. This was particularly so for Nigel and highlights again the role of experience in reflection. Although Table 7.3 does not show any definitive pattern or trend in the change of use of the reflective cycle over time, the transcripts, as opposed to simply the number of coded segments, demonstrates an increase in the quality of reflection over time. Examples of testing moved from thoughts to actions and the use of reflection became more defined and purposeful. Miranda demonstrates this point well as she reflects on her past experiences, and the risks she was prepared to take in her teaching. Thinking as she does illustrates how reflection influences the type of testing she performs, the learning she gains from it, and how reflection on that experience influences her view of future action. She no longer thinks about what she might do, she thinks about experiences that shape what she does (or will) do.

Miranda:	*4th interview*

Interviewer: If you had to teach a topic you were unfamiliar with, how would you do it?

Miranda: First thing I'd do, I wouldn't go into the class unless I was confident that I knew something about it [P 1], but I think now it's quite possible to learn something yourself so that you can go and teach it [H 1], I'd probably speak to other teachers who've taught it before and who know about it and ask them for different ways of doing things, and see if they can direct me towards different resources for me to learn something myself and to use in the classroom. Once again I'd probably rely on other staff who've taught it before then I'd go and try to learn by watching videos reading through text books, newspapers etc., so that I had confidence in the subject before I went out and tried to teach the students [S and R]. At the start of the year I probably wouldn't like to have taught something I wasn't sure [P 1] of basically because I think if you understand the subject matter, you're more confident and more able to or more willing to try different things in the classroom [H 1] and not as worried about students tripping you up knowing more than you. Now, however, during the year it probably wouldn't worry me because I've been in the situation of teaching something that I knew nothing about before I got to the school and I did all of these things, talked to other teachers, read books, looked at videos and so forth and I probably wasn't as confident as teaching it but I was happy to do so. How I got out of it I did a lot of student-centred activities, I'd let them find out things and they'd then tell me [T], I had to teach Cambodia and the Pol Pot regime and I had no idea, but it was good fun though. So no, I don't think it would phase me though I'd make sure I knew something about it before I went into the class though.

This qualitative change and its application will be examined in Chapter 8, where individuals' reflective thinking and when it occurs are explored.

Summary

Attempting to draw conclusions of a general nature about a whole TAL group with such a diversity of students is difficult. However, the purpose has been to determine whether or not it is possible to see if student-teachers employ reflection as a conscious cognitive strategy. As a result of this exploration I believe that it is possible to advance a number of valid generalizations about this group of student-teachers.

1. Although all of the participants in this study employ reflection, there is a detectable variation in the extent and degree of sophistication of its use. Nonetheless, they all reflect on their experiences.
2. The five phases of the reflective cycle are used to varying degrees by each of the student-teachers. Although the phases are not necessarily limited to a defined pattern or order, problem, suggestions and hypothesis may well comprise one distinct level of use, followed by reasoning at another level and testing at the highest (or most sophisticated) level of use. This could also be related to a developing awareness of, and skill in, the use of reflection over time.
3. The attitudes of open-mindedness, responsibilty and whole-heartedness appear to be reasonable indicators of preparedness for reflection and may also be indicators of the levels of use of the reflective cycle: open-mindedness corresponding to level one, responsibility corresponding to level two and whole-heartedness corresponding to level three.
4. Student-teachers who display the most sophisticated use of reflection are more likely to reflect on issues that are further removed from themselves. They have the ability to consider issues which may be as a consequence of matters other than their own initial actions. They can reflect on issues/ concerns that may be at a higher plane and which require a greater quality of reflection than the 'here and now'. This may also be related to van Manen's (1977) levels of reflectivity in that the more able a student-teacher is at considering issues beyond the technical, the more likely he or she is at using the reflective phases as a complete cycle.

5. In this case, student-teachers who were interviewed appear to have been markedly affected by this intervention such that their propensity for reflection has been heightened.

6. The propensity of student-teachers to reflect is linked to their need to learn about and refine their teaching; once their organized school teaching experiences are completed their perceived need to reflect diminishes.

Part 4

Reflection 'in Practice'

Chapter 8

Three Reflective Instances

Introduction

The five phases of the reflective cycle have been recognized through student-teachers' journals and interview dialogue. In each case the individual phases have been tallied to give an overall picture of the way the reflective cycle has been used by participants as they learn about teaching. This chapter is designed to explore when these student-teachers employ reflection in their teaching. In so doing it outlines some of the difficulties associated with reflection and how these are related to confidence, experience and learning from doing.

Reflection: When Does it Occur?

The interviews were designed to explore how the student-teachers thought at different times and in different situations and it soon became apparent that there were notable variations from person to person. These student-teachers thought about their teaching in different ways and at different times for different reasons. They demonstrated pre-lesson planning and post-lesson thinking; this varied depending on the individual's view of what would (or had happened) and why, and whether and/or how this might influence their students' learning. They also showed signs of thinking about their thoughts and actions during teaching episodes. These three distinct periods of thinking (pre, during, and post lesson) offer opportunities for reflection, as Miranda demonstrates.

Miranda: *4th interview*

Miranda: Before lessons, probably there's a lot [of thinking] because most of what I've been teaching I've learnt before like in school, so I've looked back on how I was taught it and when I think back on how we went through it and how we might've done it at methods [subject discipline] here, I do a lot of reflecting before classes, I do a lot of planning before classes and try to work out how things have gone and think a lot about things before class. During class is more difficult I think, it really wasn't until third round that I started to think of these things during class. First round and probably second I was more concerned with what I was doing, not so much the effects of what I was doing, or questioned whether I should be doing something better during class time but by third round I started to do that. Like I had one lesson where I thought this isn't working so I just had to change tack. I probably do most of my reflecting after teaching, I think a lot about [my teaching] before and I'm starting to do more during but it's after I've taught something I've actually got into the process of going through my lesson plans and writing an evaluation, we weren't asked to or anything though, often what the supervising teacher was saying was different to what I thought . . . probably I was more critical on myself. They'd say oh that worked well and I'd think, no it could've worked better and so I'd go and make a note of it so that if I taught something again I could look back and maybe remember that and do it differently. So I think I do most of my reflecting after class.

Baird (1990) recognized these three periods of reflection described by Miranda and labelled them as anticipatory reflection (pre-teaching), contemporaneous reflection (during teaching) and retrospective reflection (post teaching). Throughout the interviews, as opportunities presented themselves, these three reflective instances were explored to see how they influenced the student-teachers' reflection on teaching and learning.

Anticipatory Reflection

In order to teach a lesson satisfactorily there is a need to think about the content to be taught, the method to employ in teaching it and why that method is applicable. For most student-teachers lesson plans are a formal way of structuring their thinking about teaching, and as they become more accustomed to and comfortable with teaching, their use of written lesson plans tends to decrease. However, there is a difference between planning a lesson and reflecting on how that lesson might unfold, the options available in the teaching and learning environment, and the reasons for the actions adopted.

Considering the likely scenario and the nuances associated with the complexity of teaching are indicative of anticipatory reflection. This is perhaps the first time that student-teachers differentiate between simply considering an approach to teaching and genuinely reflecting on how to teach.

Pearl offers an insight into anticipatory reflection when she talks about her micro-teaching in the first weeks in the course. In the following example, Pearl illustrates how purposeful anticipatory reflection can be.

Pearl: *1st interview*

Pearl: I do that [reflect] most when I have to process something and then have to do something with it. Because I find that I come up with a whole lot of ideas but I need to sift through what's relevant and what isn't . . . a whole lot of ideas come up and a lot of them will be relevant and a whole lot will not be so then I need to take all those ideas, leave it for a while, probably write it down, then come back and say this is how it works . . .

Interviewer: Well let me remind you of a situation. When you were doing your micro-teaching did you reflect (I'll use that term because you've already used it) on what you were going to do?

Pearl: Yep. Thinking about what I was going to do. I probably spent the first three or four days just thinking about what topic I might do, why I would or wouldn't do it, what would be problematic and what wouldn't. Then it was easier to watch other people do it [their micro-teaching] and see where the problems were. Like it seemed to me to be much harder to try and just present information. I had to do some filtering of like scenarios of what would and what wouldn't work and the thing that was worrying me was the thing that I found hardest was that idea of urbanization [the topic she was going to micro-teach] to try and get that information, to try and pick it up with the video [being video taped in the micro-teaching situation] could make me sweat I think, so how, what approaches may or might not work . . . I've always done that. I think that that's one reason why I'm more conscious of it at the moment. I make resolutions about what to do or not to do.

Pearl shows that her anticipatory reflection involves an approach to thinking about her teaching in ways that allow her to make suggestions, pose problems, reason through her choices, hypothesize on what might or might not work and why, then to settle on a course of action which she can test in her teaching. Although she does not use these terms, it appears implicit in her description that this is what she is doing. She is reflecting on different approaches to teaching content, sifting and sorting the ideas that she has until she settles on an approach to adopt. This anticipatory reflection gives her an opportunity to approach her teaching in a way that is more responsive than mechanistic. By thinking about teaching in this manner she is not driven so much by a need to concentrate on the technicalities of teaching skills (e.g., questioning, wait-time) but by a holistic approach to teaching which may subsume these skills rather than be dictated by them.

Reflecting on what might be, how a teaching episode might progress, gives a greater sense of purpose to the teaching. Perry demonstrates this in his description of how he anticipates what might be. He has a purpose that drives his thinking giving purpose and meaning to his reflection.

Perry: *4th interview*

Perry: I think what if this happens, what if that happens, how will I counter that, [what's an appropriate] division of time and resources. So I think about as many different things as can happen, what's the worst thing that can happen, what's the best thing that can happen, what's my contingency plan, those sort of things . . . that obviously helps in the running of the class . . . if I have one desire, it's to make them do more of the learning and me to do less of the talking because I do, I talk too much. I'd really like to work more in a one to one [situation], or with smaller groups, or observe smaller groups.

Stephen also considers his actions in a framework of 'what might be if', hypothesizing and reasoning through possibilities so that his teaching is appropriate to his students' learning. He also briefly introduces the idea that previous experiences play a part in influencing anticipatory reflection.

Stephen: *4th interview*

Stephen: Before a lesson, I don't know if I think I'd call it reflecting but I think about what could happen in that lesson based upon previous experiences in class, OK. It is reflection . . . before or after a lesson, I mightn't do much writing [referring to his journal] I'm just preparing and collecting things I might need, and I might be thinking about it and deciding why or why not I'll use it or leave it.

It is interesting that in different ways all of these quotes have the same theme running through them. Each of the student-teachers is concerned with the 'why' (reasoning) of their methodology; the 'how' (suggestions) does not seem to be a major concern. Therefore, the likelihood that there might be meaningful learning about their teaching through anticipatory reflection is enhanced because they are planning to do more than 'survive' or 'cope' through the experience. By being committed to test their thinking about teaching, they are placing themselves in a position of learning, and from that testing, to continue the reflective cycle as proposed in Figure 7.1 as their results are an impetus for further reflection.

   This anticipatory reflection involves considering possibilities before deciding on a means of action. The ability to anticipate outcomes would clearly be influenced by one's previous experiences (as noted by Stephen), so it seems a natural progression for a thoughtful pedagogue to be interested in learning from the testing situation. Therefore, reflecting on that experience should proceed at the conclusion of the test. Hence the development of retrospective reflection.

Retrospective Reflection

Recognizing the difference between a reflective cycle as opposed to merely reviewing a teaching and learning experience is important in understanding the value and complexity of retrospective reflection.

Many student-teachers readily depart their classes relieved that they have completed another lesson. Therefore, there is a major difference between a person thinking that a lesson was either 'good' or 'bad' and a person reflecting on that experience to learn from it. Retrospective reflection should encompass learning from the experience regardless of the perceived success of the episode. The key to retrospective reflection might well be in the questions: 'Why was the lesson "good" or "bad"?' and 'How can the learning from that lesson shape my thinking about other situations?' Through these questions it is likely that reflection will be initiated.

These student-teachers demonstrate that retrospective reflection plays a part in their development as reflective practitioners and that its use influences their learning about teaching. For Andrea and Jack, retrospective reflection means learning from experiences so that they do not 'make the same mistakes twice'. Therefore, recognizing a problem would be the start of the reflective cycle. Being removed from the situation, having time to reflect after the event, is important in shaping how they might respond to the learning.

Andrea:	*3rd interview*
Andrea:	Do I think about my teaching after I've taught a lesson? Well you must in order to prepare for the next class. I do, you must. I go home and think about the class. . . .
Andrea:	*4th interview*
Andrea:	I question where I went wrong and what I'd like to have done differently. If it's something that failed I try to think why it failed if I presented something incorrectly or got into a knot with my words, or the instructions weren't clear enough, or at what point did I lose the class or at what point did I confuse some people, always trying to recap on those things before next lesson. I'd always try to avoid the same problems in the next lesson or to recap on those things.
Jack:	*1st interview*
Jack:	I guess I'm reflecting at the moment. I guess often I reflect, I go back over some notes, you just try to look behind the lines, to what's written to what they really mean, try to get to the base of it, try and get to the concept.
Interviewer:	Are there particular times that that occurs? When does it occur for you?

Jack: After most of the time, I think back over it, at the time I try and absorb it rather than make sense of it, and later on I might try and go over it a bit more closely and see what it means.

Jack: *4th interview*

Jack: I think my best reflection time is after. I think of the actual writing process that I do after as far as writing and evaluating comments from lessons and that is best after for me which is probably a couple of hours after it.

Interviewer: What impact does that have on your teaching?

Jack: You're less likely to make mistakes, or less likely to make the ones that you made in that lesson.

Finding a way into retrospective reflection so that it is more than a fleeting glance of an experience is important. As Jack demonstrates (above), there may be structured or organized ways of initiating the cycle. Seeing a need to reflect retrospectively may facilitate more formal approaches as is the case with Miranda.

Miranda: *4th interview*

Miranda: I probably do most of my reflecting after teaching, I think a lot about before and I'm starting to do more during but it's after I've taught something I've actually got into the process of going through my lesson plans and writing an evaluation, we weren't asked to or anything though, often what the supervising teacher was saying was different to what I thought a lot of the times, probably I was more critical on myself. They'd say oh that worked well and I'd think, no it could've worked better and so I'd go and make a note of it so that if I taught something again I could look back and maybe remember that and do it differently. So I think I do most of my reflecting after class.

For many of the student-teachers, retrospective reflection equates with improving the way the lesson was taught. However, understanding what improvement means is difficult. It might mean the way information was presented or how it was interpreted by the students. In some cases, reflection may encourage considering factors outside the teacher's control as the problem. Testing then becomes more difficult and less likely as the problem may be put to one side.

Sarah: *4th interview*

Sarah: After a lesson? Well of course you assess how the lesson went how you've performed, especially like did I do this right, did I do that right, and just how you think the kids enjoyed it and what

things I could've improved on that obviously didn't go down
well and perhaps why they didn't go down well. Like was it my
fault or was it to do with the environment or outside the classroom altogether or something like that, so just working out ways
of improving that.

Better understanding of one's pedagogy through retrospective reflection is possible
when the purpose of reflection allows the learning to go beyond the single teaching
episode. At one level there is learning how to teach a lesson or content area better,
but at another, there is learning to abstract the learning from one episode to another.
In either case it is through retrospective reflection that the developing pedagogue
is able to learn from and through their own experiences. Testing hypotheses about
teaching content differently requires a commitment to finding ways of being able
to repeat a teaching experience which allows the reasoned pedagogical adjustments
to be explored. Perry explained one way of doing this that satisfied his desire to
learn through reflection.

Perry: *4th interview*

Perry: [after a lesson] I'd think that could be different or that was a good
lesson, or a bad lesson. Well I'm never satisfied with my work ... I
used to consider what worked well, like I tried a lot of methods,
jigsaw and that sort of thing, and I repeated the same lesson three
times once to see what improvements I could make ...

At another level, Sabina recognizes a broader understanding of learning about
teaching by considering ways of applying thinking beyond the specific. Through
retrospective reflection she is able to consider her learning in one context so that
it might influence her teaching in a different context.

Sabina: *3rd interview*

Sabina: Well I mentally assess whether or not or how I thought the class
went whether it was a good class or a bad class and if it was bad
why was it bad and if it was good why was it good. If it was
a new activity I'd think about how the kids responded to it, and
if they responded well to it maybe you could incorporate that
more into the way you teach in different forms.

Reflection on a teaching episode is obviously important if one is to capitalize
on the learning from that experience. However, the focus of that reflection, the questions which guide and direct the hypotheses developed and the tests that might
be employed, will vary from individual to individual. To consider these guiding
questions, it appears important that retrospective reflection focuses on a concern for
pedagogical development so that learning may be from both 'good' and 'bad' lessons. The influence of the affective domain is important because a 'good' lesson can

encourage a student-teacher to reconsider the learnings from a teaching experience, while a 'bad' lesson (for some) might cause them to dismiss the episode completely and therefore limit their opportunities and pathways into retrospective reflection.

Contemporaneous Reflection

If anticipatory reflection is a starting point for student-teachers to develop ways of thinking about their approaches to pedagogy, and retrospective reflection is a vehicle for learning from attempting such approaches, then it is through contemporaneous reflection that they can learn from and about their practice in action. This is when the complex and dynamic nature of teaching may be developed so that it becomes immediately responsive to learning. In an environment where decisions often need to be made quickly, where the dominant perception is that problems and difficulties need to be resolved almost immediately, reflecting contemporaneously is not easy for student-teachers. Recognizing a need for, or the value of, contemporaneous reflection is one thing, being able to incorporate it into practice is another. So how do student-teachers address this dilemma?

Jack: 3rd interview

Interviewer: So when you're actually teaching . . .
Jack: . . . . sure, it means my teaching will be better for it because you're more in tune with what's happening, what your kids are learning. It's not easy during a lesson though because there's so much to think about. You've got to make time to reflect and not to have the pressure on you all the time as the focus.

Jack makes the point well that he needs to make time to reflect. He needs an opportunity to think about what he is doing without having to do something about it then and there. Recognition of the value of contemporaneous reflection and action from it are definitely two distinct domains in Jack's case. The ability to find time to reflect is the problem for Jack and in his mind he seems to see a need to ask the class to take 'time-out' for a moment so that he can think. This notion of time to reflect revolves around an ability to structure teaching so that time is available whilst the students are still 'on task', otherwise the prompt for the need to reflect contemporaneously may persist but be unresolved.

Sarah: 2nd interview

Interviewer: So when you were teaching were you saying things to yourself like, is this going the way I planned?
Sarah: Yes I was. Well I was trying to give them an image in their heads. Something to relate back to. While I was teaching them I just kept thinking, do something or say something

> that's going to get them to remember this class . . . I thought, give them something that it can relate to, something simple and perhaps they'll get more of a feel for it. So I was trying to get them to visualize, you know all the images I could think of . . . I just kept assessing how I was going and if I found something that wasn't working too well I'd try to work out a way to get it better, but generally the classes went as planned.

Sarah describes the difficulty in being able to respond quickly when reflecting in action. Problem recognition may have initiated a reflective cycle but her inability to quickly develop suggestions limits her capacity to develop 'on the spot' alternatives causing her to see that her classes *generally go as planned*. In this instance, Sarah may well be alluding to the fact that she has been unable to find sufficient time to resolve her problem in the class, or that she does not have enough experience to call on from which to draw suggestions in response to the problem. Therefore, the classes go as planned because, although she recognizes instances of contemporaneous reflection, the cycle begins but is not completed. The relationship between experience and time is expanded further by Sabina.

Sabina: *3rd interview*

Sabina: Sometimes, like in English, I find it easier in the classroom to assess what's going on and I think more quickly about how I'm going to change it and why I'm going to change it and have alternative strategies where I can change the pace. But something like history I find really quite difficult because it's so knowledge reliant as a subject and just personally at the moment I find it takes me a lot longer to think up ways that knowledge can be imparted through the kids being involved in the learning more. So that if something is not working in the classroom in history I'm less likely to come up with something quickly to change that but it might reflect on how I might teach that same unit in future.

Sabina outlines how her ability to reflect contemporaneously is closely linked to her understanding of the content knowledge; the better her content knowledge the better her 'response time' for changes in pedagogy in action. She also raises another point which is consistent with her approach to retrospective reflection. She says, 'It might reflect on how I might teach that same unit in the future.' Sabina is putting forward the idea that she learns from her attempts at contemporaneous reflection so that she might well be honing her skills when reflecting in action through doing. Also, her store of suggestions and hypotheses pertaining to certain pedagogical problems is being increased even though testing may not necessarily lead to resolution of the problem on each occasion.

The relationship between retrospective and contemporaneous reflection is important to recognize because although attempts at contemporaneous reflection may not be satisfying for the student-teacher, the opportunity to go back over them is offered through retrospective reflection. By learning from retrospective reflection, contemporaneous reflection may be enhanced. Pearl explains this well as she articulates the links between learning and reflection while still noting some of the difficulties associated with finding time to reflect in action.

Pearl:	*4th interview*
Pearl:	. . . before is the easiest because it's the easiest to do, you know, like you're trying to make sense of something that happens, not sure what's going to happen, then there's a strong push to actually engage in it. And that's where planning starts, you know, like partly reflection partly working out what works . . . Part of it though is extracting from past, past experiences now.
Interviewer:	Do you do that?
Pearl:	. . . yeah I have to create space for me if I want to reflect, I mean I actually actively say you will now have 2 minutes where you're not the person who is determining what will happen, where you can work out what they say, because I can't do it while I'm just responding. And unless, and unless I'm very comfortable I can't say, 'Hang on I just need to time off to reflect'. Afterwards, depending on how badly it's gone, I don't think about it first, it's like absolute shut down on it.
Interviewer:	What do you mean the worse it is the less likelihood it is that you think about it?
Pearl:	Well I can't think about it, like it's like scolding yourself every time you think about it. You know what I mean, like it's just like you think you're going to die, I'm going to die but I haven't but then there's a delayed time before coming back and you're trying to work it out. And you try to work it out, just what was going on and the way I do that is to try and get into it again and work out was happening, like why the responses and did I actually do that? And then I would carry that through until the next time. So before I teach again I go back, revisit all this stuff I've figured, does that make sense?

Contemporaneous reflection is, then, a challenge for student-teachers. It may be threatening or uncomfortable to recognize a need for alternative approaches to pedagogy during practice. The difficulty is also increased by not having suggestions on hand to reason through in order to address the problems in the teaching and learning episode. Pearl talks about her approach to learning in practice by reliving the event, vicariously placing herself back in the 'action present' to hypothesize about how she might have acted. Perry was able to recognize an opportunity to learn through contemporaneous reflection, the immediate threat of uncertainty about how to act being lessened by the recognition of the value of the learning for his students. The learning was so powerful that it encouraged him to continue to incorporate contemporaneous reflection more and more in his teaching.

Perry: *4th interview*

Perry: Like one of the best learning episodes that we had in the class was when I stuffed up on the board. All of a sudden the kids saw this as a chance to explore their knowledge. They were going what if this affects that and the inflation affects aggregate demand etc. The kids saw an opening for new ideas and new thoughts and it was really good so I didn't worry about not having the answer and I let them think on because I could feel the vibes from behind me. As I looked at the board I was reflecting. It might have only been half the kids but they were really challenging their knowledge and understanding of the information.

Interviewer: What allows you to do that sort of thing?

Perry: I guess it's based on my confidence . . . reflection I know I do it in the class, and I'm sure that most people do, it's just that they don't isolate it, and it's partly because of this study I tend to think about it. Like it's just, I think to myself well I've reflected and that's why I'm going to do this, and partly because I'm conscious of this study. That obviously helps in the running of the class. Like I feel comfortable in the class that I can change around in class, I don't feel bogged down by my lesson plan, when your supervisor comes in and they want a copy of your lesson plan I always feel more restricted and I've had to go up and say look I'm going off my lesson plan now and that's because of this, this and this.

Perry's description of learning about and through contemporaneous reflection is punctuated by references to this study. There is little doubt that being interviewed throughout the year about his views on teaching and learning was an intervention in the 'normal' process of his pre-service education course. However, the intervention was of a form that did not mandate ways of thinking or acting. I attempted to model an approach to thinking about teaching and coupled this with my probing of each individual's thoughts and views. Each student-teacher was able to make up their own mind about how much (if any) of what was happening to them needed to be incorporated in their own practice and, as the excerpts (above) demonstrate, there is a difference between individuals in the way that they have explored for themselves an understanding of contemporaneous reflection.

Overview

This chapter was designed to illustrate that student-teachers reflect about their practice in different ways and at different times. The point made by Perry that his thinking has been influenced by being a participant in this study is also important as it again highlights the value of the interaction between myself and my student-teachers in ways that go beyond their 'expected' class participation. There is ample evidence to suggest that modelling reflection has influenced both the participants' views of, and practice of anticipatory, contemporaneous and retrospective reflection. Miranda draws attention to this in her third interview and explains her practice, understanding and valuing of reflection.

Miranda:	*3rd interview*
Miranda:	I suppose to good teaching you should add thinking about it before during and after.
Interviewer:	Had you always thought that?
Miranda:	No, probably not. I know that you've said that in class, but I think it's true though.
Interviewer:	Why do you think it's important?
Miranda:	It's obviously important to plan and be thinking before a class, but it's important to be thinking about what you're doing during class so that as I said if you need to change tack you can do that, then after class you need to look back and see if something didn't work and ask why it didn't work rather than just throw it away and say I won't do that again. Just look at other ways you can improve it next time.
Interviewer:	Can you learn to do that? How do you learn to do that?
Miranda:	I think you have to be aware of it. I found that once you said it I started to think about it and started doing much more of it on the second teaching round than the first. The first was just, oh good it's over, next class. But second teaching round I'd take a step back after the class and think, go through my planning again and think about what I would do differently next time.
Interviewer:	Why?
Miranda:	Because I wasn't learning anything. Like first round was just survival. But the second round was exploring different things . . . like you should be ready to accept that things don't always go to plan but work out why and then think of other alternatives.

Interviewer:	Why do you think that?
Miranda:	Because you often say things in class like this isn't working or whatever
Interviewer:	Why do I do that?
Miranda:	You're doing that to tell us your thought processes so that hopefully we'll emulate them and think about it ourselves and I found I was doing that on teaching rounds . . . I may have realized the need for it myself but it definitely helps when you say those things.
Interviewer:	Is it easy to do?
Miranda:	I found it increasingly easy to do, it had a lot to do with confidence and knowing your subject matter and knowing your students and knowing that they're not going to think any less of you. So I don't think it's so hard now as long as you've got alternative strategies.
Interviewer:	Were you in lessons where you thought, I need to make a change now but I don't know what to do?
Miranda:	Oh yeah. I had one lesson where I needed to make a change but I didn't know what to do because I didn't have any alternative strategy. I ended up turning it into a revision class — I suppose I did have an alternative strategy.
Interviewer:	What about when you finish a class, what happens then?
Miranda:	I found that I'd talk to my supervising teachers then I'd sit there and go through my lesson plan book again and say, oh yeah I didn't quite do that the way I wanted to.
Interviewer:	Why do you do things like that?
Miranda:	I think it's important so that next time I don't make the same mistake twice, the kids wouldn't be learning anything by it and it's important for my teaching as well. Otherwise teaching would be very boring if you had your own little formula and you didn't change it or alter it at all.

Even though deliberate deception seems unlikely, one of the problems with interviews is that the ideas espoused by the participants cannot readily be verified or validated against their practice. Therefore investigating my student-teachers' reflective practice in their classroom teaching is a natural consequence of this study as it led me to follow my student-teachers into schools on their third (and final) school teaching experience so that I could observe them in action, and explore when and how they reflected on their practice.

Chapter 9 places in context the thoughts and actions of practice in action of the four student-teachers who volunteered to be video-taped teaching, by presenting that data through case-studies. Chapter 10 builds on the case-studies by analysing in detail the influences on their anticipatory, contemporaneous and retrospective reflection.

Case-studies

Introduction

This chapter focuses on the thoughts and actions of four of the student-teachers during their final school teaching experience. Through the intensive interview-observation-interview schedule it was possible to compare the student-teachers' 'thinking' about practice with their 'actual' practice. In each case the participant was interviewed by me three times in respect of the observed lesson, with the third interview being conducted immediately after the second. The first interview was before teaching the lesson. The purpose of this was to ascertain what he or she intended to do in the lesson and why. The lesson was then video-taped. During the lesson, specific instances that may have portrayed the influence of reflective practice were noted by me. Some of these instances may have been as a diversion from the plan, others could have been as a result of the planning.

Immediately after the lesson the student-teacher was interviewed a second time. This interview was designed to determine such things as the individual's ideas about how he or she viewed the lesson, did it go as planned, why or why not? Observation of the video-taped lesson followed next during which the third interview was conducted. As the video was replayed the instances noted during the lesson were 'unpacked' to determine why certain actions were taken or not taken as the case may be. Finally, any other instances that I had not noted but were raised by the student-teacher were also fully explored.

In each case, the participant was interviewed for up to 50 minutes pre-teaching, then the lesson was video-taped (also lasting approximately 50 minutes). This was followed by the post-teaching experience of interview, video observation and interview, which lasted up to 120 minutes. This was an extensive time commitment by all of those involved and consumed much of the student-teacher's day.

In essence, this chapter attempts to develop an understanding of these four student-teachers, their approach to, and thinking about, their teaching. This is done by presenting case-studies which demonstrate the 'data of narrative inquiry' (Connelly and Clandinin, 1990). Case-studies have been adopted as they best portray the form of inquiry conducted as well as the type of practitioner–researcher relationship necessary to develop such rich data.

> Narrative inquiry in the social sciences is a form of empirical narrative in which empirical data is central to the work. The inevitable interpretation

that occurs, something which is embedded even in the data collection process, does not make narrative into fiction even though the language of narrative inquiry is heavily laced with terms derived from literary criticism of fiction. (Connelly and Clandinin, 1990, p. 5)

The case-studies give details of the interview-observation-interview sequence described above, and some broader background for each student-teacher. The case studies represent an account of the interview-observation-interview sequence and is then further analysed in Chapter 10.

Individual Case-studies

The four case-studies that follow have been constructed from: journals; the individual interviews conducted through the year; the intensive interview-observation-interview cycle of the video-taped lesson; and, my understanding of each individual from my viewpoint as both their teacher educator/researcher. The case-studies represent the type of teaching–learning relationship (which is equally important with respect to researcher–practitioner relationships) so important to this type of study. Noddings (1986) described this relationship as occurring when 'we approach our goal by living with those whom we teach in a caring community, through modeling, dialogue, practice and confirmation' (p. 502). The insights possible through these case-studies are the result of a relationship built up over the year of the pre-service program where the student-teachers and I learnt with and from one another in a variety of teaching and learning environments.

The case-studies have been written in an effort to portray a holistic view of each student-teacher in action. This is important as it places the student-teachers in context and enhances an understanding of the analysis of the observation-interview-observation cycle that follows in Chapter 10.

The format adopted (parallel columns of case and commentary) for presenting the case-studies is similar to that used by Malcolm (1994) and is designed to enhance the reader's understanding of the issues being raised. The first column is the case-study itself and the second column serves as a commentary on the case-study. There are two purposes for this commentary: one is to elaborate on context (from the participants' perspective as well as mine), the second is to point to issues, events and episodes that are important for the research. The commentary column therefore strengthens the case-studies by overtly highlighting some of the theoretical aspects which underpin data analysis of this nature. It also signals those issues which will be examined in more detail in Chapter 10.

The commentary in the right hand column is organized so that it occurs next to the issue being raised by the case study. Therefore, the commentary columns do not always align with the start of a paragraph in the case-study column.

Case 1: Perry: Of Thoughts and Actions

Perry had been working as an accountant for a couple of years before enrolling in Dip Ed but had become dissatisfied with the routine nature of his work. He was a 'weekend warrior' — a Captain in the Australian Army Reserve — and enjoyed the authority that accompanied the position. He also saw himself as a capable communicator and leader.

Perry's successful Army Reserve experience inadvertently caused him to blur the distinction between training and teaching. He later recognized that the difference would be important in shaping his approach to teaching.

Perry's schooling was interesting as he had experienced 'success without the sweat'. He had attended a large Independent Boys' school before completing a bachelors degree in Economics, but rarely felt as though he needed to work hard to understand the content he was learning. 'I suppose it's because I have like a photographic memory,' he once explained when talking about studying for exams.

He recognized that his academic achievements were primarily as a result of applying rote learning techniques.

An outstanding and observable characteristic was his ability to plan for both the expected and the unexpected. He attributed this to his Army training. He often said, 'You have to be prepared for everything.'

Perry was adept at thinking about and developing alternative approaches (suggestions) and recognizing possible problems.

Perry saw himself as being able to 'read' people so teaching looked to be a career that could be more challenging, and more appropriate, to his way of life than accountancy had been. He thought that he'd waltz in to DipEd and pick up the bit of paper that would give him the credentials to teach and everything else would fall into place, just as it had been so often the case in the past.

Perry expected to be trained in the skills necessary to be a teacher of high school students. Once he had those skills he would be ready to work as a teacher.

Things did not quite go to plan though. As the DipEd year progressed he became more and more intrigued by teaching. 'This is not as easy as knowing the right things to do. You can't give us a recipe for teaching can you?' he once said. Perry found himself trying to understand more about learning and trying to apply his new found knowledge to his teaching. He often thought about his teaching and was unusually articulate about his own learning. By his second

The difference between training and teaching became apparent, he

school teaching experience he was speaking about the lost opportunities from his first classroom venture. He was keen to experiment and try out strategies that might be 'risky' on his next foray into the classroom.

recognized it as a problem which caused him to reconsider what learning to teach really meant.

By the third school teaching experience there was little doubt that he would volunteer to be involved in the video-tape experience. It was obvious that, to him, any chance to learn more about teaching was an opportunity too good to miss. As far as he was concerned, being involved in research gave him the chance to understand better how to learn to teach. He might be helping the researcher but first and foremost he was helping himself.

Perry was always seeking to learn more about teaching. By this time he no longer held the view that there were a finite number of skills to learn.

It was a bright sunny morning the day John arrived at the school to meet Perry to video-tape his lesson. Perry was anxious and excited. 'I thought about ringing you last night to change the lesson that you were going to see. My Economics method lecturer from Uni. came yesterday and she wants me to sort of test the kids. I don't really agree with her but I've got to do it. I think I've got an interesting way to do it, I'll use an essay format, but I didn't know if it's the sort of thing you would want to video-tape and talk about. Then I thought you probably wouldn't mind anyway so I decided not to ring,' he said. 'That's fine,' said John as they wandered off to the staffroom to talk about the lesson.

Even though he was a confident student-teacher, he still had an underlying concern about wanting to be seen as performing well. A problem had been imposed by his supervisor, he had developed suggestions in response to the problem.

Perry was typically well prepared. He had an incredible array of options for how to teach the lesson. He had a point form list of the advantages and disadvantages for each approach and his preferred action plan. It resembled a dichotomous key which a botanist might use for the classification of plants.

His anticipatory reflection was detailed.

Hypotheses were readily tested by imaginative action.

'Goodness, do you always set out pages of planning like this?' asked John. 'No, not really. I normally do it all up here,' he said pointing to his head. 'I just thought I'd better do it like this today so I didn't leave out anything when talking to you. I thought it would be helpful for you and save you having to transcribe so much from the cassette,' he said with a wry grin.

The opportunity to know the extent of Perry's anticipatory reflection was greatly enhanced through the methods adopted in this research.

It was obvious to John that Perry's idea of each student doing a concept map then using these to construct one on the chalkboard with the whole class would challenge his understanding of the use of concept maps, but it was not apparent to Perry. He was seeing his strategy as a way of 'forcing' the students to think about their understanding of economics, yet he intended to finish with one 'right' concept map from the whole class. A curious paradox was apparent. Perry wanted divergent thinking from his students but wanted a convergent response as the final outcome.

Perry's understanding of concept maps would be challenged. A problem was looming that he could not yet see.

John quizzed and probed Perry's thinking as he tried to create a picture in his own mind of what underpinned Perry's ideas for the lesson. 'What sorts of things have affected your planning for today? How does this lesson fit in with yesterday's? How does it fit in with tomorrow's?' he asked as he searched for understanding.

Perry's reasoning was extensive but was affected by his lack of experience in the use of concept maps.

Perry had all the bases covered. His only concerns related to issues of timing and whether or not the video camera would be a distraction for some of the students. 'It'll be a successful lesson,' he said. 'I'm confident about that. I think it'll be useful for them. It'll help them with their revision and I want to see them get good marks on their essay and I think this'll be a good tool for that,' he said as he collected his books, chalk box and duster before wandering off to class. 'I want to get there a bit early to put some of the stuff on the board. It might save some time,' was his final comment as John turned off the cassette player, grabbed the video camera and tripod and struggled along behind him.

Anticipated problems were generally related to organizational matters. He did not see any major concerns related to pedagogy or learning occurring.

The students nonchalantly sauntered into the classroom. Perry reminded them of the purpose of the lesson and quickly summarized the activities they would be doing. The students started working on their own concept maps while Perry moved around the room quietly talking to individual students. Occasionally he would call for attention and explain a term or further clarify the task, but generally he seemed happy with the way things were going. After about fifteen minutes he started to construct a class concept map on the board. For the first time in the lesson it was obvious that Perry was working hard to get the students to understand the purpose of the activity. He selected different individuals to write terms on the board and to fill in their link terms. Unexpected responses were rife and Perry was conscious that time was slipping away from him. He appeared to be caught between the need to slow down and make sure that students understood the work, and the need to get finished because they would be using all of this information for tomorrow's essay test. Perry seemed uneasy but he battled on continually trying to address the competing needs.

Here was the first sign that Perry had recognized a problem with his understanding of the use of concept maps. Contemporaneous reflection was initiated.

Two different types of problem are occurring. Timing (organizational) and the consequence of this use of concept mapping (teaching and learning). Suggestions are difficult to develop 'in action'.

As the bell sounded for the end of the lesson, Perry quickly summarized the purpose of the lesson and how it was meant to help each student know what to study for the essay. As the students left the room, Perry sighed and looked disappointed that his lesson was not as exciting as he had previously hoped. 'I try very hard in TAL, and when you're on the spot, you can't always be as good as you'd like. You had an affect on the way I worked,' he said with an apologetic tone. 'Unenthusiastic, not really a hot lesson, hey? It was too slow moving. Did you notice that I lost my sheet of answers and that it put me on the back foot a little? I started to think that it was boring so I tried to pick up the pace but it was still reasonably slow. I think the way I structured it made

The difference between imaginative testing in anticipatory reflection and covert testing in action is apparent. Context and time influence reflection.

Retrospective reflection is triggered by problem recognition.

it too easy for kids to turn off after they'd done their bit,' he said to no-one in particular as he seemed to be thinking aloud.

John and Perry headed for the staffroom to discuss the lesson. As they sat down, John asked how the lesson would be taught if Perry was to repeat it. Immediately Perry started to explain how he needed more time to do all of the things he wanted to do. He felt as though he had his students thinking and learning but that it was only a start to it, the need to test them was getting in the way of their learning. Perry said, 'I was thinking as I was writing on the board and sometimes as I was moving around the class. I knew what was happening but didn't really know what to do about it, except move faster. I thought I'd have been better able to deal with it.' Through much of the post-lesson interview, Perry spoke about how he tried to adjust to unexpected events during the lesson.

Organizational aspects of teaching consistently influence the structure of Perry's lesson.

The influence of experience in making suggestions during contemporaneous reflection is apparent.

Perry was keen to know what John thought of the lesson but John avoided a direct answer by deflecting it in his transition to the next interview phase. John spoke about wanting to know more about Perry's thinking. 'Tell me about some of these instances,' he said turning on the video. Perry reeled off reasons for his actions with ease. He quite enjoyed the experience of reliving what he had done and why. He was able to give full accounts of his thinking for things ranging from classroom management to the students he chose to answer questions.

Anticipatory reflection had a large bearing on his teaching. Most of the actions went according to plan.

He was in control of every move. Then an interesting instance came up. It revolved around one of the terms on the concept map. John asked what was happening at that point and Perry's response was slower and much more considered than anything he had previously explained. 'Well,' he said slowly, 'I'm just elaborating on that point, working through it with the class and I realized that it was only the person who was directly up at the board who was actually working. The rest can slack

A different type of problem occurs. Student learning is affected by the lesson structure and simultaneously a content issue also arises.

off. Then aggregate demand comes up. There it is now,' he said pointing to the television. 'I'm not sure of it myself. It's the most wishy-washy area of my knowledge so I thought they would probably be the same. I go in now,' he said watching himself in action, 'and modify the kid's work. In this case I thought the group's needs overrode the individual kid's needs. I had to change what he'd done.'

Contemporaneous reflection is enhanced by his own experience of learning. He overtly tests his hypothesis.

John sat back in his chair, his eyes darting between the television and his notes from the class. 'How did you judge that?' he asked.

'Well he's resilient, but the class don't seem to be with him. People didn't seem to understand commodity pricing and I didn't understand why,' Perry explained. 'I assumed they'd understood it when I taught it last lesson, but they show now that they don't,' he said shaking his head. 'It caught me off guard. It seemed so obvious but when you had to think about it and you were the one in the hot seat, it wasn't so obvious at all,' he said, recognizing how difficult it was for some of the students to explain some of the concepts he had been teaching.

The thinking that influenced his contemporaneous reflection is articulated.

The problems, suggestions, reasoning and hypotheses that influenced the testing are all explained giving the researcher access to important data which is usually difficult to uncover.

John leaned forward and asked Perry to watch the next section carefully. 'I can see you thinking,' he said. 'You're thinking something. What's happening here?' was the quizzical prompt put forward.

The ideas were flashing through Perry's mind. 'I was conscious that I'd said this would be a low teacher-centred lesson, yet I'm working like a traffic cop. I'm really concerned about this export index. It's a diversion from the plan but I feel I really need to clarify it. Then I realize that he's finished his work,' he said pointing to a student in the front row. 'He's copied it down and I haven't had any time to think, so I rub out the wrong line. I'm trying to get lots of think time because this is really complex. This is the classic thing in this subject, like the questions you normally ask in our

Contemporaneous reflection is a considered purposeful process. In this instance, the problem is a

interviews, like how do you learn something. I know that if you increase the exchange rate that your exports go down and your imports go up, and I can trot that out, but I don't like to teach it that way because that's the way I learnt it, and that's the way my supervising teacher does it. It's just a string, they will only know it by rote, that's all. I always have to work through it myself. So I referred to the picture we did last time to try and trigger it off in their minds again.

'But I have to work through it while they have the picture in front of them, so they go through it quicker than me because I'm processing it. See they can just say it, but they don't under-stand it, so I feel that I need to teach it to them my way otherwise they won't understand it. If they forget some of the details, they can work through it and work it out, but if it's a string they can't. They either know it or they don't,' he explained.

Perry continued to point out other instances that illustrated his frustration with trying to link his understanding of learning with his devel-oping skills in teaching. By the time they had finished watching the video Perry was keen to review his thoughts about the lesson.

'You know what I realize now?' Perry asked rhetorically. 'It was not having a really really good knowledge of the material made it hard to teach it. I was struggling with it and the kids were struggling with it, too. I now know more about learning it because that's what I've just done. I think I could teach this much better now,' he said. 'Well now it's over, what do you think?' he said turning to John for a response. 'And none of that evasive stuff. Tell me what you really think. I can take it.'

John drew his breath and responded in a slow, thoughtful manner. 'I think perhaps what we've

content issue. But, to convey the content in a meaningful way Perry needs to reason through and de-velop a way of trying to teach for understanding rather than for rote learning. His previous experience as a learner is now influencing his understanding of what it means to teach and this is causing him to reflect on the way he approaches his work.

He does not want his students to simply know the information he wants them to be able to under-stand it.

Perry's retrospective reflection is enhanced by viewing his teaching which helps him to better recount and reflect on his thinking at the time.

Content knowledge influences pedagogical approaches. Through better understanding the content, teaching and learning can be bet-ter aligned and this influences the extent to which reflection might be employed.

Reflection can be enhanced by learning from others' experiences. Perry is also displaying open-mindedness.

been watching is you trying to learn for the kids. You seem to be taking all of the responsibility for the learning, almost as if it's your problem not theirs. You just told me that you have now understood this work, learnt it. I wonder how you might teach it so they could do that too.'

The same episode can display problems which can be interpreted in different ways. Experience can influence such interpretations.

Perry mulled over John's response as they packed up the equipment. 'Thanks for that. It's given me a lot to think about. See you back at Uni. next week,' he said, as John opened the staffroom door to leave. 'I need a rest. That's really taken a lot out of me,' he thought, as he wandered off for a cup of coffee.

Reflection does not always lead to resolution of a problem (Figure 7.1, p. 92). Perry's retrospective reflection about the lesson is influenced by revisiting the problem from a different perspective.

Case 2: Sociable Sarah

Sarah was an energetic, outgoing student-teacher who never did anything by half. She was either fully involved in what was happening or else she gave it a wide berth. Things either sparked an interest in her or were immediately 'obvious' and required little further exploration.

Of the nine student-teachers who were interviewed, only Andrea displayed a lower frequency of open-mindedness (Table 6.1, p. 83).

As was her nature, her recollections of school were full of joy and praise or disdain and criticism. Stories of her Catholic Girls' School upbringing were always vividly described. Her favourite teachers were fantastic and held a special place in her heart. They did things in ways that she hoped to emulate. Those that she disliked were 'awful'. In her mind they had no right to be teachers because they did not care enough about the lesser lights in the class. She saw them as unnecessarily strict, narrow — minded and unfair in their treatment of students, particularly their treatment of her.

An important factor which influenced her view of learning was her understanding of teachers. She thought that some people were born to be teachers and those who were not were usually bad teachers. This emphasis on teacher and teaching as opposed to learning is also demonstrated in Table 6.3 (p. 86). Her journal entries were dominated by teaching issues, no learning issues were raised in her journal.

Sarah was not backward in coming forward. She had no difficulty expressing her opinion and did so on most occasions. In fact, it would be hard to imagine a topic in which she did not have a strong view one way or the other.

Sarah tended to make decisions quickly. She often saw solutions to problems from one of two competing perspectives rather than from a range of possibilities.

Being enthusiastic and keen to display her teaching skills to her tutor, Sarah was quick to volunteer to be video-taped on her third school teaching experience. When John arrived at the school Sarah bounded into the front office to greet him. The school was now her domain and she was confident and as exuberant as ever. 'So what's planned for today?' John asked as they headed for the staffroom.

'Well, today we're starting a new topic which I think explains why I've done it the way I have. We're looking at explorers and exploration so it's basically a sort of comprehension lesson. Firstly I'll be getting up and just chatting to the kids to see how much they know and to try and draw out information from them, give them a few clues like prompt them with a few questions. I don't know how well that's going to go because they're a pretty excitable group,' she responded quickly.

Sarah's interpretation of a new topic was that the students had no knowledge in that field. Her role as a teacher was to give them that knowledge.

This was a sign that classroom management was looming as an important shaping force in her teaching.

Trying to determine the extent of her planning and the reasons for her approach, John asked, 'Do you have anything in particular you want brought out?'

Attempting to determine the influence of content on the pedagogy she would adopt.

With barely enough time to draw breath she answered, 'Right yes, definite points. The first one is about why they want to explore, like the curiosity about what was around and a lot of beliefs about the world being flat and people wanting to challenge that, so we're not getting into specific explorers at this time we're just looking at why people wanted to explore. Another point is the overcrowding of the land and cities, things like that, more population stress leading them to need to find more land. Then there was the trade, spice and gold, so greed comes into that a little and seeing as it's a Christian school I thought I'd better include the missionaries and convert-the-heathens sort of thing. Lastly, the new colonies to increase the country's sphere of influence. So they're the main points that I'd like to bring out. If the kids have got anything else to bring out great.

Her lesson would revolve around a number of key points that she thought the students needed to know to understand the topic.

To Sarah, her role was to bring the students to know the content she had to deliver. The teaching

I'll be trying to guide them towards what I want them to say. If they bring out a valid point that's great too.'

John quizzed her a little more. 'So tell me about the thoughts you had in planning this.'

'Well, I'm taking it for granted that they know very little and I think they need to have some sort of basis for what they're studying and I think the best way for them to learn is for me to tell them initially rather than have them read it all from a book. We can discuss it a bit and then they can give me their own ideas and hopefully they can remember it and understand it a little bit better. Just to get them used to it a bit more. Following on from that I have two very short paragraphs to write up on the board because knowing this group they're going to be jumpy and if I give them something to write down straight off they're hopefully going to settle down,' she said.

John pursued this point with her a little further. The longer the conversation continued the more obvious it was that the lesson was organized with two specific points in mind. The first was to try and involve the students in the work, but this was to be counter-balanced by a need to keep them under control. Classroom management was an important issue. Most of her planning threw up the apparent dilemma of trying to conduct a student-centred lesson which would be highly teacher directed. It would be interesting to see how she managed the class and whether she would recognize her predicament.

Sarah continued to talk about the lesson all the way to the classroom. She spent some time discussing her options for dealing with the class if they were rowdy but she was not really sure how she would react in the hurly burly of the classroom.

The students entered the room on mass. They resembled a swarm of bees as they collectively buzzed around the room. One at a time they

skills revolved around how well she could get this content across to the students.

Sarah's approach suggests that she equates learning with acquiring information. Suggestions to address the problem of getting the students to know hinge on her skills in telling. Despite this she recognizes that the learning may not be intellectually challenging for the students, classroom management is again signalled as a concern for her.

If this was anticipatory reflection it barely extended beyond problem and suggestions.

She is not able to link the problem of classroom management to the form of teaching she is using. She has not reasoned through her pedagogical approach.

Suggestions for organizational matters were not so difficult for her to think up. This was in stark contrast to suggestions for teaching and learning.

broke from formation to find a seat. Finally they were seated and some were paying attention as Sarah had already started giving instructions.

Because of the puzzled faces and continued low-level chatter Sarah repeated most of what she had already said. The interaction between Sarah and the students was at a frenzied pace. When she was concentrating on one student she was almost oblivious to the rest. She spent most of her time poised and ready to add another important point to the growing list on the chalkboard.

Her teaching followed her lesson plan almost regardless of what happened around her.

At one stage she moved amongst the students impatiently directing their reading, continually searching the sea of faces for the next person to read aloud. Within arms reach was Nigel. He had a pencil case which he must have been making in woodwork. He spent most of the lesson sanding it off and paid little attention to what Sarah was teaching. Strangely, he did not seem to be too perturbed by her presence, nor she by his actions.

Sarah appeared to be consumed by the need to get the information across, little else influenced what happened in the lesson.

By the time the bell sounded Sarah should have been exhausted but she appeared as lively as ever. Most of the lesson had revolved around her and so much had been happening that she truly deserved a break. But without a second thought, she whisked John off to another room to go through the video and discuss her lesson.

'I thought it went pretty well, I was happy with it,' she said as they sat down. 'The kids weren't too bad although I do have to be firmer on them. I'm not really much of a dragon, I didn't really yell that much, I thought they worked fairly well. They gave some really good ideas just based on their own knowledge and bringing up different points which was really good. They kind of rolled with the work although they didn't get through as much as I'd hoped. But we did do a lot of reading, and I made the mistake of choosing one person who I knew wasn't a terribly good reader and I shouldn't have,' she continued at break-neck speed.

The students' ideas were interesting and almost surprised Sarah, but it did not cause her to reconsider what this could mean for her teaching.

She saw her choice of student as a problem rather than the type of exercise being conducted. She could not view the problem from another perspective.

Trying to slow the pace a little, John gently enquired as to why she had chosen someone who she knew could not read well. Her response started mid-way through the question. 'He seemed eager and I can't resist an eager person and I think students like that really do need a bit of encouragement. I probably didn't encourage him by changing readers halfway through but he does respond really well to a bit of attention. I would've liked to ask more questions of a variety of students although I tended to stick to the ones that I knew instead of sharing the questions around more,' she said.

Sarah recognizes some important problems in her approach to the class and although she has some suggestions, she does not reason through her thinking or consider testing any alternative hypotheses.

Sarah spoke for quite some time about the lesson. She did not need a lot of prompting and she initiated most of the discussion. Interestingly, there were two issues about the lesson in her mind. One was time, the other was classroom management. She said, 'I could've saved time by being a bit harder, it's one of the hardest things I find with teaching, not getting the discipline of the kids. Like just from that noisy stage to the quiet stage. Like just that little bit is really hard for me and I really don't like yelling or threatening too much and I don't think I raised my voice terribly much in that lesson, although I did yesterday and there was an instant reaction so they really do respond to it. But I find that extremely hard to do. It's something I really have to work on.' She readily demonstrated an ability to recognize problems, but tended to gloss over them rather than to seriously reconsider her approach.

The type of issues that prompted Sarah to reflect were usually about organizational or structural features of teaching. Suggestions tended to be of ways of minimizing problems rather than determining the cause of them.

As they watched the video together, the discussions suggested that her actions were more a result of lesson planning than responses to a change in the situation. 'I think a lot of the time students take things down but don't think about what they're writing,' she said. 'I'm very aware that a lot of them would've taken down the notes and thought, oh they're just notes. So I thought if I go through it with them then they might remember it a bit more, take more notice of it. I always planned to do it. Look, there,' she

No substantial examples of contemporaneous reflection were evident even though interesting prompts were evident.

Her view of learning dramatically influences her teaching. She believes that if she tells the students they will learn.

said pointing at the video, 'I'm just checking to see who's following and who's doing something else. I really wanted everyone to follow it and to think about what they'd written and I thought I just needed to have them check it through.'

'See what Nigel's doing?' John said pointing at the pencil case and sandpaper. 'Yeah. I don't like holding my book like that, it's sort of like a security blanket. I don't think I need it but I like to have something in my hand to refer to, I wasn't particularly worried,' she responded, glossing over the point John was referring to. 'That Bianca's a little sly one,' she added. John asked why she thought that. 'She'll look at you and the minute you turn your back she'll do something else, she's very um,' the answer was lost in her thoughts for a moment. 'I had her in for detention not long ago. I gave her extra homework last night and she said her baby brother threw up all over it. I mean, what can you do? She probably thinks I'm a push-over because I haven't chased her up on that work. I should've settled that. I just think it's so artificial being a student-teacher. They're not really your class and they give you some measure of respect but it's certainly not as much as they'd give their own teacher. They know you're only there for three weeks and so you can't get any established discipline or any real rapport going with the students. It's so fake and superficial. I think if this was my own class, they'd probably be different because they'd know how far they can go and I'd set more strict guidelines. I'm taking it seriously, of course, but because they're not my kids I'm not chasing up on them like I would be if they were my kids. So in that way I'd like to have my own class,' she concluded.

At one point she seemed to recognize how her actions affected different students. 'I'm thinking that's an awful thing to do, cut him off like that,' she said noting how she stopped a student from reading. John said something about

Her major concerns revolve around her delivery of information and this continues to mask other events in the classroom.

Instead of confronting problems, Sarah has a habit of suggesting reasons for avoiding them. She tends to use alternative scenarios to justify her actions in the present situation. Is this a way of avoiding reflection and rationalizing one's actions?

teachers needing to be aware of students' feelings and being able to respond to more than just the lesson. But she continued undeterred. 'But then again I shouldn't have chosen him in the first place. The others were getting restless and I could hear them telling him the words that he was having trouble with which showed that they were reading it, but, it's a bit disruptive to the others. You can see now that Rachel is reading and it immediately quietens down.'

At times Sarah gives the impression that she is trying to repress her thinking rather than exploring it.

John pointed out another instance that was of interest to him. Sarah was explaining her actions before he finished the question. 'I wanted to get them to talk about some of the difficulties in that paragraph, so I was hoping we'd get into it and I'd write it up on the board, you know, the notes that I had prepared and what they were saying, try to tie it all in together. I had a look through their workbooks and they really do not have many notes in their workbooks. I really do think they need something to base their study on. I mean sure, group work and activities are fun, but you need some basic facts to back it up. Apart from management issues that's another reason why I planned the lesson the way I did so that they'd have some notes in their books that they could go back to. I'm really conscious of them having work in their books.' Her response was barely complete when another instance came up on the screen. 'You never have everyone giving you their attention the whole time,' she said, picking up on another instance. 'As you can see, I have Vicki in the corner there. She looks like she's falling asleep. I hate to say it but she's a dim wit. I get really frustrated with her,' she added. 'Dim wit!' John said to himself. Her words echoed in his mind as he thought about some of the stories she had told about her own schooldays.

Another opportunity to reflect on actions was being offered, but the invitation was not accepted. Sarah does not appear to be able to stand back from situations in which she is personally involved. This may be an impediment to reflection.

Sarah was not really able to take 'risks' in her teaching, she was not prepared to challenge her approach to pedagogy.

As John packed away the video he asked one last question. 'Is there anything in that video that you did differently from what you planned to do?'

An attempt to determine what might prompt her to reflect retrospectively.

'I think I stuck to plan. I sort of have a visual plan of what I want to do in a lesson before I do it. No, that's more or less the way I'd planned it to go. I think it all went quite well. I've still got a little bit of room for improvement, but no, I thought it went quite well,' she said.

Her anticipatory reflection controls her teaching. It appears as though the key to teaching for Sarah is in refining the delivery of information.

John thanked her for her time, help and cooperation then packed the equipment into his car and headed back to work.

Case 3: Whispering Jack

Jack was a quiet and perceptive young man who was well respected by his peers. He thought about what he had to say and always paid attention to others' points of view. His nature was such that one came to trust in him very quickly. This was a student-teacher who genuinely embraced the notion of 'learning to teach'.

Jack was an open-minded person who could see things from multiple viewpoints.

Throughout the year his interviews with John were very different from anyone else's. There were pauses between sentences, he did not answer questions just for the sake of having something to say. Everything he said was carefully considered and his calm, quiet manner reinforced the view that he meant what he said.

Jack was not only in John's TAL class, but was in both his Science Method class and an additional integrated science program class as well. He was with John in many different contexts and happily volunteered to be video-taped on his third school teaching experience. He saw it as an opportunity to extend himself in his teaching and to use John as a 'sounding board' for his actions. His journal gave an amazing insight into his thinking and demonstrated how conscientiously he applied himself to his work. Teaching and learning were important to him and his journal was extensively dotted with questions and explorations which examined the interdependence of each. His journal writing

Jack's journal writing demonstrated the depth of his thinking about topics. Through his journal writing he reflected on his learning. This was an early sign that he was used to reconsidering events, that he employed retrospective reflection.

reflected how he thought about his teaching and learning and that of his teachers, lecturers and supervisors. He did not describe situations in his writing, he analysed them, constantly looking to enhance his understanding.

When John arrived at the school, Jack was at the front office waiting for him and was soon talking about the science lesson John would be observing. The unit he was teaching was called 'forces at work', and the students were trying to work out practical ways of measuring speed. The previous lesson they had tried to measure the speed of cars and today they were going to try to measure the speeds of other objects. Jack expected the students all to know the objects they would be using as it had been their home-work problem from last lesson. If they did not have an object, Jack had a few spares 'up his sleeve' just in case. Each group of students would be given a sheet to fill in with their predictions for each object's speed. He also thought that he might get them to write down any likely problems. Jack thought time might be a limiting factor but said they would just have to organize themselves properly. They would be working with ticker-timers and he thought perhaps a student could explain it to the rest of the class to refresh their memories. Then they would all work out the speed at different points on the tape and try to convert it to kilometres an hour.

Anticipatory reflection allowed him to recognize and prepare for possible problems.

Organizational and structural aspects of the lesson were not a major concern to him.

Jack was aware of, and comfortable with, most of the organizational and classroom manage-ment issues. Fitting the activity into the time was his only real concern. He was not really sure what he would do if they ran out of time but thought he would deal with that when or if it arose.

Jack was confident that he could think on his feet if confronted with this type of problem.

Jack seemed to be confident with his planning, the way the lesson was linked to the previous lesson and how it would lead on to the next, so when John asked, 'So you feel confident that this will go well, that the learning you want to

Anticipatory reflection gave Jack a structure for his teaching but it

137

happen will happen?' He was a little surprised by Jack's answer. 'I'm not sure, it's sort of a risky lesson. I'm not sure how effective it is going to be,' he said.

Jack thought that the students did not really think about what they did in class. 'They just do it,' he said. 'And something else that'll affect the lesson is the background and language of the kids, most don't speak English very well so I've tried to make the worksheet fairly clear and I've got to explain things in a number of ways so that they all know what they have to do. Also because of that, their general ability level isn't as high as others I've had so that affects the way I plan it. I'm not all that confident with using the ticker-timer machinery myself so that could be a problem, there is some difficulty with the likely timing. And there's no way of knowing how it will work out with all of the gear and things they plan to measure so I could end up with a lesson that could be a disaster, but I'm prepared to try that. Come on, let's get up to the class before the bell,' he said, leading John down the corridor to the science room.

The lesson seemed to go quite well but it was difficult to pick up many of Jack's reactions as most of his time was spent with small groups of students, out of ear shot and away from the close-up view of the video camera. The few points of interest that John noted had more to do with 'feelings' about how Jack was thinking rather than clearly discernible instances, but knowing Jack as he did, he fully expected Jack to outline his thinking about his actions.

As they walked down the corridor together, Jack said, 'I was really conscious of making decisions this time because I knew you were there. I don't think it affected the actual decisions that I made but I was more conscious of them.'

To John, this was a very interesting line. He wondered why Jack felt that way. Did he make

was a start to his thinking, not an end.

Anticipatory reflection led Jack to recognize problems associated with learning. He had reasoned through his thinking so that his actions were purposeful.

Because he has reasoned through his approach, the risks in the lesson are diminished.

There were non-verbal cues that suggested that Jack used contemporaneous reflection but this needed to be checked after the lesson.

Jack was conscious of reflection and it was a deliberate act.

Jack feel as though he was being 'judged'? He quizzed Jack for an answer saying, 'Say a bit more. Unpack that for me.'

Jack spoke briefly about seeing his teaching as becoming more responsive to 'where the students were at'. He related his thinking and decision making to that which John had been doing with the TAL class. 'Like you do with us,' he said. 'I was conscious of why I was doing something. Like you do with us. Different to you but the same, you know what I mean?' he said, looking to John for some cue to acknowledge understanding. John nodded and smiled, then they turned down another corridor and walked into the room where Jack had a video and television set up for them.

The thinking aloud John had been doing in TAL had been a positive modelling experience for Jack, it influenced the way he approached his teaching.

Jack spoke honestly about his reactions to the lesson. He was concerned that the lesson might not have been challenging enough for the students. 'Maybe I could've got them to do something else, I don't know what, I just don't know if it was challenging,' he said. He continued on to explain how a couple of groups could not do what they had intended but this was not the same as being scientifically challenged, or challenged by the concept. This gave John an opening he had been waiting for. 'Well, you'll repeat this lesson tomorrow, how will today's lesson affect tomorrow's?' he asked. 'Are you going to ask these questions again after the video?' was Jack's reply. 'Perhaps,' replied John wondering what Jack was getting at. 'Because I was thinking I'd probably be able to tell you more about it after I've seen the video. I don't know yet that I'd do anything all that differently. I'd like to see it and think about it. Other times with teaching the first class, I have changed a little bit, like organizational things like asking them to have one spokesperson per group getting that person to report back whatever they found rather than getting each person to do it, sometimes I have explained a concept better or in more ways a second time knowing the first time that they

Retrospective reflection revolved around the quality of the learning for the students.

Jack displays responsibility in thinking about his teaching.

Retrospective reflection gives Jack greater understanding of some of the general organizational and structural aspects of teaching.

weren't too clear about it or something. I think it went quite well because they didn't need much help from me which was quite good. I don't think the video affected them, they seemed to act normal enough. Perhaps they were just engrossed in what they were doing I think they were genuinely interested in doing the task. Let's watch the video,' he said, motioning to John to turn it on.

According to Jack the first few instances John had noted were all actions which were planned. Things went fairly well according to plan and his comments demonstrated a thoughtfulness about his actions. As they viewed some of the episodes Jack openly and honestly questioned what he saw himself doing. He easily explained why he did things but also suggested alternative approaches, particularly when he was not satisfied with what he had done.

Anticipatory reflection led to actions being performed as planned.

Jack had the ability to 'stand back' from the situation and reflect on his actions.

The longer they watched the video, the more Jack initiated the conversation. Many of the instances were not readily apparent through the video so it was interesting to hear his thoughts as the lesson unfurled. 'See what's happening here?' he started. 'I have to explain it to be sure they know what they're doing. The thing about constant speed is important, so I decided to get somebody to explain it to everybody else. See there, I don't know whether to make them stop and listen to me or just say what I've got to say, will they listen? I'm worried here about the problems they might have, you can see that they're thinking about accuracy with speed but they're on the wrong track. I tell them because they didn't know what I was on about it. It takes a while to get to know these kids too, it takes a while to know what they're on about. Their abilities differ, some of them have genuine problems knowing what you mean. I was thinking here about the order of my instructions. Whether they were being coherent, structured. I wasn't getting much feedback,' he said, taking John through the video replay.

Video observation as a methodological tool for initiating reflection worked very well for Jack. He readily relived the teaching experience in a non-judgmental manner.

Contemporaneous reflection is often triggered by problem recognition.

Reviewing the video enhances the quality of retrospective reflection, as actions can be observed directly.

Next came a segment that John had highlighted in his notes. While Jack was explaining a couple of points to the class a student walked up next to him and started getting the equipment he needed for the prac. Then, while Jack was still talking, a second student came forward to do the same thing. Jack seemed oblivious to the first student but noticed the second. 'He doesn't know what you're telling him, why he has to sit down,' John said. Jack explained, 'That must be why he was upset. I didn't even notice this first guy, I didn't pay any attention to him. That's amazing, he's got what he wants and I haven't even noticed and look how unhappy the other kid is, no wonder he was upset later on.' 'He must've carried that grudge throughout the lesson, that's what the link is,' he said finally recognizing why the student was surly for the rest of the lesson. 'I wonder how Sarah would have responded to something like this?' John thought to himself.

Through reviewing the episode Jack is able to link events and make more sense of what was happening. Reflecting on the episode will influence his actions in future lessons.

Sarah did not readily display this skill in her post-teaching interview.

A number of instances came and went and Jack continued to explain his actions objectively. He had the ability to stand back from the situation and respond to it rather than just defend his actions. 'Now you're about to go through speed and you pick a kid. Take me through that,' said John. Jack responded, 'I'm asking for volunteers and no-one says anything. I could've waited longer I suppose, did I ask a couple of times? I looked at him and thought he's the one, he'll be able to come up and explain it. Now I was wondering how they'd done it before, had they just measured between two dots, three or five or something. They should've known that, it surprised me that he didn't. We discuss it for a while and then I say I'll let you work it out. I just couldn't think. I made this bit up. I don't know why. I wasn't really confident about teaching this bit. Why they should do it over 5 dots not just over one, I mean like it's more accurate or something, I wasn't sure, I didn't explain it very well.' This was the first time that Jack's understanding of

Jack has to make time to be able to reflect contemporaneously.

Contemporaneous reflection is influenced by understanding of content-knowledge.

the content knowledge seemed to be affecting his teaching and he noted it. 'As they were going out, I realized that they had all gone through it and it was far too rushed, I hadn't really asked them if they had any questions so as they were leaving I tell them to ask me any questions at the door, that was to try and compensate for it, but they were in a rush to get out so they probably didn't pay any attention to me,' he said, recognizing the lack of understanding apparent on the students' faces.

Problem recognition initiates contemporaneous reflection but suggestions are difficult to think of under pressure.

The discussion continued well after the video had finished. Jack was concerned with his difficulty in explaining something that he was not really sure of himself. He put forward a number of suggestions for different ways to teach the same lesson again but had not settled on one over another. He needed to think about it some more before he made a decision.

Retrospective reflection may comprise revisiting an episode a number of times and reasoning through different suggestions over time.

As they walked back down the corridor John thanked Jack for his help. Jack said, 'That's OK. It's interesting to see myself that way. I got to see what I really did, not just what I thought I did.' The last thing he said was, 'It's funny about how I told Dan off for walking around and not the other guy; how I didn't see him at the time. I could've gone and seen Dan, seen if there was a problem. Funny isn't it? The things you miss can make such a difference. I need to see Dan.'

The constraints of time are largely removed in retrospective reflection, increasing the opportunities for more considered hypothesis testing.

As John sat at the traffic lights waiting for them to change he thought about Jack's approach to teaching. 'Funny isn't it,' he mused, 'what a difference it makes to teaching. Learning from what you do not just coping with what you do.'

The quality of reflection, and the learning from it, is influenced by the nature of the problem under consideration.

Case 4: Pearl: In Search of Purpose

From day one Pearl was an impressive student-teacher. She was doing DipEd for a reason. She wanted to 'learn to teach' and, for her, meaning was something that came from thinking and did not occur by 'osmosis'. She thought about and questioned most things in a deeper, more intense and open way than most of the others in her class. Everything had a purpose, and Pearl wanted to know and understand the purpose in everything she did. To some extent she was disappointed if others did not have a need to know, or took things on face value alone.

For Pearl, learning was enhanced through reflection.

Her journal ended up as a 'three volume classic' and uncovered a social conscience which directed her learning. Learning was power, and such power should be available to everyone, not just society's elite. She read widely and, not surprisingly, was particularly taken by the writing of Freire.

It was no accident that she chose to spend two of her school teaching experiences in schools in the industrial suburbs of Melbourne which were 'disadvantaged' both socially and economically. The students she taught came from backgrounds which most of her classmates may have read about but rarely had firsthand experience of. Where she taught, she would make a difference, she would try to help those less fortunate than herself share in the power of education.

Pearl displayed whole-heartedness. Her actions were as a result of substantial thinking and reasoning.

Everyone respected Pearl, perhaps none more than Perry. He saw her as someone worthy of the responsibilities of a teacher because she 'thought about her actions'. In Perry's eyes, Pearl asked the 'hard' questions not only of others, but of herself as well. In fact her thinking in some instances intimidated Perry because of the strength of her conviction and the depth of her thinking. Neither of them really 'suffered fools lightly', but each for different reasons. Pearl did not like to see individuals squander their own opportunities to learn whereas Perry did not like to see students' learning opportunities trivialized by thoughtless approaches to teaching.

Pearl's reflective nature was apparent to her peers.

Although Pearl was unsure exactly what she was putting herself in for by being video-taped

A chance to learn from experience demonstrated her open-mindedness.

on her third school teaching experience, she nonetheless volunteered to be involved.

When John arrived at the school he was surprised to hear that Pearl was nervous about the visit. She had spoken to Perry the previous night and his description of his time with John had sown a seed of doubt in her mind. For some reason Perry had rethought his approach to teaching since John's visit and this unsettled Pearl a little because she saw Perry as being very confident and sure of himself. 'So what might your visit do to me?' she asked rhetorically.

John tried to set her mind at ease about the visit as they headed off to the staffroom. He also made a mental note to be attentive of Perry and to try to follow it up if the same thing came up in his final interview at Monash after the school teaching experience.

In the short time it took Pearl and John to get settled in the staffroom, she was already explaining what she was going to teach and why, what factors had contributed to her planning and how her lesson fitted into the whole unit she had devised. 'I did an affective values thing and a lot of them were all over the place in what they think of refugees and stuff, so I made sure they knew the difference between physical and political refugees, then they're doing a lot of mapping work, one that shows refugees and one that shows where famine and war are. Then on a blank map they have to correlate the information to see if there's a relationship between the two,' she explained with a passion that showed the importance of the issue to her. 'They will also do a small activity on who's a refugee and who's an immigrant, then do a list of political and physical factors, I've already put up things that they think might cause refugees, during the next couple of lessons we're going through whether what they think is what actually happens. So to do a bit more of that in detail

Her anticipatory reflection demonstrated an integrated approach to teaching rather than a disjointed lesson-by-lesson approach.

She had worked through a number of suggestions and had tested her ideas through imaginative actions.

Anticipatory reflection that encompasses a holistic view of learning the content.

and then to go into the mapping work, which is mainly to do as individuals but then to bring them back as twos or threes for discussion. If I've got time at the end, then there's another question I want them to do for that affective stuff which is to write a paragraph about who they'd accept as African refugees into Australia, to see if that changes a little bit, but I'm still not sure if I have time to do that,' she said.

Her planning seemed to be quite complex as she spoke about what she was doing and the ideas that underpinned her approach. John was surprised to hear Pearl say, 'I plan out everything that I want to do and then when something happens to change it, it throws me, takes me off course. This unit has been changed two or three times now, I'm just at the point where I'm about to put it together but one of the things I've found difficult is just how to get across the basic concepts, how to get them across,' she repeated to herself, still thinking about her problem. 'I haven't had enough time to work out how I want to do that,' she concluded more to herself than to John. This interested John because he saw Pearl as being confident in herself and able to respond to the changing demands of teaching, yet clearly, although she was responsive, it was not something that she took 'in her stride'. Like Perry, planning was important in directing her thinking and she did not like to teach in ways that were not carefully thought through. She did not like to lose sight of the aim of a lesson nor did she purposely 'pad out' them out.

Their discussion continued to throw up interesting lines which prompted John to revisit an idea he had been mulling over for some time. He was beginning to see that the more 'good student-teachers' thought about their teaching, the less sure they were about the best way to do it. 'Perhaps this was a sign that they were reflecting on their teaching, moving beyond some technical approach to the job,' he thought

She readily recognizes problems as she is planning her work. This causes her to reconsider her actions.

Anticipatory reflection is a deliberative and ongoing process.

The quality of anticipatory reflection is influenced by the topic prompting it. Issues associated with student learning and developing students' understanding are intellectually demanding and difficult to simply resolve.

to himself. This was reinforced by Pearl's response to his question about what she thought the students would learn from her teaching. She said, 'I suppose it's too vague, but to have an understanding of what causes refugees and where they go, and I want them to be able to do that by seeing it visually on the map and drawing their own conclusions from that. But I'm still not sure how I think I'm going to have that happen.' She stopped and thought to herself for a moment then continued, 'I don't even know if I'll know if it's a good lesson. I'm just not sure that I've given it enough. I like to be one hundred per cent certain about what I'm doing before I do it and I'm not, so it'll be difficult. I've been worried about doing it.'

Although she has decided on particular pedagogical approaches she is predisposed to learn through testing her hypotheses.

Pearl glanced over her shoulder to the clock on the wall. 'I'd better go,' she said. 'I'll pick you up here again after this lesson and then we'll go to 8C. OK.' 'Sure, no worries,' John replied as Pearl ducked out of the staffroom and into the mass of students already milling around between periods. 'I wonder what sort of pressure I'm putting her under?' John asked himself as he sipped his coffee. This would be Pearl's second class for the day, then she had the one which John would observe. 'All this before lunchtime. She's right into the real world of teaching now,' he thought.

Is there a relationship between physical well-being and reflection?

In John's mind the lesson went according to plan. Everything seemed to go well enough and Pearl had been attentive to her students. She had a reassuring nature and the students responded well to her efforts. John had struggled to find many instances during the lesson which he thought were worth discussing. Like his experience with Jack he would need Pearl to fill in most of the gaps. It reminded him more and more of the value of his 'thinking aloud' in TAL. It gave his student-teachers access to his thinking so that their discussions about pedagogy were based on knowledge about actions rather than assumptions. 'I need to know

Without the video-tape of the lesson and Pearl to explain her

her thinking. The problems she saw and how she resolved them. What was going on that I couldn't see?' he asked himself repeatedly during the lesson.

They sat down to watch the video of the lesson together. Pearl was pleased with the way things had gone. She thought it went quite well especially as the class had a couple of students who were very disruptive for other teachers. She did not think that they had learnt as much as she had expected and that an understanding of refugees had not 'completely sunk in yet'. She saw the next lesson as an opportunity to do some case-studies which would help resolve the issue for them.

When John asked how she would teach the lesson if she had to do it again he was surprised at her quick response. 'When I was thinking about doing it, the other option I was thinking about was starting with a couple of specific countries that had refugees and making up some cards that had basic information and stuff and getting them to work out from that, maybe having questions about the conditions in the country and things like that, doing the same distinction with the drought and war and that, but I decided not to do that because it's probably too complicated. I don't know if maybe in that lesson it would be good to lead into it because it was very backwards and forwards. I'd like to work out a way of doing it where it wasn't so much but I'm not sure how I'd do that.'

Before John had time to question her further, she added, 'I don't like spending so much time doing something on the board and them copying it down, I should get them to copy it down as I go, but then some don't participate so I don't know, maybe I should try it the other way. Maybe with that profile thing, who's an immigrant and who's a refugee, I was thinking maybe I should've done that in more of a spoken way, but then I'm not guaranteed that

thoughts and actions, gathering research data on contemporaneous reflection would be extremely difficult.

Much of her anticipatory reflection had positively influenced her teaching.

Detailed anticipatory reflection illustrating an abundance of possible suggestions.

Reasoning influences the actions to be tested.

Recognition of a pedagogical problem.

Retrospective reflection does not necessarily resolve a problem, it may be a catalyst for further problem recognition which may then influence hypothesis formation.

they'd all do it so I still don't know that I would do it that way.'

It amazed John that she had so many different options in her mind. She could readily recognize problems, reason through them and develop hypotheses to test in an instant. 'How does this happen?' he asked himself. At the same time another thought quickly ran through his mind. 'I really am hearing her think. This must be her reflective conversation,' he said to himself as a grin of recognition, like an ocean wave, gently rolled across his face.

Pearl's approach to reflection readily demonstrated the five phases described by Dewey (1933).

Many of the instances they discussed demonstrated how Pearl had learnt from her previous experiences and was applying that to her teaching. Her ability to test ideas or alternative approaches to action was apparent as she explained many of the episodes they watched together.

Reflection on practice demonstrably influenced Pearl's teaching.

At one point a student reminded Pearl that the lesson was ten minutes shorter than normal. John stopped the video and asked Pearl to explain what happened in her mind in that split second. 'I'm just trying to work out what it means for my timing, do I do five more minutes now or do I do it at the end. Also, I'm thinking I need to re-organize, do I do that, do I do something else, do I throw this out, come up with another ending perhaps, I'm going to have to make something up,' she answered. 'So what did you decide?' he asked. 'Well, it's only ten minutes shorter, so the activity stays, I cut down the answers to question one so I reckon I can fit it in. That happens to me all the time at this school', she said articulating the thinking that was not obvious on the video-tape.

During contemporaneous reflection Pearl works through different scenarios — imaginative testing.

Pearl pointed out other instances which showed the complexity of the thinking behind some seemingly simple actions. Her concern for students' feelings and desire to help them learn was obvious. She had a soft spot for Jesse who never seemed to make sense of what was going on. She pointed out one such instant. 'Well,' she

Most of the examples of contemporaneous reflection were to do with ways of enhancing student learning.

started, as she thought about his answer to one of her questions, 'I could've just dismissed it but he's just had a shocking report, he has an awful home life and he always sneers in class and opts out of the work, so when he says something, it's quite amazing that he would suggest anything, so I wanted him to see why his suggestion wasn't right but that I valued his input anyway. If he's not participating and I jump on him it doesn't help at all,' she said, as the video continued, then added, 'I then went down to the back of the room to talk to him a little about it because of that and because I needed some thinking time to work out how to respond to him.'

Pearl has to consciously make time in class to be able to reflect contemporaneously.

Throughout the video she pointed out instances which indicated how much she monitored what was going on in the class. She was acutely aware of individuals and conscious of trying to ensure that the thinking she started with them in class continued after the bell. 'Is there anything I can do to stop it so as it stays in their heads or will they just say oh well it's over?' she said, directing the question more towards herself than John. This concern was particularly highlighted by her annoyance at the way she finished the lesson.

Pearl's teaching is driven by a desire to improve her students' learning.

She felt as though she would have to rethink how she would approach the next lesson, scrapping what she had planned, otherwise the unit would not hang together properly. John did not necessarily agree with all of her conclusions but was pleased to hear her describing the thinking which influenced her teaching.

Retrospective reflection triggered by pedagogical concerns.

As John leaned forward to turn off the video he asked Pearl what she thought about the lesson now that she had seen it and talked about it. She quite honestly and openly spoke about the difficulty she found watching herself in action. She was not really sure whether the students had learnt what she hoped they would learn. 'How do you find out?' she said. 'I can't tell just from that, there are no strategies there

Pearl was able to stand back from the situation and reflect on her teaching. The process was not threatening, it was an extension of her normal approach to retrospective reflection.

to tell me that except for when I do the discussions on refugees, so I don't know. I need to do something about that. What do I do?' she said. The look on her face suggested that she was already working through the question in her mind.

The discussion about how the outcomes of the lesson would affect the rest of the unit continued for some time, then, almost out of the blue, Pearl said something that both pleased and worried John. 'Now I'm not so sure that I want to be a teacher,' she started. 'Why's that?' John asked, almost as a reflex to the statement. 'Well, you think about it. How do you get to a point where you are good? In fact I'm not even sure I know what good is now. I just think about what you learn and how you learn and how that affects the way you teach and am I doing it well enough.' John was taken aback but subconsciously pursued the point further. 'So what's this process with me done to you?' he asked. 'It clarifies that to be good is not so easy. I don't think anything dreadful happened but I don't know that anything good happened either. So you think, well, what have I done that's different and I don't know. Then part of me thinks it's got to do with understanding and maybe it's just not happening, and I don't know if it will and that's what worries me. It's muddy isn't it?' she said. She thought for a moment longer then finished by saying, 'You quiz us quite a bit you know, so I probably focus more on it, you don't let us push it away to one side, we have to think, that makes it hard. There's so much I want to learn but it's really hard, you have to try it out and this has made me conscious of lots of things that I might've pushed to one side. You make me worry more about what and why. There's a lot to think about.'

'You are showing me the value of reflection to your learning about teaching. You're doing just fine, just fine,' John said as much to reassure himself as to reassure Pearl.

Retrospective reflection as a cycle where suggestions are reasoned through in a variety of ways.

Pearl did not see teaching as a set of skills to be acquired. Teaching is a complex task.

To make sense of an experience requires reflection on action.

Being involved in this research project has been a catalyst for reflection.

As he drove back across town to the University a number of questions kept popping up. He had an image in his mind. He could see Dick saying, 'You do not learn from experience. You learn by reflecting on experience.' He hoped that this was what he was doing with his student-teachers, but there was a lot to think about. A lot to understand.

A research project of this nature not only influences the thoughts and actions of the participants, it also influences those of the researcher. Learning is not a one-way process.

Summary

Each of these four student-teachers thinks about their teaching in different ways and at different times for different reasons. Their pre-lesson planning shows that they have reasons for the teaching approach adopted, and each of them are able to articulate these. The nature of their post-lesson thinking varies but is dependent on the individual's view of what happened and why, and whether or how this influences their students' learning. The complex nature of teaching and the lack of extended teaching experience combine to make thoughts and actions during a lesson more problematic for student-teachers.

Overall, the case-studies have been designed to demonstrate that three distinct periods of thinking occur (pre, during, and post, lesson) and that each student-teacher approaches them differently. During these periods there are opportunities for reflection and to varying degrees, and each student-teacher demonstrates this.

The case-studies have been written to give the reader a context for how each student-teacher approaches their teaching. This context is important in helping to develop an understanding of how and why each individual varies in their approach to reflection. Chapter 10 develops and extends the links between these three reflective instances for each of the four student-teachers described in the cases above.

Understanding Reflective Practice

Introduction

Reflective thinking can be described as the 'Active, persistent, and careful consideration of any belief or supposed form of knowledge in the light of the grounds that support it and the further conclusions to which it tends' (Dewey, 1933, p. 9). Understanding such thinking in pre, during and post teaching experiences is a guide to how reflection influences practice. To explore these periods of reflection the four student-teachers' interview-observation-interview episodes from the video-taped lessons were analysed. However, it is important to remember that these times of reflection are very much context dependent. Context embraces domains such as: content knowledge, experience, time, action, feelings and self-confidence. All of these vary in different situations. Understanding the context for each of the four student-teachers is important in understanding the analysis of their reflection and how it influenced their thinking and practice. The case-studies in Chapter 9 illustrated how each student-teacher approached their teaching. The context in which they functioned was different and the focus of their reflection varied accordingly.

This chapter aims to explore the anticipatory, contemporaneous and retrospective reflective practice of each of the student-teachers within the context of their teaching experience. All of the interview data quoted in this chapter are from the interviews associated with the student-teachers' video-taped lessons.

Anticipatory Reflection

Anticipatory reflection is the first and most common form of reflection and embraces the question, 'How might I approach teaching "this" particular content/lesson?' If this question is the entree to anticipatory reflection then it should be a guide to how one reasons through and develops a pedagogical approach that might be tested in practice. Therefore the reflective cycle offers opportunities to imaginatively work through and test suggestions and to make purposeful pedagogical decisions about a course of action to be embarked upon.

As the case-studies in Chapter 9 demonstrate, each of the four student-teachers uses anticipatory reflection. However, there are notable differences in the focus of that reflection and the reasons for its use.

Table 10.1 shows the reflective phases data from the interview-observation-

Table 10.1: Number of coded segments for each of the reflective phases for anticipatory reflection from the interview-observation-interview cycle from the video-taped lessons

Student-teacher	Suggestions	Problem	Hypothesis	Reasoning	Testing
Jack	12	7	6	7	3
Pearl	9	5	3	2	2
Perry	8	5	6	7	3
Sarah	9	2	3	3	1

interview cycle for anticipatory reflection and are drawn from their reflection before they taught the particular lesson being observed. The value of these data is not so much in the number of coded segments per phase but in the relationship between the phases and the issue/concern which prompted the reflective cycle.

For each of the student-teachers, the number of coded segments in the testing column (Table 10.1) is directly proportional to the number of issues/concerns which influenced their thinking. Jack's anticipatory reflection was in three cycles related to issues of classroom management, content-knowledge and the language problems of his students; most of his students were not native English speakers. Pearl's anticipatory reflection was in two cycles, the first concerned her content-knowledge and the second related to her pedagogical approach. Perry's anticipatory reflection was in three cycles related to issues of content-knowledge, pedagogy and student learning while Sarah's single (extended) reflective cycle hinged solely on classroom management.

The differences between the student-teachers' use of reflection are, in part, comparable to the results in Table 7.3 (p. 98). In Table 7.3, concerns about teaching prompted the majority of the reflective thoughts in their journal writing, but Sarah was the only one of the four whose second most predominant concerns were related to 'self'. Table 6.2 (p. 85) shows that these concerns comprise issues of classroom management and discipline, and personality traits, concerns or perceived weaknesses. Table 7.3 also shows that although Jack, Pearl and Perry substantially reflected on learning, Sarah (surprisingly) did not reflect on this issue in a written form in her journal. These varying concerns seem to have differentially influenced the student-teachers' approach to, and use of, reflection and, therefore, their teaching practice.

The pre-lesson interview data (described in Chapter 9) supports this notion. The tests that each student-teacher has worked through as a thought-experiment (imaginative testing) are the focus of the reflective cycle and give a 'practice run' of the lesson. For Sarah, the only test she is concerned with is related to keeping the students quiet and on task, while the other three student-teachers pursue tests related to their understanding of the content-knowledge, teaching, and learning. This difference is borne out in both the number and nature of the phases of the reflective cycle (suggestions, problem, etc.) for each of the student-teachers and also influences their retrospective and contemporaneous reflection.

One problem related to comparisons between individual student-teachers in their use of, and approach, to reflection is that qualitative differences are perhaps best understood if they are bounded by similar parameters. Although the complex nature of teaching and learning does not make it possible to 'control the variables' so that each may be studied one at a time, some comparison can be drawn if similar conditions apply. In this case, I shall present the analysis according to the themes which prompted anticipatory reflection so that reasonable comparisons can be made between each of the student-teachers. The following sections reflect this thematic approach to data analysis.

Classroom Management

Jack's anticipatory reflection revolved around three issues: classroom management, content-knowledge and his students' language ability. In the pre-lesson interview, these three issues continually surfaced at different times as he explained how his lesson was organized and why. A major difference between the classroom management issue for Jack compared to Sarah, was that he considered his teaching approach might lead to classroom management problems because his students would be free of his direct control. On the other hand, Sarah was concerned with teaching in a way that might suppress her students, keeping them under her control so that classroom management problems might not arise. The following excerpts illustrate this point.

Jack: . . . it should be interesting [the lesson]. I feel reasonably comfortable in controlling this class, if it was a more difficult task I might not try it, there's quite a lot of scope for kids to muck around and for things to go wrong, but I'd like to try it anyway.

Interviewer: What do you see as possible things during the lesson that you'll be keeping an eye out for?

Jack: Well it's going to be hard with kids outside as well as inside. I don't know how much I'll have to go outside or look through the window to supervise them because I don't just want them to go off kicking the football and stuff, we won't have time if they're going to do that. They've used ticker-timers before so they know how to set them up, they shouldn't need me to tell them what voltage to use on their power pack and all that kind of thing.

Interviewer: So the organizational things you're comfortable with, it's just fitting the activity into the time?

Jack: Yeah, I think so.

Although classroom management problems may arise as a result of Jack's teaching approach, he reasons that he can deal with likely problems because he has already considered the impact they might have on the students' behaviour. Consequently, later in the interview, he is able to put forward suggestions for dealing with some

of the problems he foresees, and how he might overcome them so that classroom management issues do not 'get in the way' of his teaching. Sarah's focus
on classroom management is very different to Jack's as her reflective cycle is concerned with suggestions and reasoning designed to control the students. The teaching
approach she adopts is a test of her hypothesis: 'if students are kept busy they will
not be disruptive'.

Sarah:	. . . I have two very short paragraphs to write up on the board because knowing this group they're going to be jumpy and if I give them something to write down straight off they're going to settle down hopefully . . . The third thing I want to get on with after that is to read a short passage from the text books. I thought I'd read the first paragraph and then select students to read on from there. If that's not going well then I'll read the rest myself because sometimes these kids like to take their time or act silly or whatever so I'm going to be specifically choosing the students that are more capable of reading, more so than those that aren't, because as the lesson's shorter I've got a lot to get through.
Interviewer:	The lesson's shorter and you're still going to try and fit the same amount of work in in less time?
Sarah:	Well I'm confident I'll get it all in. The only thing is as I said before the class might be jumpy because I told them you were coming and they like the idea of being on video so I threatened them that I would tolerate no misbehaviour so I don't know how much yelling's going to be going on. I think they're going to test me to see if I really carry out my threats so it could be quite a loud lesson but I'm looking for things that are going to settle them down . . . so I'm doing it to settle them down because you're here and because the other lessons I've had have been quite free and easy and I need something a little more structured to start the topic off. So that's my rationale for doing that. So they've got a bit to read from the book, and then we're going to write some points up in a table as we go through the paragraph they've read. They have to break it down and tell me the reasons why exploration was difficult and they're all in the passage so we'll discuss the passage thoroughly and write the points on the board which of course they take into their books. That should just about bring us to the end of the lesson . . . I think they will be a little bit jumpy because you're there with the video plus today is their drama day, they're having their drama plays after lunch so they're all excited about performing and there are a lot of performers in this class, could be jumpy.

> *Interviewer*: Is there anything in the lesson that you're not sure of how it will go, or concerns or worries for you?
>
> *Sarah*: No, I think it should go pretty well. They're really good at discussions this group. They like to have their say, they like to get a bit loud in the process. But they do think, there are a few slow students there but they just take a bit of prompting and they're OK. But, no, I've designed it so that I can get the maximum amount of work from them, hopefully with the least amount of yelling from them but it is purely a management lesson.

Because Sarah's anticipatory reflection is largely concerned with controlling her students she does not yet seem to recognize the influence of pedagogy on student behaviour and, ultimately, the implications of this for her students' learning. As her case-study shows, the bulk of her time is spent reflecting on her students' behaviour. This seems to limit her ability to recognize likely teaching and learning problems and inhibits reflection on these issues. This may in part be due to her low-level use of the attitude of responsibility compared to that of Jack, Pearl and Perry; as shown in Table 6.1 (p. 83). As Dewey (1933) explains, this can restrict 'consistency and harmony in belief. It is not uncommon to see persons continue to accept beliefs whose logical consequences they refuse to acknowledge. They profess certain beliefs but are unwilling to commit themselves to the consequences that flow from them. The result is mental confusion' (p. 32). So, for Sarah, even though she has suggestions about how she might teach the lessons to follow, she nonetheless will likely ignore these ideas as she continues to struggle to resolve this one issue. This is not to suggest that classroom management is an insignificant issue for a student-teacher, even one so close to completing her course, but when it is the major issue it may mask the development of other teaching skills that are equally important or even the most appropriate response to a management concern.

This absence of recognition of the problem, aligned with a denial of the consequences (even though it may well be sub-conscious), is an impediment to Sarah's learning from reflection. Her anticipatory reflection is characterized by reasoning of this type.

> *Sarah*: Well I think this whole lesson was planned to specifically get them under control and to calm them down because they have had a few rowdy lessons I suppose. Not that they've been out of control but I think the whole lesson is aimed at getting them to settle down, do quiet work and I'll really be pushing them, I tried the three minute's silence yesterday, it worked really well, first one who spoke got work to do so I think I'll be doing that one again. At the moment I'm just trying to work out for myself what sort of punishments are appropriate. I've tried lines and my supervisor agrees with that, but another supervisor who came in when he was away said that she found that inappropriate so I'm just juggling

a few different sorts of punishments and seeing which ones are the most effective so I can't say I'm going to do this this or this. So I'll see how the class goes and if I get an idea in my head of some good threat to carry out then I'll probably do it.

It would appear that until Sarah is able to recognize problems in areas outside the classroom management domain, her anticipatory reflection will be characterized by cycles that are predominantly level one (suggestions, problem, hypothesis; see Figure 7.1, p. 92), minimizing the importance and learning from the use of reasoning and testing (levels two and three). Her reflection continues to be restricted to one major area of concern so that her reasoning does not raise other issues beyond the immediate problem. As will be documented in her retrospective and contemporaneous reflection, Sarah does not reason that the mundane nature of her lesson, although designed to keep the students busy and quiet, might also lead to boredom or lack of intellectual challenge and therefore initiate further classroom management problems.

The multiple issue approach to anticipatory reflection is demonstrated in the data on content-knowledge, teaching and learning from Jack, Pearl and Perry. For each of them, their reasoning in one area is linked to the hypothesis testing they contemplate for another so that reflection on one issue influences the nature of reflection on another.

Content-knowledge, Teaching and Learning

Concerns with their own understanding of the content to be taught were raised by Jack, Pearl and Perry. In each case it was a cause for anticipatory reflection and it influenced the structure and organization of their lessons. There was, however, a difference between the type of content-knowledge problem Jack and Perry experienced compared to Pearl. Pearl's problem was related to challenging students' values about refugees (affective domain) whereas Jack and Perry were concerned with their own understanding of the content (cognitive domain) they were to teach. The impact of these on their thinking created a different atmosphere and approach to reflection and testing was a way of learning more about the problem rather than necessarily attempting to solve the problem.

Pearl: ... then there's another question I want them to do for that affective stuff which is to write about who they'd accept as African refugees into Australia, to see if that changes a little bit ... [to do that] next [lesson I have] a video on a South African talking about why they were forced to flee the country. So [we need] to do some talking about why that happens then to come back in at the end to find an activity that correlates I suppose in the end why people leave, but I'm not sure ... They're a good class, I'm just not sure that I've given it enough. I like to be 100 per cent certain

about what I'm doing before I do it and I'm not so, it'll be difficult with the video, I've been worried about doing this . . . I was
trying to work out how to do more P.O.E. [prediction, observation,
explanation; White and Gunstone (1992)] stuff and that but I couldn't
so I threw it out because I didn't have anything definite but I've
been trying to think of how to do that throughout the whole unit.

In this instance, Pearl is reflecting on how to challenge her students' values in an
attempt to unsettle their pre-conceived ideas so that they might be able to empathize
with refugees. Her reasoning encourages her to take a risk in her teaching. She does
not have a lot of suggestions for possible courses of action, and although she is
not sure what her testing will turn up, she is prepared to persevere in an attempt
to better understand ways of probing students' values. Anticipatory reflection in
this instance is likely to lead to retrospective reflection, and, because Pearl does
not appear threatened by her lack of understanding of how the lesson will progress,
might also encourage her to reflect contemporaneously.

Jack's lack of content-knowledge for his unit of work on force and motion
raises problems that are of concern to him. Perry similarly notices difficulties in his
understanding of economics. However, as they reflect on the likely scenarios they
are also prepared to accept the risk associated with their approach to their teaching.

Jack: Also, other things about planning the lesson, I wasn't sure whether
I should get them to do a graph and what depth to do it in, whether
I should get them to get the acceleration, or a velocity versus time
graph or that kind of thing. If they mention that it's faster in the
middle than at the start, do I mention acceleration, greater detail
than that? . . . Also, I'm not all that confident with using the ticker-
timer machinery myself so that could be a problem, there is some
difficulty with the likely timing and there's no way of knowing
how it will work out with all of the gear and things they plan to
measure so I could end up with a lesson that could be a disaster,
but I'm prepared to try that.

Perry: In terms of external policy, I never even understood it at Uni. I
didn't do Economics in HSC [final year of high school] and I
only did one unit that relates to the economics I'm teaching [now],
and whilst we covered far more than the Year 12 course, I wasn't
sure that I really understood it, the learning wasn't important to
me [then], so consequently I come here and have to teach external
policy and I knew I was ignorant but I thought I could cope with
it when it came about, and it has, but I was continually reflecting
on what I'd said when we'd had our talks [interviews] and that's
the way I learnt it, I fleshed it out, and I'm still adding flesh now.
I've been constrained in how I've presented the information, which
I wouldn't have been if I had my own class, because of the
supervisor and we're working through the text book.

The difference in the anticipatory reflection of Jack, Pearl and Perry compared to Sarah is in the way that their reflective processes branch out and link up across different issues or concerns. They see the relationship between teaching and learning and how their understanding of the content to be taught influences these factors. As a result, their lessons are designed with a learning purpose in mind. They have pedagogical hypotheses to test as reflection on one issue interacts with reflection on another. These combine to give a holistic approach to their lesson planning.

Jack: Something else that'll affect the lesson is the background and language of the kids, some don't speak English very well so I've tried to make the worksheet fairly clear and I've got to explain things in a number of ways so that they all know what they have to do. Also because of that their general ability level isn't as high as [students I taught at another school] so that affects the way I plan it . . . So the first thing I'm going to do is put them back in their groups and ask them what they're going to do and I've got a sheet for them to fill in their predictions . . . I might get them to write down what problems they may anticipate . . . If they can't do it then they'll have to think about it, why it didn't work. Then we'll come back in groups, I might get somebody up . . . to do it just to refresh their memory. Then I'll get them to work out the speed near the beginning of the tape, then in the middle and near the end so they can see if there are any changes . . . I've used worksheets before, it's good because it helps them see what they have to do, to put their ideas down on paper so they know exactly what they're doing, it's a good way for them to write down their recordings and things . . . it's sort of a risky lesson I'm not sure how effective it is going to be.

Interviewer: What's the risk?

Jack: That the kids don't really think about what they're doing. They just do it.

Jack prepared his lesson in a way that he hoped would aid student learning. He built in practices that would take into account his students' difficulties with language while working within a framework directed towards getting his students to think about their learning. His lesson was planned to encourage his students to take more responsibility for their learning. His concerns about his understanding of the content-knowledge did not detract from his recognition of the learning issues. He could see that he could not get his students to be responsible for their own learning if he was directing it. If his concerns about his own content-knowledge had over-shadowed his concerns about student learning, he might have decided to give the students only the information he was comfortable with or confident about. Instead, he developed a lesson that allowed his students to explore and think about the topic so that they could learn from their own experiences. At the same time he was able to learn more about this approach to teaching by testing it in action with his class.

Perry articulated his anticipatory reflection in minute detail. As noted in his case-study, he went to the trouble of outlining all of his thoughts about his teaching. His thoughts were a labyrinth of interconnected ideas through which each issue/ concern triggered reflection. His thinking, like Jack's, was apparently directed towards one major purpose. He adopted a teaching approach that he thought would enhance his students' learning.

Perry: Students should be able to identify interrelationships between economic variables relating to external policy by completing a personal concept map forming part of the summary of external policy . . . I didn't want to reinforce any misunderstandings that they'd had . . . I had this thought in my mind when I did a jig-saw activity [cooperative learning strategy] at [another school] where the kids were really enthusiastic about it and then when I tried to pick it up again next lesson, it never really got off the ground the second time. So I'm a little bit concerned that it might fall flat . . . I felt the need to get all students involved so what I did was I got them to do their own personal concept map first, then I moved them into groups of 4–5, then we're going to move it onto a board type correction. Possible ways to correct it [lists a number of suggestions] . . . I also want the kids to assume responsibility for the activity which they had done last lesson. Time will have to suffer for better learning . . . It's the best way I can see of bringing all of the concepts together because they're so interrelated, because I know that the way I learn this suits my style because it shows the relationships in a concrete fashion . . . Those that learn through more written, normal means should already understand I suppose . . . Concerns, I hope they take up the challenge because I really hated that feeling when the jig-saw method fell on it's face last time. In terms of how much I've prepared for it, I don't think I've prepared for it any more than had you not been coming so I don't think it's a put on . . . it depends how much I think the kids are getting out of it at the time as to when I'll move them on, and also how deeply I'll go into each point . . . I might go into examples of them so that I reinforce in my own mind that the kids know what it means rather than just knowing my buzz words . . . basically up 'til now we've examined separate relationships as in two variables and how they relate, now this is getting to the point where we're trying to look at complex interrelationships of variables and I think it's a very useful summary tool . . .

Because of the detail of Perry's explanations about his anticipatory reflection, the full extent of his reflective cycle is able to be unravelled. Perry wanted his students to do more than learn the content, he wanted them to understand it. Because of this, he was reminded of the gaps in his own content-knowledge and what he needed to do to address these deficits. Reflection on this point led to a reasoned pedagogical approach so that teaching and learning were intertwined, valuable and meaningful. He related the way he learnt the content to the way he wanted his students to learn the content. This reasoning led him to believe that his pedagogical approach would enhance the students' understanding of the content. The culmination of his planning led him to see the lesson as:

> *Perry*: I picture the strings on a bag and this is drawing them in as the culmination of the three weeks and this is the method that I chose to do it. Once I selected the method it was a matter of making sure that I had all the interrelationships right because this is a perfect example of teaching something that I wasn't really sure of.

The thinking that underpins the anticipatory reflection of each of the student-teachers demonstrates that reasoning is important in learning through the use of reflection. Considering the factors which might influence a particular course of action can give the student-teacher specific points to focus on, and learn from, through retrospective and contemporaneous reflection. Their reasoning gives purpose to their testing and is an indication of their conviction to the course of action to be implemented.

Overview of Anticipatory Reflection

Chapters 6 and 7 were drawn from the student-teachers' journal writing which encompassed attitudes and reflection. One proposition derived from those data was that the student-teachers might be able to be categorized in terms of their use of reflection. If this is the case then two instances stand out when comparing the results of Tables 6.1 (p. 83) and 7.1 (p. 90) with the anticipatory reflective data outlined above.

Table 7.1 illustrates that Sarah recorded much fewer journal entries on reasoning and testing than either Jack, Pearl or Perry. This suggests that her use of reflection would be lower than the other three. Her anticipatory reflection documented here supports this proposition and suggests that her reflective data, through journal writing, is indicative of her reflective thinking generally. However, journal writing as a form of documenting these thoughts is slower and more cumbersome than speaking so although trends in reflective phases may be similar, their magnitude is lower.

Table 6.1 shows that Jack and Pearl record significantly higher scores for the attitudes of responsibility and whole-heartedness than Perry and Sarah. This suggests that Perry, like Sarah, may in fact not yet recognize the consequences of what he is 'really' doing. He certainly believes (and from his transcripts and observing him in action there seems little reason to doubt) that his teaching was designed to encourage students to be responsible for their own learning. Considering the obvious differences in approach to anticipatory reflection by Sarah and Perry, it is interesting to ponder how their similarities in attitudinal data might be explained. Perhaps their approach to retrospective reflection might shed more light on this apparent dilemma. Perhaps there is a dynamic interplay between attitudes and reflection that is not readily apparent in anticipatory reflective data. Exploring how the thoughts and actions of anticipatory reflection are followed up through retrospective reflection is therefore important in understanding this relationship further and in determining the influence of learning from, and through, reflection on practice.

Finally, van Manen's (1977) three levels of reflectivity may also help to shed light on some of these data. It could be that Sarah is operating only at the first of van Manen's (1977) levels. Her focus is at a technical-practical level as she pursues ways of thinking about, and experimenting with, classroom management strategies. Jack, Perry and Pearl appear to be operating predominantly at van Manen's (1977) second level where their understanding relates to the quality of the educational experiences they construct for their students. This does not however preclude operation at the first level (Jack's data demonstrates some reflection at this level), but suggests that they have overcome some of the uncertainties which still perplex Sarah. What this anticipatory reflective data shows is that there does appear to be a distinction between Sarah, and Jack, Pearl and Perry in both the focus of their reflection and their approach to it. How this is played out in their retrospective reflection is considered in the following section.

Retrospective Reflection

Retrospective reflection is initiated by questioning what happened and why in a teaching episode. Interview data from the student-teachers' attempts to answer these questions are the key to their retrospective reflective thoughts and processes. Two sources of retrospective reflection were available. The first was from the interview conducted immediately after the teaching episode, the second was from the interview conducted after viewing the video of the teaching episode.

Table 10.2 shows the number of coded segments of retrospective reflection from the student-teachers' post-teaching interviews. The number of reflective cycles is proportional to the number of coded segments registered in the testing column, as was the case in Table 10.1. For each student-teacher, retrospective reflection centred on the concerns expressed, and the tests they had planned, through their anticipatory reflection. Jack reflected on classroom management and student learning, Pearl was concerned with content-knowledge and her pedagogy, Perry reconsidered his teaching and his students' learning, while Sarah was again only concerned with classroom management.

It would seem reasonable to propose that retrospective reflection would be initiated in response to the actions embarked upon as a result of testing hypotheses and teaching approaches devised through anticipatory reflection. The extent to which retrospective reflection might be entered into is likely to be influenced by the

Table 10.2: Number of coded segments for each of the reflective phases for retrospective reflection from the post-teaching interviews

Student-teacher	Suggestions	Problem	Hypothesis	Reasoning	Testing
Jack	8	3	5	3	2
Pearl	7	5	3	3	2
Perry	7	3	3	2	2
Sarah	4	4	2	3	1

issues/concerns which prompted reflection in the first place. As the section on anticipatory reflection (above) demonstrated, there is a variation in these issues for these student-teachers. It is therefore logical to conclude that the nature of the retrospective reflection for each student-teacher will also vary in line with their initial concerns, and to some extent, by their recognition, perception, and interpretation of other events occurring during the teaching experience.

Each student-teacher was given the opportunity to retrospectively reflect on their teaching immediately after their lesson, then again in a more informed way after viewing and discussing the video-tape of their teaching. The resultant retrospective reflection from this process demonstrates individual differences in the student-teachers' ability to see what occurred and why, as well as its influence on their use of the reflective cycle.

Classroom Management

Sarah and Jack were both concerned with classroom management but their concerns were for different reasons. Their retrospective reflection illustrates a marked difference in their ability to hypothesize and reason through this issue. Consequently, the influence of retrospective reflection on their thinking about future teaching is also different.

Interviewer:	Just tell me first of all what you think about the lesson, the types of ideas you've got in your mind.
Sarah:	I thought it went pretty well, I was happy with it, the kids weren't too bad although I do have to be firmer on them. I'm not really much of a dragon, I didn't really yell that much, I thought they worked fairly well . . . They kind of rolled with the work although they didn't get through as much as I'd hoped for by reading, and I made the mistake of choosing one person who I knew wasn't a terribly good reader and I shouldn't have.
Interviewer:	Why did you do that?
Sarah:	Nigel seemed eager [interviewer is surprised. Nigel had been sanding his pencil case all lesson, had she recognized this?] and I can't resist an eager person and I think students like that really do need a bit of encouragement. I probably didn't

encourage him by changing readers halfway through but he does respond really well to a bit of attention . . . I would've liked to ask more questions of a variety of students, I tended to stick to the ones that I know . . . They seemed interested. It's harder though today because the lesson was shorter and you being there and being the drama finals day so they were a bit jumpy but they weren't uncontrollable, they did their work so I was pretty happy with them . . . I stuck to my plan almost exactly. Except perhaps I didn't give them enough time to discuss the first bit, why they thought explorers explored, I think I changed that and went into the writing sooner because I realised that I wasn't going to have enough time. So long as you get the basic points out [that's really what matters] . . . I was very conscious of the time running out, I thought it went well and I thought the kids followed pretty well.

Interviewer: Would you do anything differently if you were teaching that class again?

Sarah: I don't think I would do anything differently, I thought it went pretty well. There weren't any major hiccups in my mind, and although it might have been more of a boring class and the kids did get a bit restless here and there, especially with dictation and writing on the board [each of these were predominant parts of the lesson structure]. Some students finished faster than others so for those students who hadn't finished they take a bit of time, but I think it was good . . . I wanted to settle them down and get them used to doing some written work. So for my purposes I thought it went well and it was good. I think they took to it pretty well.

Interviewer: Any other impressions of the lesson?

Sarah: Not really. I just wish I'd had more time. Like an extra five minutes does make a lot of difference, we could've got at least a start on the second lot of work that I wanted to get done. Possibly discussed it a little bit more, but no I thought it went pretty well. I mean I could've saved time by being a bit harder, it's one of the hardest things I find with teaching is not getting the discipline of the kids but just settling them down initially. Like just from that noisy stage to the quiet stage. Like just that little bit is really hard for me and I really don't like yelling or threatening too much. I don't think I raised my voice terribly much in that lesson, although I did yesterday and there was an instant reaction so they really do respond to it. But I find that extremely hard to do. It's something I really have to work on.

Sarah's initial reaction to her lesson revolves around her concerns about classroom management. She had planned to teach the students in a manner that would keep them busy so that they would be subdued and quiet. She recognized a problem that she had created by asking Nigel to read. She realized that stopping him from reading could have had negative consequences for his learning, but as she was driven by the need to control the class she did not dwell on the problem. This opportunity to consider a problem, to seek out alternative suggestions and to engage in reflection is bypassed because it does not 'fit in' with her major concern: classroom management. Her overriding need to be able to control the class seems to limit her ability to respond to other issues so her reflective focus tends to be uni-dimensional.

Sarah also notes time as an issue. She felt as though she could have completed more work if the lesson had been a little longer. The problem with Nigel did not trigger reflection and neither did the problem of time. It is possible that she sees the problem of time being linked to classroom management, rather than being related to, for example, aspects of student motivation or learning. It may be that one of her hypotheses is: more work is able to be completed in a lesson if a class is 'under control'. Noting time as an issue may in fact support her hypothesis rather than initiate reasoning beyond that issue alone. It could be that Sarah believes that the better she manages to control her students, the more propositional knowledge she can transmit per lesson and that this is a sign of good teaching.

Clearly her retrospective reflection revolves around her perception of how well she can control the class. This perception influences her view of the success of the lesson, consequently she sees little that she would change if she were to teach the lesson again.

The case-study of Sarah in Chapter 9 depicts a student-teacher who is racing through a lesson desperately trying to avoid classroom management problems, often seemingly unaware of many of the things happening around her. Because of her focus, she seems blind to many of the other issues occurring around her in the teaching/learning situation. So how might her reflective processes be affected by seeing herself in action from the video-tape? The following transcript demonstrates her understanding and how her pre-conceived ideas continue to influence her thinking.

Interviewer: Now that you've seen the video, how do you feel about the lesson?

Sarah: I still think it was all right. I can see though that I should've been harder on them. I've got room for improvement there. But I'm still happy with it.

Interviewer: What about the pen incident [one student threw another student's pen out to the front of the classroom] tell me about that?

Sarah: Well as soon as I saw who it was, Glen, he's a very capable student, and I know that he wouldn't do something like that and just the look on his face was horror that he'd done it and I knew that it wasn't intentional. When I said to him I want to see you at the end of the lesson his face just dropped.

He came up to me and apologized and I pointed out that he
had to be careful and all that. I decided it was OK., but if
it was Nigel or Michael or some of the girls I would've
really gone to town.

Even though she is given the opportunity to see her lesson from a different perspective it does not seem to influence her reconstruction of the events. As she shows
with the discussion about the pen being thrown across the room, she has decided
on a course of action. The data she takes in is the data which supports her view,
not data which might challenge her to consider things from another perspective.
Nigel, Michael, or one of the girls, would not have been dealt with in a similar way
if they had been the culprits and they had feigned innocence. She has a view about
Glen and that view controls her response to his actions. She does not have any
alternative suggestions, nor does she recognize any other problems as a result of her
actions (such as whether or not her response is consistent with her general approach
to classroom management, or whether the rest of the class would see her response
as being fair).

Sarah's retrospective reflection is extensively linked to the thoughts and actions
she planed in her anticipatory reflection. Through retrospective reflection she does
not attempt to question what happened and why, rather it is an attempt to see how
closely her teaching performance aligned with her planning. Successful teaching
in her mind seems to be related to the fidelity of implementation of the teaching approaches in the episode rather than as a response to it.

Interviewer: Is there anything in that video that you recognize that you
did differently than you'd planned to?

Sarah: I think I stuck to plan. I sort of have a visual plan of what
I want to do in a lesson before I do it anyway, but no, that's
more or less the way I'd planned it to go.

On the issue of classroom management there is a noticeable difference in approach
to retrospective reflection between Sarah and Jack. As Jack reflects on his lesson
(immediately after teaching it) he displays an ability to reconsider his actions in a
detached manner. He neither jumps to conclusions nor judges his actions, he tends
to reflect on them by offering suggestions, proposing hypotheses and considering
issues from different perspectives. Jack's thinking shows that he sees a number of
links between issues where Sarah did not. Also, Jack gives a reason for assigning
some degree of success to his lesson by connecting the perceived risk in the lesson
structure to the students' behaviour and their learning.

Interviewer: Tell me about the lesson. How did it go?

Jack: I think it went quite well. If I thought it was risky before,
I think it went quite well considering those risks and they
had chances to muck around and that kind of thing. I'm
wondering if it was challenging enough for them because

they had done that sort of thing before (recording simple motion), maybe I could've got them to do something else, I don't know what, I just don't know if it was challenging, but then again a couple of groups couldn't do what they intended so I suppose it was a bit of a challenge in that way but not scientifically, or concept wise. But that was good because it was a practical exercise and that was one of the objectives to see if they could actually do it . . . I was wondering how often I should go out to the groups outside. I suppose that'll come up on the video . . . I think it went quite well because they didn't need much help from me which was quite good. Perhaps they were engrossed in what they were doing. I think they were genuinely interested in doing the task.

Jack also demonstrates open-mindedness as he responds to a question about how the lesson he had just taught might affect his approach to subsequent lessons. He with-holds judgment and says, 'I think I'd probably be able to tell you more about that after I've seen the video.' Jack is ready to '*see*' his lesson so that he does not block other avenues to retrospective reflection.

After observing his actions Jack 'sees' things that he did not notice during the lesson and he reconsiders the influence of time and classroom management on his teaching in a very different manner to that of Sarah. He brings more reasoning to bear on his retrospective reflection as he considers the issue of time in concert with student learning. He also reconsiders his approach to classroom management from two different perspectives — his and his school teaching supervisor's.

Jack:	. . . it's funny about how I told that guy off [Dan] for walking around and not the other guy, how I didn't see him at the time.
Interviewer:	Is there anything in how you handle things that makes you think you could've done it differently.
Jack:	I could've gone and seen Dan and seen if there was a problem, but at the time I'd forgotten that I'd told him off before [Dan did not contribute to the class again after being chastised by Jack]. Because we were rushed, I didn't ask for any questions from them, and if they didn't offer anything maybe I could've asked questions of them because a lot of the time they probably do have questions but they're probably too afraid to ask, you've got to be quite pushy, but then again I was conscious of pushing on through . . . I probably [need to] keep my eye on the time more, to make sure that they do have enough time to go through the activity. I wonder if I should be a bit harder on them in terms of discipline, like I'm fairly slack compared to other teachers,

> particularly when Shane [supervising teacher] teaches. He
> makes the point that you have to act it up and act mad but
> I find it hard to do that, I don't even know whether you
> should. I mean it went fairly well today I don't think there
> were any instances where I could've been harder, but my
> style is quite relaxed I don't get flustered by too many
> things, I don't know if I should.

Jack's approach to retrospective reflection is one of questioning and reconsidering his position. Although he does not always have alternative suggestions 'at hand', or hypotheses to test, he does have the ability to pose the problem and to consider it from different perspectives.

Jack and Sarah are both exploring classroom management yet their approach to testing and their responses to their actions are very different. This is well documented in their retrospective reflection and shows that even though the issues may be similar, the influence of reflection on their thoughts and actions produces different outcomes. In comparison to Jack, Sarah appears much more limited in her retrospective reflection; she is seeking to test 'the answer' while Jack is attempting to explore a multitude of possibilities as he reconstructs his learning experiences in an attempt to develop new meaning and understanding.

Content-knowledge, Teaching and Learning

Jack, Pearl and Perry all used retrospective reflection as a way of refining their teaching by learning from their previous experiences. However, the extent to which the different phases of the reflective cycle were used varied for each. The issue which prompted reflection also influenced the extent to which the different phases were employed. At an organizational or structural level, an implicit confidence in one's ability to make appropriate adjustments to future lessons was readily apparent with all three.

> *Jack*:   Other times with teaching the first class, I have changed a little
> bit [when teaching the second class], like organizational things
> like asking them to have one spokesperson per group getting that
> person to report back whatever they found rather than getting
> each person to do it, times where I might have explained a concept
> better or in more ways a second time. Having known the first time
> that they weren't too clear about it or something.

But when retrospective reflection focussed on more complex issues such as the relationship between pedagogical approach and enhancing student learning, much less confidence was apparent — suggestions for action were limited and hypotheses were more difficult to articulate. Consequently, although problems might be acknowledged, possible courses of action are not able to be reasoned through and tested with the same confidence as occurs with less complex issues.

Pearl demonstrates this when discussing other ways of teaching her lesson. Her retrospective reflection on the lesson incorporates her views from her anticipatory reflection. However, although she has suggestions and possibilities for other teaching approaches, she is not convinced by her own reasoning. The complex nature of the issue does not lead to immediate problem resolution.

Interviewer: How would you teach that lesson if you had to do it again?

Pearl: When I was thinking about it, the other option was starting with a couple of specific countries that had refugees and making up some cards with basic information and getting them to work [things] out from that with questions about the conditions in the country and things like that, doing the same distinction with the drought and war, I decided it was probably too complicated. I don't know if maybe in that lesson [the video-taped lesson] it would [have] been good to lead into it more because it was very backwards and forwards. I'd like to work out a way of doing it where it wasn't so but I'm not sure how I'd do that.

Pearl and Perry demonstrate that the issues of content-knowledge and teaching and learning cause them to reconsider their teaching episodes through retrospective reflection. In so doing, they mentally reconstruct the episodes and try to find new meaning that might help them to reshape their teaching. Even though they are able to recognize the relationship between these issues and their understanding of teaching, they struggle to resolve their problems. Their approach to retrospective reflection is such that understanding the issue is initially more important than determining a course of action to test. However, it does appear as though hypothesis formation is occurring even though it is not immediately verbalized. Accordingly it may be that other phases of reflection may be occurring in a subconscious manner and that they are simply being delayed until an acceptable understanding of the problem, or suggestions, or reasoning is realized. The following account from Perry is an example of this:

Perry: I don't think it was as educating as I'd hoped it would be . . . My teaching was dictated by getting through the work objectives . . . I don't think there was anything so much wrong with the lesson, it was [just] that not having a really really good knowledge of the material made it hard. Like you can't be unsure of the material and enjoy it at the same time, and be positive and outgoing and flowing, and brilliant questions. I was struggling with it and the kids were struggling with it too. It would've assisted me if I had a better knowledge of the learning, and I think I might have been able to put a bit more pizzazz into it and that would've made me feel better about it.

Perry appears to be thinking about a number of issues concurrently even though he is only able to verbalize one at a time. He did not see the lesson as being so 'wrong' but he was not particularly happy with it. He had conducted the lesson according to his plan, but his lack of understanding of the content stood in the way of him being satisfied with his teaching. He readily acknowledges the problem but does not suggest a solution, yet it is obvious that he needs to do more about understanding the content better if in future he is to be satisfied with his efforts. So a hypothesis is available but is not articulated. When it is articulated it is likely that he will reason through his thinking and develop a course of action to test. This suggests that in some cases retrospective reflection may require more 'thinking time', rather than being an immediate progression through the reflective phases. Although Jack does not articulate his retrospective reflection to anywhere near the same extent as Pearl and Perry, he also appears to require extended 'thinking time' for his reflection. His responses to questions were not immediate and he often said he did not know '*yet*', suggesting that he believed that over time he would come to a reasoned position.

It is likely that the reflective cycle may persist over an extended period of time. If so, then progression through other phases may not be initiated until satisfactory resolution of preceding phases is achieved. Pearl gives a hint that this may well be an influencing factor in her approach to retrospective reflection.

> *Pearl*: I was thinking about getting them [students] to do some different things but it would've required more synthesis of things [that] they haven't got. At the moment, they have little information about refugees and I want to give them some that they can check back against and I'd hoped that they'd be able to do that when they have the factual stuff so how do I get through that I don't know. It takes me a while to think about it.

In this instance she is able to reason through the problem but is not able to resolve it. She does not explicitly state a hypothesis even though one is able to be deduced from her statement. She can reason but cannot think of alternative suggestions, she can see a problem but does not know how to address it. She needs time to think, time to reflect. Examples similar to these abound, different phases are apparent but may not be linked together to complete a reflective cycle.

> *Perry*: ... going around and asking one person to contribute the answer, as soon as you've asked that person they tended to switch off ... those that I asked first could effectively switch off because they didn't think I would ask them any more questions ... that was a problem ... when kids put down their answers [I didn't know] whether to leave them in their uncorrected form or to interject and give a more succinct answer.

There was a lot of learning taking place, kids were quiet, if they weren't learning anything I think they would've been more distracted and they'd be mucking around more, looking out of the window more, but they were actually looking through their notes, correcting their diagrams, trying to listen to what was said . . .

I really would have liked some time before I launched into the essay. It really seemed like it was just tacked onto the end, I should've spun the lesson out for the whole period and not gone on to anything else, perhaps set them some problems or something like that. But the problem is this is my last contact before my last lesson so I had to get those instructions out so that was a limitation, I would've liked more time to go over the essay.

I'd like to have some means that they [students] were more prepared. Perhaps I could've gone round last lesson and selected one relationship that they had to present to the class as a presentation for two minutes and do it that way. But then again it might've allowed them to slack off because they never knew who was going to be next and which relationshi ps were left. That could've saved a bit of anxiety and I wouldn't have to run around like that.

Pearl: I think [the lesson was] quite good . . . [though] I'm not sure that they did very much, whether much was accomplished.

Getting at knowing what refugees were, I don't think that's completely sunk in yet, that's why looking at the case-studies [is important] and that's why it'll be good to do that more specific stuff on Monday. I think that building stuff isn't going to make much more sense until we do that . . .

. . . I don't like spending so much time doing something on the board and them copying it down, I should get them to copy it down as I go, but then some don't participate so I don't know, maybe I should try it the other way. Maybe with that profile thing, who's an immigrant and who's a refugee, I was thinking maybe I should've done that [in] more a spoken way but then I'm not guaranteed that they'd all do it so I still don't know that I would do it that way.

I really don't know [if the students learnt what I wanted]. How do you find out? I can't tell just from that, there are no strategies there to tell me that except for when I do the discussion on refugees, so I don't know. The colouring in and that, I can't tell really 'til I see their work.

> *Interviewer*: How does this lesson effect what you'll do next lesson?
> *Pearl*: Now it pushes it all back, they need to finish this. I can't say just leave this otherwise I'm telling them that it's not valuable, it's just so difficult.

The phases of reflection need not occur in a fixed order but a reflective cycle is when the phases are able to be linked together to work through an issue. The more complex the issue under consideration, the longer it may take to complete a reflective cycle; in terms of research, the more difficult it may be to detect and document.

The relationship between retrospective reflection and time also applies to the dilemma regarding attitudes and reflection. Perry and Sarah both had lower scores for responsibility and whole-heartedness compared to Jack and Pearl. One conclusion proposed from Table 6.1 (p. 92) was that attitudes were a guide to a student-teacher's preparedness to reflect, yet the reflective data (anticipatory and retrospective) for Perry and Sarah clearly demonstrate fundamental differences in their approach to, and use of, reflective process. It appears then that just as reflection may be developed and extended over time, so might attitudes. The key to this coincidentally focuses on Perry. If his lower score in responsibility (Table 6.1) is a guide to his ability to 'really see' what he is doing, then it could be expected that, like Sarah, he may not be fully cognizant of the consequences of his actions. But his anticipatory and retrospective reflection does not accord with that notion. However, when one recalls the closing moments of his post-teaching interview (as outlined in his case-study in Chapter 9) he thought the questions he was being asked were probing for something more, something he might not have recognized. The abridged version of that transcript (below) gives a subtle clue to this recognition.

> *Interviewer*: Did the lesson run smoothly? [Perry responds . . .]
> *Interviewer*: If you had to do this again, how would you do it? [Perry responds to this question . . .]
> *Interviewer*: What are your other reactions? [Perry adds a little more to his previous statements . . .]
> *Interviewer*: Anything else?
> *Perry*: You make it sound as if there should be [something else] and I've missed it.

This dialogue led Perry to pursue the issue further after the interview so that he knew what I was thinking, as described in his case-study: 'I think perhaps what we've been watching is you trying to learn for the kids. You seem to be taking all of the responsibility for the learning, almost as if it's your problem not theirs. You just told me that you have now understood this work, learnt it. I wonder how you might teach it so they could do that too?'

The attitude of responsibility encompasses seeing the consequences of one's actions from different perspectives. It may be that Jack and Pearl would have drawn the conclusion (described above) themselves if they had been in a similar position to Perry. Perry's scores for responsibility in Table 6.1 do not suggest that he is as 'responsible' as either Jack or Pearl, rather that, like Sarah, he is more likely to pursue actions related to beliefs from which he does not really see or acknowledge the logical consequences. Perry did not recognize the apparent paradox between what he intended to do for his students' learning through his teaching, and what he was actually doing through his teaching. Nevertheless, once it was pointed out, he was able to retrospectively reflect on it in a meaningful way. Sarah did not show that (at this stage) she could make this transition. This notion of transition was quite unexpectedly uncovered in Perry's final interview for the year at Monash and is an important link between the video-taped lesson and his learning through reflection.

Perry:	*fourth individual interview*
Perry:	Do you know what the biggest learning experience was that I've had on this course?
Interviewer:	No.
Perry:	Well it was when you came out to video-tape me and I think the fact that it was H.S.C. [final year of secondary school] brought this to a head. Up to that point I felt that I had to present all of the information . . . no matter what I said, I did feel ultimately as though I was the font of wisdom. When you said [referring to the discussion about the video-taped lesson] that I was virtually doing H.S.C. [for the students], bang, it sounded totally right to put the responsibility back on the students. Even though there was only two or three days to go after you left, I really enjoyed the classes from then on because I enjoyed watching them learn rather than them watching me learn. It gave me the opportunity to go around to those that needed the work, to still supervise, but the responsibility for the work was with them, not me.
Interviewer:	So what are you saying made that happen?
Perry:	Well it was basically your highlighting the situation, but I just saw myself on this video running around like I'd almost fly.
Interviewer:	So you saw yourself?
Perry:	Yeah, I just recognized it and thought shit, this isn't what I want to do, this isn't my ideal teacher, but it was only once I saw myself and particularly through your questions . . . I'm trying to justify why I did certain things in the class. It was just why did I do that, oh I'm not going to do that, oh, oh, I did it. That was probably the biggest thing, and because it was quite a long session it really set me back in my

tracks for the rest of the day. I was thinking about it all night and that sort of thing. I won't forget it, it's been a learning episode and it'll stick in my mind.

Interviewer: There may be something in that, I only did video-tapes with a few people. You saw what happened, others might not. You see what you want to see happening, so I wonder why are you able to recognize those things?

Perry: I guess I'm always looking to improve on my teaching. I think at the start of the thing, on my first teaching round I thought I was reasonably good. But the further I went, the more I can see that I learnt. I think at that stage I said to you, well basically I need the piece of paper, but I think I can learn a lot along the way. Well now I think I could've done teaching at the start but all I would've done would be the by-product of all the teaching experiences I had at school, and I think I'd have become the way they teach at [his old school] without any problem. I could've taken on that luggage fairly easily. But now I realize that I want to, and I guess this is what the course has given me through dealing with things, it's not just the written curriculum it's also the unwritten curriculum, now I can see how I can change and adapt teaching to what I want rather than just accepting everyone else's opinions and that sort of thing.

Interviewer: What makes you think that?

Perry: There's a lot more freedom within the course, more than any other course, but the thing you run the risk of is that some people come through and they don't get anything from it, untouched. You know, they manage to survive the whole year and they still don't think very much from it, which is the negative. But I wonder if the positive might outweigh that. Like if you [John] had've used more conventional teaching things, well you would've lost me for a start. I would've gone into my slack mode and I would've got through but I wouldn't have tested myself. It's sort of like when I went to that next year's DipEd thing [an information session for prospective students] I wanted to tell them how they could get the most out of the course. Yet, when I mentioned some of the things I'd said to other people around here, they're going, 'what like in school!' and it's amazing you can have such highs and lows in the one exposure to the same teaching. But I guess it just didn't fit in with what they were after.

There was approximately six weeks between the video-taped experience and the final interview. In that time Perry had reflected on his experience a number of times.

His initial retrospective reflection, a consequence of the interview-observation-interview experience which acted as a catalyst to his application of responsibility to his thinking, led him to restructure his teaching. The net result of retrospective reflection over an extended period of time was a re-analysis of the affect of the course on his learning, as well as enhanced valuing of pre-service education in shaping his learning about, and actions in, teaching.

This very rich example from Perry demonstrates the complex nature of reflection and why it can be a difficult area to research. Undoubtedly, time is one crucial factor in the development of attitudes and reflective processes.

Overview

Understanding content-knowledge inevitably has a bearing on the way the student-teachers teach. The type of teaching approach used in a lesson obviously has a bearing on the way students learn the content. Therefore, the student-teachers who recognize these issues, and the relationship of one with the other, ultimately become involved in complex reflective processes.

Pearl and Perry show that they are beginning to build on and learn from the experiences that will give them greater access to suggestions, problem recognition, hypothesis formation, reasoning and testing for their retrospective reflection. Hence, their retrospective reflection may be a process which continues over an extended period of time until the different phases are linked to one another. When this occurs they are then more likely (and able) to initiate new pedagogical approaches to test.

In both anticipatory and retrospective reflection, time is readily available for the student-teacher to consider the options available and to work toward some form of problem resolution. The much more urgent and immediate nature of classroom teaching does not afford the same opportunity for one to dwell on an issue in a correspondingly 'relaxed' manner. This change in available time and its effect on reflection during teaching is explored in the nature of the student-teachers' contemporaneous reflection in the following section.

Contemporaneous Reflection

Contemporaneous reflection is where the 'action-present' is the impetus for reflection. It is reflection that is immediately responsive to the learning environment and may be seen as shifts in pedagogical approaches and behaviours which may be either anticipated or unexpected. This is where the complexity of the teaching moment may enhance the dynamic nature of reflection. Therefore, contemporaneous reflection is a most demanding and highly context dependent action.

Contemporaneous reflection leads to learning from testing during a teaching episode and requires a personal acceptance of the risks involved. Student-teachers who, by virtue of their position, lack extensive classroom teaching experience, could find contemporaneous reflection to be a frustrating, difficult and perplexing experience as they strive to understand and learn more about teaching through reflection. The lack of experience to draw on, the difficulties associated with attempting to respond quickly to changes in the teaching episode, combined with the pressure of trying to develop suggestions for addressing problems are all added pressures associated with contemporaneous reflection. A student-teacher may well recognize problems but be unable to respond appropriately or confidently, therefore opportunities for contemporaneous reflection may be presented but remain unattended.

Analysis of the discussions while viewing the video-taped lessons suggests that two forms of contemporaneous reflection are identifiable. One is a thoughtful approach to a perceived problem during practice and is able to be reconstructed and explained by the student-teacher without too much difficulty. The other is an almost subconscious action which 'just happens' and the student-teacher has difficulty explaining why. Consequently, tallying the contemporaneous reflective data for Table 10.3 was much more difficult than was the case for anticipatory or retrospective reflection. It was harder to decide what data 'really' comprised reflection. The recognition that these two forms of reflection were occurring made the assignation of reflective phases much more context dependent, and called for an understanding of the student-teacher's thinking-while-acting which went beyond the transcript data alone.

The difference between these two forms of contemporaneous reflection and how it influenced analysis is perhaps best illustrated by comparing two sections of transcript from Pearl's lesson. The first demonstrates a thoughtful, well organized approach to contemporaneous reflection where she had already anticipated a problem derived from her learning through retrospective reflection. She links that problem to her current practice and so has a way of working through it during her lesson. It shapes her approach to teaching.

Pearl: Do you remember my tape analysis [TAL assignment after first teaching round: linking learning from that to the present situation as a result of retrospective reflection], well they [students] said three kids were away and I never picked it up and so they didn't ever grasp any of what was happening [problem], so now I'm quite paranoid about finding out who's missed out. And because people are always sick, I want to know who's up to where [suggestion]. Just so I know where to start, otherwise it'll throw me if some of them don't know what we're up to, so I can address it as I go this way [reasoning].

Interviewer: You get a response, what effect does it have on your actions?

Pearl: It had quite an effect in the beginning because there were not any that were not there last week, like I had down [lesson plan], check who's here and who's not, if there are people who were not here, bring them up to it and explain it. So I didn't have to do that so I could go straight into recapping the subject not catching up on other stuff [testing]. Also

there are some kids who've been away for a couple of weeks
so I had to decide what I'm going to do with them [hypo-
thesis: when a student is absent the teacher has to help
him/her catch up on the work missed or the student will be
disadvantaged].

In this example Pearl has reasons for her action, she has thought about what to do
and why and quickly reviews these thoughts as she is teaching. Her contemporaneous reflection is thoughtful and logical and is performed in action. This is in
contrast to another instance in which she acted without really knowing why.

Interviewer:　They're working quietly again and I didn't see any cue for
　　　　　　it but you said OK, we've had enough.
Pearl:　　　Sandy and these boys back here they had actually finished,
　　　　　　the non-verbals told me that they had finished pretty quickly.
　　　　　　I still don't know what to do when some finish too early com-
　　　　　　pared to others. I just decided to stop them.

The class consisted of twenty-four students, six had finished the work. From this
Pearl decided to stop the rest of the class from doing the task and to move on. She
recognizes the problem that she does not know what to do when some students
finish earlier than others. She responds to this problem but does not really know
why she decided to act in the way she did; it just happened. Examples similar to
this are also apparent in Jack and Perry's transcripts, but not in Sarah's.

Jack:　　It just occurred to me, I thought that was important.

Perry:　　I don't know why I did that, it was just an instantaneous thing.

Therefore, problem recognition leading to action does not always follow the same
thoughtful pattern of Dewey's (1933) reflective cycle but may be an indication of
the beginnings of reflection-in-action[1] as described by Schön (1983). The distinction between reflection-on-action and reflection-in-action is important. As Munby
and Russell (1989) point out, in this case the term reflection can be confusing.

Schön's argument is easily misread if we focus on reflection rather than
on action. 'Reflection' typically suggests thinking about action, but the
crucial phrase, on our reading, is 'in-action'. The reflection that Schön is
calling attention to is *in the action*, not in associated thinking about action.
(p. 73)

In Pearl's case, she recognized that she did not know what to do when some
students finished earlier than others while Sarah is much less responsive to the pedagogical moment (van Manen, 1991a) than Jack or Perry, while Pearl is the most
responsive of all. Table 10.3 illustrates differences in the way each of the student-
teachers approaches contemporaneous reflection.

Table 10.3: *Number of coded segments for each of the reflective phases for contemporaneous reflection from the interview-observation-interview cycle from the video-taped lessons*

Student-teacher	Suggestions	Problem	Hypothesis	Reasoning	Testing
Jack	12	6	1	4	1
Pearl	13	9	8	9	7
Perry	15	6	3	4	3
Sarah	6	3	3	5	1

Sarah's contemporaneous reflective cycle revolves around one aspect of her lesson format: the amount of notes she expected the students to write. She also developed hypotheses and reasoned through different aspects of her understanding of classroom management, but did not decide on actions which she could overtly test during the lesson.

Jack's contemporaneous reflective cycle related to his need to know whether or not the students understood the content. Although he had a number of suggestions related to other problems which he recognized during the lesson, he only performed one test. So although he displayed thinking which illustrated phases of reflection with regard to other aspects of his teaching, he only completed one full reflective cycle *during* the lesson.

Perry was also aware of a number of problems during his lesson which prompted him to reflect contemporaneously. His thoughtful considerations led him to perform three tests during the lesson. The first was a test of an approach to class-room management, the second was an attempt to challenge his students' thinking, and the third was in response to his own perception of his teaching during the lesson.

Pearl was by far the most responsive to both her teaching and her students' learning during the lesson. This could have been influenced by the nature of her lesson and the type of students she was teaching (her students were generally described as low-achievers who tended to be disruptive in the majority of lessons). Four of her contemporaneous reflective cycles centred on organizational issues associated with the structure of the lesson, the other three focused on aspects of student learning.

The major difference between the contemporaneous reflective cycles documented was that some were in response to problems which were anticipated in advance, and some were in response to problems which arose (and were recognized by the student-teacher) during the lesson. The following section gives analyses of instances of contemporaneous reflection based on the these two categories.

Anticipated Problems

Each of the student-teachers recognized problems which they had predicted could occur and were therefore ready to address during the lesson. Their contemporaneous reflection was then a response to something which they were in some way prepared for.

Their preparation varied from initiating pre-determined actions as a response to the stimuli of problem recognition during the lesson, through to simply raising their own awareness of a possible problem without considering it any further. In the latter, they were withholding thoughts and actions until the problem presented itself, confident of being able to work through the necessary thinking during the lesson. Jack illustrated this in his pre-lesson interview when he was talking about how his approach to the lesson might be affected by the time needed to adequately complete the task.

> *Interviewer*: If they do not complete that [work], how will it affect the lesson?
>
> *Jack*: I'm not really sure yet. That's probably something I'll decide at the time. Hopefully they will get it all done, what they don't they should be able to do for homework, if they've got the data they can do the calculations.

In this instance, Jack is able to see a problem that might arise during the lesson. He knows that if the students do not complete all of their experiments they are less likely to capitalize on the learning experience the way he has planned. Despite this, he does not have a plan for what to do if this occurs, rather he will 'decide at the time'. When the problem does arise (as will be seen in the next section), his response is very different from the type associated with implementing a pre-determined action plan.

Initiating a pre-determined action plan is the way that Sarah approached her contemporaneous reflection. She had ideas or approaches that she had reflected on which influenced how she might react during her teaching. This type of contemporaneous reflection is heavily influenced by anticipatory and/or retrospective reflection and involves re-igniting the reflective cycle in response to problem recognition. Sarah shows how this happened in her lesson when she saw an appropriate time to act in a given way.

> *Interviewer*: Tell me what's happening now.
>
> *Sarah*: I was checking up on how far people have got while taking the notes. I was pretty sure most of them had [taken them down] because they're fairly good workers there's only a few there that I thought might've been a bit slow and I knew who they were. Just to see how they were going taking the notes down and besides I really do like walking around the class just to give a presence [suggestions] so that they know I'm around . . . I can't stand the teachers who sit behind the desk or sit at the front, I can't do that.
>
> *Interviewer*: Then you go through what's written on the board, why do you do that?
>
> *Sarah*: Because I think a lot of time students take things down but don't think about what they're writing [hypothesis] and as

	I'm tutoring a Year 7 student and that's his major problem so I'm very aware that a lot of them would've taken them down and thought, oh they're just notes [problem]. So I thought if I go through it with them then they might remember it a bit more, take more notice of it [test].
Interviewer:	When did that thought occur to you?
Sarah:	From the beginning, I always planned to do it.
Interviewer:	Now you're reading out the notes. Had you originally planned to be the person reading these?
Sarah:	Yeah, although I really should've had silence, there are a lot of kids who weren't following or were doing other things, which I was aware of . . . I really wanted everyone to follow it and to think about what they'd written and I thought [it would help] just to have them check it through [reasoning].

Sarah anticipated the problem that during note-taking students copy the work without processing the information. Because she was aware of this she had a course of action which she thought would help address the problem. The feedback that she was getting from the students triggered her to reflect contemporaneously and to initiate her pre-determined plan in response to recognizing that the problem had arisen.

This approach may be indicative of learning about the use of contemporaneous reflection. Having already reflected on the problem when sufficient time was available, the confidence to respond and reflect again in class is enhanced so that one is primed for contemporaneous reflection. In Sarah's case this appears likely, particularly as she seemed unaware of other problems which arose during her lesson. For her, contemporaneous reflection was not initiated by unexpected problem situations, but more so by the recognition of expected problem situations.

This difference between being prepared to respond to expected problem situations and being able to respond to unexpected problem situations is the essence of contemporaneous reflection. It seems that some student-teachers are able to recognize and respond to unexpected problem situations in an environment (the action present) where reflection could be thwarted by other simultaneous and competing events. Jack, Pearl and Perry demonstrate that they are capable of responding to both the expected and the unexpected as well as displaying greater confidence in their use of contemporaneous reflection. Even though the extent of contemporaneous reflection varies amongst each of the student-teachers, they do demonstrate a level of use which seems more advanced than that used by Sarah.

Unanticipated Problems

An important difference between contemporaneous reflection initiated by unanticipated problems as opposed to anticipated problems is related to the 'withitness' (Kounin, 1977) of the student-teacher. As the term suggests, withitness refers to how well a teacher knows what is happening in all places at all times during a lesson. It is characterized by phrases such as, 'Having eyes in the back of his head,' or 'She [the teacher] knew what I wanted before I asked my question.' Therefore, the greater the degree of withitness student-teachers display, the more perceptive they are to the goings on in their classes.

Although opportunities for contemporaneous reflection may arise during a lesson, that does not mean that they will be recognized or acted upon. The more sensitive student-teachers are to feedback from the teaching and learning environment, the more likely they are to seize the opportunity for contemporaneous reflection. The way that these student-teachers recognized and responded to these opportunities is an indication of their sense of *awareness* of the nuances of the teaching and learning environment, as well as their ability to *adjust* to the omnipresent demands of classroom teaching. As Sarah's case-study portrayed, she did not appear to be as 'withit' as Jack, Pearl or Perry. Consequently, she did not overtly display signs of contemporaneous reflection to the same extent as the other three. This section shows how Jack, Pearl and Perry approached the opportunities for contemporaneous reflection that they recognised.

The following excerpts, derived from transcripts while observing the video-taped lessons, are indicative of how each of the student-teachers were confronted by different problem-situations in their lessons. The fact that they actually recognized these is important as it demonstrates that they are able to 'reframe' (Schön, 1983). These reframing experiences may present opportunities for contemporaneous reflection.

Interviewer: . . . you go through the questions, what's happening here?

Jack: Well it's partly a language thing. I have to explain it to be sure they know what they're doing. The thing about constant speed is important, so I decided to get somebody to explain it to everybody else. See there, I don't know whether to make them stop and listen to me or just say what I've got to say, will they listen? . . . I'm worried here about the problems they might have, you can see that they're thinking about accuracy with speed but they're on the wrong track I actually meant practical problems with how to do the prac. so I tell them because they didn't know what I was on about. It takes a while to get to know these kids too, it takes a while to know what they're on about. Their abilities differ, some of them have genuine problems knowing what you mean.

Interviewer: You're going through the answers and you're happy then you stop at this one and work it for some time, when do you decide you've made the point that you wanted them to understand?

Pearl: I'm worried about their answers, I don't want to put their answers down and I'm hoping that we can work towards a common understanding rather than them seeing me as giving them an answer that is just my point of view. Jesse's happy because it was his point that I was using, Sarah over there gives a bit of recognition that it can be tricky that it's not always straight forward. I don't want to get bogged down but I want them to follow.

Interviewer: What's happening here?

Perry: I think I'm just elaborating, you know how I said if I had time I'd go into a bit of a summary type thing. What he [student] hadn't done was indicate with arrows up and down what the affect was going to be. I'm just working through it with the class, I've realized that it was only the person who was directly up that was in the hot seat and others could slack off so I started throwing questions out to everyone else to try and get them, I later ask a question of John because he's starting to stare out and not pay enough attention.

Jack, Pearl and Perry each display an ability to see what is happening as they teach. They are responsive to their students' overt and covert feedback and in so doing enable their teaching to be influenced by the pedagogical moment, helping it to be a two-way process rather than a static unidimensional presentation of knowledge or skills.

This interplay of 'withitness' — conscious reframing of the problem situation and pedagogy — appears to be a key to contemporaneous reflection. It is something that Sarah does not seem as conscious of while Jack, Pearl and Perry are not only conscious of it, but also respond to it. The following extract demonstrates this difference. A major theme of Sarah's case-study was her inability to really 'see' the opportunities for reframing. Instead she appeared intent on pursuing her structured plan, seemingly unaware of the feedback of her students. Thus she bypassed the opportunities to reframe problem situations.

Interviewer: See what Nigel's doing all the time, sanding off his pencil case.

Sarah: Yeah . . . I don't like holding my book like that, it's sort of like a security blanket almost. I don't think I need it but I like to have something in my hand to refer to.

Interviewer: Now why do you choose Nigel. Had you planned to?

Sarah: No. He asked where are we up to and so I thought I'll choose him but I shouldn't have done it. Well looking at this I chose Brett. From the very start he was going can I read, and I know that he's a very capable student.

Interviewer: You listen to this and tell me what's going on? [Nigel's reading is slow and disjointed, Sarah stops him quickly dismissing him for another student.]

Sarah: I'm thinking that's an awful thing to do, cut him off like
            that, but then again I shouldn't have chosen him in the first
            place . . . The others were getting restless and I could hear
            them telling him the words that he was having trouble with
            which showed that they were reading it, but it's a bit dis-
            ruptive to the others. You can see now that Rachel is read-
            ing and it immediately quietens down.

Sarah's understanding of this episode is limited during the lesson because her focus
is largely dominated by a desire to get her students to complete a set amount of
work. This restricts her thinking in other directions to such an extent that she does
not attend to Nigel because it might slow the process of information dissemination.
The possibility of seeing Nigel's actions in a different light by reframing the problem
situation is missed.

Recognizing problems during a teaching episode is a catalyst for contemporaneous reflection. Through the thoughtful reconsideration of the pedagogical
moment a better understanding of one's own teaching practice (and the students)
learning may be developed. The thinking which comprises contemporaneous reflection may vary with time as the ability to draw on suggestions, and to develop hypotheses to reason and test will be influenced by the type of problem and the context
of the situation.

Pearl demonstrates one way of giving herself time to reflect contemporaneously.
At one point in her lesson, after spending some time developing ideas with the
students about why people might become refugees, she is confronted by a problem
situation.

Interviewer: . . . you ask about a natural disaster and he [student] says a
            car crash. You've spent some time talking about it and he
            suggests a car crash, but he's serious, so what were you
            thinking?
Pearl: Well I could've just dismissed it but he's just had a shock-
            ing report, he has an awful home-life and he always sneers
            in class and opts out of the work, so when he says some-
            thing it's quite amazing that he would suggest anything, so
            I wanted him to see why his suggestion wasn't right but that
            I valued his input anyway because if he's not participating
            and I jump on him it doesn't help at all. I then went down
            the back to talk to him a little about it because of that and
            because I needed some thinking time to work out how to
            respond to him.

Amidst juggling the interactions of an interpretive discussion (Barnes, 1976) Pearl
recognized a problem situation. She hypothesized that the student would not interact
further if she did not show that she valued his response. She could have dismissed

his suggestion as inappropriate and selected another student, but instead she re-framed what she was seeing and hearing, brought additional information to bear on her reasoning, then made time to determine how to act. She found a way of making time to reflect during her teaching. Pearl had recognized an opportunity for contemporaneous reflection and had accepted the challenge that was unfolding before her.

The influence of time is important in terms of thinking and possible responses for testing. Pearl showed how she was able to make space during the lesson to think and respond. There was an obvious lag between problem recognition and response. Her discussion with the student gave her additional time to develop suggestions and reason through her actions. However, in the context of the total lesson, her actions were relatively quick.

On the other hand, Perry had an ongoing problem which he struggled to respond to throughout the lesson. He was continually confronted by his own lack of understanding of the content he was teaching. Because of the teaching strategy he had decided to implement, the problem returned time and time again as the lesson unfurled, continually confronting him as he struggled with subordinate problems stemming from his content-knowledge problem. Although Perry did not resolve the issue during the lesson, reframing the problem situation allowed him to see more of what was happening from perspectives other than just his own. Contemporaneous reflection did not immediately lead to problem resolution but was the impetus for further consideration, reasoning and testing. Ultimately, his contemporaneous reflection influenced his learning about teaching.

The following edited compilation of excerpts derived from watching the video-taped lesson with Perry shows how his contemporaneous reflection extends over time.

Interviewer: What are you doing now?

Perry: I'm looking for my answers. It's a bit of a panic. I took them [papers] to one side to get out of the way. I was conscious that I was intruding into the exercise, but I needed my sheet, it's getting to the desperation point.

Interviewer: But what is there on the answer sheet that you don't know anyway?

Perry: I wanted to make sure that I got all of the interrelationships because there's 21 of them, and so I could easily forget one. So I was hoping to tick them off as I went, like that was in my plan. I could see it getting further and further out of hand, see there, I was thinking to myself, I wasn't listening to a word she said, I'm thinking, I left them on the table in the staffroom and so I abandoned hope of finding it, so I'll just have to wing it . . . I thought I know most of them, so I'll just try and rely on my knowledge rather than the security blanket of the piece of paper.

Interviewer: So did that affect the way you went about it?

Perry: Yeah I had to think on my feet a lot more. Make sure the relationships that they were suggesting, like the terms of trade one which comes up later, I saw it and it takes me a little while to twig to it then I found that what they had on the board was incorrect so I had to put in a bit of an explanation which wouldn't have happened, I would've recognized it quicker if I'd have had the sheet.

Interviewer: Aggregate demand comes up and you spend a long time on it.

Perry: It's because I'm not sure of it myself. It's the most wishy-washy area of my knowledge and I guess I assumed that it's the same for them . . . it caught me off guard, that was the thing. Because it seemed so obvious but when you had to think about it on the hot seat, it wasn't so obvious.

Interviewer: I can see you thinking about this now, you've drawn it up on the board, you're thinking something.

Perry: I was conscious that I'd said this would be a low teacher-centred lesson, yet I'm working like a traffic cop. I'm really concerned about this export index, it's a diversion from the plan but I feel I really need to clarify it. Then I realize that he's finished his work, he's put it down and I haven't had any time to think, so I rub out the wrong line, I'm trying to get lots of think time because this is really complex . . . I have to work through it and they have it in front of them, so they go through it quicker than I am because I'm processing it . . . I wasn't sure how many more relationships there were to do, not having my sheet, I knew I had about 21 and there are 17 kids in the class, and they'd all done one and I could only see one extra one. Like some are less important than others, so I was trying to decide because I could only see one that was missing. God it's slow isn't it? . . . I asked Jimmy and he didn't seem to have a concept of fixed interest, then I asked a couple of people and they said the exchange rate alters but it doesn't because it's fixed, so I'm trying to recreate the episode from when I taught it . . . It is a brain strain this subject.

Perry was continually confronted by the problem-situation as he struggled to determine how to respond in the short-term during class, but also in the long-term in relation to developing his pedagogy. Jack found himself with a similar problem but, as time was limited, he acted in a way that he recognized did not really address the problem. His response was interesting because, as outlined earlier, he had anticipated this problem arising. He was confident that he would be able to respond appropriately at the time, yet when the problem presented itself he struggled to adequately address it.

Interviewer: You get them working, then you realize it's two minutes to the bell.

Jack: I was wondering what do I do, but I couldn't think of anything except to tell them to move it. Here [looking at the instance on video] I decided that they should try and convert these to kilometres an hour, then as they were going out, I realized that they had all gone through it and it was far too rushed, I hadn't really asked them if they had any questions so as they were leaving I tell them to ask me any questions at the door, that was to try and compensate for it but they were in a rush to get out so they probably didn't pay any attention to me.

Jack's need to act made him respond to the perceived (and anticipated) student learning problem without being able to reason through his thinking. However, because he recognized the ineffective nature of his action, his contemporaneous reflection spilt over into post-action thinking. It then influenced his retrospective reflection and might therefore have bolstered his ability to reflect contemporaneously in similar situations in the future.

An important aspect in all of these episodes is that there is recognition of a problem situation *during* teaching. In each case the student-teachers are able to stand back from their own teaching and reconsider what they are doing. They are teaching and reflecting on their teaching as it unfolds. They are developing and refining the art of contemporaneous reflection.

There are numerous examples of how Jack, Pearl and Perry showed that they could view events from different perspectives. As a result they were able to learn more from their teaching episodes as they actively sought to engage themselves in their learning about teaching. They were able to meaningfully reconstruct their pedagogy. The major difference for Sarah was that she appeared unable to approach her teaching in this manner. She did not display discernible approaches to teaching that incorporated contemporaneous reflection in the way that Jack, Pearl or Perry did.

Overview

Contemporaneous reflection is a most demanding and context dependent form of reflection. This chapter demonstrates that student-teachers reflect contemporaneously when confronted by anticipated and unanticipated problems during their teaching. Unanticipated problems tend to create a greater sense of urgency in the individual than do anticipated problems and each of the student-teachers show that they are developing ways of dealing with this.

The key to the development of contemporaneous reflection appears to be related to the ability to reframe the problem situation. It is important that individuals are able to stand back and (in effect) observe their own actions if the thinking processes involved in contemporaneous reflection are to be initiated.

The more reframing occurs, the more likely it is that one's confidence in the use of contemporaneous reflection will increase. Learning about one's own pedagogy through reflection may lead to a greater store of ideas and suggestions about actions for teaching in different contexts. Therefore, the more often the process is employed, the more comfortable one might become with its use leading to a cycle of learning through doing. Like the Meno paradox, the initial search might be for something one can neither do nor see, but eventually, seeing comes with doing. In this way, it may be that one's use of contemporaneous reflection becomes more and more refined. This could be an indication that Schön's (1983) reflection-in-action, described as occurring spontaneously within action, is an elegant form of higher order reflective processing that may once have been more conscious and deliberate, but through experience, has become more refined and less time dependent. Perhaps that is what Perry was coming to grips with during his lesson.

> *Perry*: I was thinking that if we run out of time, I still want to go around and hand out the homework, then here it is, I have to justify giving them an essay. So while they're complaining about it I'm thinking bad luck, they have to do it, they need the practice. Then I suppose that's part of the reason why I went over to get those sheets of paper, because going through your old answers, you lose a bit of planning on the work yourself, so we should go through it in a more structured way in class. But this essay is a worry, this is something I hadn't thought would happen before . . .

Perry's reflection is in the action, but in this case it also carries on after the action.

> *Perry*: . . . now seeing [watching the video] I realize how bad it really is, when I got up there and planned it on the board, they've gone away with only half the information.

As Perry demonstrates, reflective cycles can continue over extended periods of time, enhancing both confidence and skills in reflection and ultimately, shaping teaching practice. This is a most important attribute to foster and develop in student-teachers and can not be done in isolation. That is why I see the need to explicitly incorporate modelling of reflection in my teaching practice for my students.

Conclusion

This chapter has been designed to demonstrate the student-teachers' use of the three forms of reflection: anticipatory, contemporaneous and retrospective reflection. Each of the student-teachers approached and used reflection in different ways as they were influenced by the context of their teaching experience and by their disposition towards reflection. It is clear that there are differences in the nature of reflection amongst the four student-teachers and that these differences extend over the three forms of reflection.

Contemporaneous reflection stands out as being a most demanding form of reflection for student-teachers and is influenced by both anticipatory and retrospective reflection. In fact it may well be that the more overtly the three are linked to one another, the more valuable the experience is as a learning tool for developing pedagogy.

Finally, it is difficult to envisage an approach to researching reflection that is not in itself an intervention process. The research method used in this study has indeed been an intervention, yet, like reflection, it is still a matter for each individual to decide how much and in what ways the process might influence his or her thoughts, deeds and actions. Perhaps the research approach has heightened my student-teachers' awareness of their own teaching in ways that might not have been as readily accessible without a video-recorder and my interviews, but an individual still only sees what he or she is ready and willing to see. That is their choice and, as this chapter has demonstrated, the responses vary regardless of any single outside influence. The major influence still resides within the individual.

Interviewer:	Now watch this. This kid wanders over to get his stuff while you're talking and then this second one comes . . .
Jack:	I didn't even notice that kid . . .
Interviewer:	Watch this, he doesn't know what you're telling him, he does not know why he has to sit down . . .
Jack:	That must be why he was upset. I didn't even notice this first guy, I didn't pay any attention to him. That's amazing, he's got what he wants and I haven't even noticed and look how unhappy the other kid is, no wonder he was upset later on . . . That other kid must've carried that grudge throughout the lesson, that's what the link is.

Deciding how to respond, or even whether to respond, is dependent on the individual's understanding of the pedagogical moment.

Note

1 The transcripts shows that other situations such as this arise but are not probed in ways that help resolve the categorization one way or the other. In retrospect, it is clear that these were lost opportunities to explore reflection-in-action and highlights why some researchers suggest that documenting reflection-in-action is difficult and that strategies to do so need to be developed (Russell, 1989).

Chapter 11

Conclusion

The work of Schön (1983, 1987) has been a catalyst for the recent resurgence of interest and research on reflection and varying conceptions of the nature of reflection have been well documented. Zeichner (1983) and Tom (1985) described some of these: teachers as action researchers, inquirers, problem solvers, hypothesis makers, self-monitors and analysers. It is little wonder then that teacher educators have sought to introduce and develop reflection in pre-service education courses; student-teachers should be encouraged to develop along the lines of these descriptors.

Through my teaching practice I hope to encourage my student-teachers to develop the pedagogical habits, skills and attitudes necessary for self-directed growth, and in so doing better understand the development of their reflective processes. Therefore being able to uncover the extent to which this occurs is important and is why I see the reflective cycle as outlined by Dewey (1933) as an appropriate lens to view my student-teachers' thoughts and actions in the development of their reflective practice.

Erickson (1988) poses the dilemma that confronts many teacher educators as they attempt to facilitate student-teachers' learning about teaching, and hence, learning about reflection.

> Reflection that occurs in the context of 'the giving of reasons to the learner' . . . must also be mediated by a consideration of what is 'reasonable' in a particular learning situation. And it is precisely in this mediation process between these two principles that Shulman [1988] claims 'the traditions of technical rationality . . . and reflection and action must come together. These are not competing principles.' (p. 196)

Trying to map a path in pre-service education that would allow this mediation to occur is what led me to develop the approach to modelling that I use in my teaching. I believe that if student-teachers are to learn about reflection, they need to continually be given opportunities to view it in action. As reflection is a cognitive process, access to such thinking needs to be possible in ways that allow it to be observed and understood across a range of teaching and learning contexts and in a number of observable forms: thus the incorporation of the 'thinking aloud' approach in my teaching, and my open and honest personal reflections on the teaching and learning in my classes as described in my journal. It is also important to me that individuals are able to draw their own conclusions about the use, value, and development of reflection on practice.

An interesting pre-cursor to preparedness for reflection which needs to be kept in mind when considering the development of reflection are the three attitudes of open-mindedness, responsibility, and whole-heartedness. I have suggested that the greater the frequency of these attitudes (as detected in their journal writing) in an individual, the more the individual would be likely to demonstrate the five phases of reflection. It would therefore seem reasonable to suggest that these attitudes should be fostered in student-teachers through all aspects of their teacher education program.

It also appears as though throughout a pre-service education program, there is an increase in the use of the five phases of the reflective cycle (see Figure 7.3, p. 98) which leads me to the notion that the frequency of phases recorded relates to a student-teacher's development in their use. Using this assertion it seems as though student-teachers are readily able to recognize problems, develop suggestions and hypotheses to test, but that reasoning through the situation and then pursuing the test do not so readily occur. The first three phases occur most often. Then, over time, reasoning and testing increase, suggesting that student-teachers learn to use these two phases as they gradually incorporate the use of the individual phases into a reflective cycle.

Dewey (1933) proposed that the five phases need not occur in any set order or pattern. At the start of their teacher education course this does not seem to apply as student-teachers (generally) have not developed their reflective processes in the context of *teaching*. However, after some teaching experience (in this case two school teaching experiences) the ability to apply the five phases to their thinking about teaching is better realized. Following this realization, I believe that the application of the five phases subsequently does not follow any particular order as student-teachers have a more developed and refined approach to reflection.

In the development of a student-teacher's reflection, the ability to apply the phases may come in stages (see Figure 7.1, p. 90) until a fluency in the use of reflection is achieved. Again, relating these phases to the three attitudes, a similar pattern applies. The ability to recognize a problem, to develop suggestions and hypotheses, appears to parallel one's ability to apply the attitude of open-mindedness. To be able to recognize the consequences of the deliberation of these phases calls on an intellectual responsibility which parallels that of reasoning, thus the close relationship between the attitude of responsibility and the reflective phase of reasoning. To perform a test developed through reflection also requires the ability to whole-heartedly pursue that test while accepting the consequences of the actions. This relationship between testing and whole-heartedness is the final link in the chain of reflective thinking and attitudes that enables the student-teacher to perform the actions developed through reflective thought. It signals the emergence of the developing reflective practitioner.

Learning from and through experience is important for student-teachers in the development of the skills of reflective practice and is very closely linked to their teaching experiences. Enhancing reflection in student-teachers through teacher education programs is then most likely if there is an overt link between reflection and *their* teaching experiences. There appears to be a strong relationship between reflection and *their* practice which becomes much more internalized when it is focused on the individual's *own* thoughts and actions.

Finally, the ability to develop student-teachers' reflective processes is also related to the concerns that influence their thinking and learning throughout their pre-service program. As student-teachers become more at ease with their role as a teacher, there may be a shift in their concerns as the focus moves from themselves to their students. Hence, their concerns move toward the relationship between their teaching and their students' learning (as well as their learning from and through their own teaching). At this time, their ability to reflect, and the quality of that reflection, noticeably improves and the influence of this reflection on their teaching practice is at an optimum.

In modelling reflection for my students, both thinking aloud and journal writing depend heavily on a trusting classroom environment and good tutor–student–teacher relationships. Even so, both serve their purpose well in demonstrating that teaching, and learning about teaching, are enhanced through reflection. Giving student-teachers immediate access to my thoughts and concerns during teaching demonstrates for them that even experienced teachers continue to find teaching problematic. Student-teachers often perceive experienced teachers' lessons as moving smoothly and methodically from an introduction to a conclusion. To them, it may sometimes appear as though each step, including students' responses and actions, are known in advance to the teacher. By being privy to the thoughts that influence my practice this belief is demystified as they see and hear my pedagogical struggles (both cognitive and affective) with their learning about teaching.

One of the most heartening aspects of this modelling is how it encourages my students to be comfortable with similar struggles with their own pedagogy and helps them to realize that this is an important part of teaching. It also highlights for many that even though their fellow class members are party to the same pedagogical experiences, they do not experience the same learning outcomes from those experiences. This is important for two reasons. The first is that it parallels the position of their students' learning when they are teaching, and it also demonstrates that there is not one way to teach particular content (or one way to learn to teach).

Both of these points are important when considering the development of student-teachers' views of reflection. In the case of their teaching and their students' learning, they can see, by experiencing it themselves, that to enhance learning across the range of students in a class, pedagogy must be responsive to different learners. To do that, reflection on practice is fundamental. The second point is important in terms of their own view of their development as teachers. There is an old saying that a teacher can have ten years' experience, or one year's experience ten times. The student-teachers in my TAL class had little doubt that they would learn from their experiences through reflection so that they had (at least) ten years experience.

'How do student-teachers develop in their use of reflection?' must be an important question for teacher educators who hope to develop reflective practitioners through their teacher education programs. It is clear to me that the use of the three times of reflection (anticipatory, retrospective and contemporaneous) varies depending on a number of factors, but that development of reflection is increasingly complex from anticipatory, through to retrospective and finally into contemporaneous reflection.

In the rush and bustle of classroom practice, what student-teachers (and perhaps teacher educators) say about reflection and what they do about reflection are sometimes two different things. However, an important link between saying and doing is seeing. Student-teachers who become accustomed to seeing their experiences from different perspectives, and who are able to be more detached from their personal feelings about their teaching, tend to develop their reflection more readily than those who do not. This seeing becomes a most important issue as it opens up new avenues for thinking about teaching and new ways of learning from experience. It is also an important aim of modelling, which in this case, through the method adopted, attempted to encourage student-teachers to recognize the need for teachers to 'see' and for them to then apply that to their own teaching experience. However, as my student-teachers are not (and should not be) forced to apply all of the lessons from the modelling experience to their own practice, the ability to 'see' situations in different ways at different times varies from individual to individual. Importantly though, for me, this is to be expected as I believe teaching should lead to greater divergence of outcomes rather than simple convergence.

The relationship between student-teachers' concerns and their use of reflection is also important. These concerns shift throughout their pre-service education program and inevitably influence the three times of reflection, how they are used, and to what extent they are employed in practice. As student-teachers move from concerns about self to concerns about their students' learning, they become more able to reflect on their practice as their recognition of problem situations encourages them to respond. This is most apparent during teaching when opportunities for contemporaneous reflection are recognized and seized so that teaching practice can be more responsive to student learning.

The distinction between reflection as a deliberate, purposeful act (similar to Schön's reflection-on-action) and reflection as a spontaneous perhaps subconscious act (similar to Schön's reflection-in-action), may well be related to how well student-teachers develop, adapt or become more at ease with contemporaneous reflection. As their repertoire of suggestions, experiences of problem situations, hypotheses, reasoning and testing skills increases, their ability to reflect during teaching is enhanced. Through so doing, the amount of time and the extent of thoughtful deliberation necessary to overtly reflect on practice might be reduced (and then it perhaps resembles something like reflection-in-action) as it begins to emerge as an extension of this important pedagogical skill.

The conceptual framework which I proposed (see Figure 2.1, p. 22) suggests that through the social and artifactual tools of a pre-service education program, together with explicit modelling of reflection on practice, student-teachers would better learn about teaching and more likely apply that learning in their own practice. This understanding of learning about reflective practice in the context of the student-teachers' own teaching and learning situations is fundamental to the view of learning from, and through, experience that I hold dear in teacher education. I firmly believe that student-teachers should not simply be told the mechanics of reflection then be trained in such methods to apply them generally to their pedagogy. They must experience reflection as a part of their own learning about learning and teaching; then they can, and will, decide how to apply it in their own practice as they better understand how their pedagogy is shaped by the context of the teaching-learning environments in which they work.

Reflection is something that when understood and valued (by teacher educators and student-teachers) can be developed through teacher education programs where teacher educators practice what they preach. By approaching teaching in pre-service education in this manner teacher educators will encourage their student-teachers to do likewise.

I have often heard experienced teachers say that good teachers can take any group of students and shape their learning. I believe the same applies to teacher educators. Students are influenced by their teachers' values and the application of the conceptual framework (Figure 2.1) which is the basis of my approach to teaching about teaching and learning can lead student-teachers to be similarly influenced by their teacher educators.

Throughout this book, I have attempted to include my student-teachers' voice. Their voice is part of the understanding which emerges as they, through their journals and interviews, attempted to communicate meaning to me. It is this aspect of inquiry that in this case best portrays how I understand my student-teachers' development. Although I did not initiate my work with a particular view of research that I needed to adhere to, it would appear as though it has developed into narrative inquiry. As Connelly and Clandinin (1990) describe it, narrative inquiry is 'derived from field notes of shared experience, journal records, interviews, story telling, letter writing, and autobiographical and biographical writing' (pp. 5–6). I have used most of these to portray the results of my exploration of the development of my students' reflective practice. This book has depicted their learning from and through experience as they individually developed their own approach to reflection as a result of their involvement in a pre-service education program which attempted to model reflective practice.

Bibliography

BAIRD, J.R. (1990) 'Individual and group reflection as a basis for teacher development', in HUGHES, P. (ed.) *Teachers' Professional Development*, Australian Council for Educational Research.

BAIRD, J.R. and MITCHELL, I.J. (1986) *Project for the Enhancement of Effective Learning (PEEL): An Australian Case-study*, Melbourne, Monash University Printing.

BAIRD, J.R. and NORTHFIELD, J.R. (1992) *Learning for the PEEL Experience*, Melbourne, Monash University Printing.

BARNES, D.R. (1976) *From Communication to Curriculum*, Harmondsworth, Penguin Education.

BEAN, T.W. and ZULICH, J. (1989) 'Using dialogue journals to foster reflective practice with preservice content-area teachers', *Teacher Education Quarterly*, **16**, 1, pp. 33–40.

BERLINER, D. (1986) 'In pursuit of the expert pedagogue', *Educational Researcher*, **15**, 7, pp. 5–13.

BOUD, D., KEOGH, R. and WALKER, D. (1985) *Reflection: Turning Experience into Learning*, London, Kogan Page Ltd.

CLARKE, C.M. (1988) 'Asking the right questions about teacher preparation: Contributions of research on teacher thinking', *Educational Researcher*, **17**, 2, pp. 5–12.

CONNELLY, M.F. and CLANDININ, D.J. (1990) 'Stories of experience and narrative inquiry', *Educational Researcher*, **19**, 5, pp. 2–14.

DEWEY, J. (1933) *How We Think*, New York, Heath and Co.

DOBBINS, R. (1990, July) 'Developing critically reflective practitioners', A paper presented to the 20th Annual Conference of Australian Teacher Education Association, Adelaide.

ERICKSON, G.L. (1988) 'Explorations in the field of reflection: Directions for future research agendas', in GRIMMETT, P.L. and ERICKSON, G.L. (eds) *Reflection in Teacher Education*, New York, Teachers College Press.

FERRO, 'S.C. and LENZ, K.B. (1992, April) 'The pre-service teacher log: A useful pedagogical tool'. A paper presented at the annual meeting of the American Educational Research Association, San Francisco.

FULLER, F.F. (1969) 'Concerns of teachers: A developmental conceptualization', *American Educational Research Journal*, **6**, 2, pp. 207–26.

FULLER, F.F. and BOWN, O.H. (1975) 'Becoming a teacher', in RYAN, K. (ed.)

Teacher Education: The 74th Yearbook of the National Society for the Study of Education, Part 11, Chicago, University of Chicago Press.

GOODMAN, J. (1983) 'The seminar's role in the education of student teachers: A case study', *Journal of Teacher Education*, **34**, 3, pp. 44–8.

GOODMAN, J. (1984) 'Reflection and teacher education: A case study and theoretical analysis', *Interchange*, **15**, 3, pp. 9–26.

GRIMMETT, P.P. and ERICKSON, G.L. (1988) *Reflection in Teacher Education*, New York, Teachers College Press.

GRIMMETT, P.P., MACKINNON, A.M., ERICKSON, G.L. and RIECKEN, T.J. (1990) 'Reflective practice in teacher education', in CLIFT, R.T., HOUSTON, R.W. and PUGACH, M.C. (eds) *Encouraging Reflective Practice in Education: An Analysis of Issues and Programs*, New York, Teachers College Press.

GUNSTONE, R.F. and MACKAY, L.D. (1975) 'The self perceived needs of student teachers', *South Pacific Journal of Teacher Education*, **3**, 1, pp. 44–51.

GUNSTONE, R.F., SLATTERY, M., BAIRD, J.R. and NORTHFIELD, J.R. (1993) 'A case study exploration of development in preservice science teachers', *Science Education*, **77**, 1, pp. 47–73.

KEMMIS, S. and MCTAGGART, R. (eds) (1988) *The Action Research Planner (3rd ed.)*, Geelong, Deakin University Press.

KOUNIN, J.S. (1977) *Discipline and Group Management in Classrooms*, Krieger Publishing Co, Huntington, New York.

KROGH, S.L. and CREWS, R. (1989, March) 'Determinants of reflectivity in student teachers' reflective reports'. A paper presented at the annual meeting of the American Educational Research Association, San Francisco.

LABOSKEY, V.K. (1993) 'A conceptual framework for reflection in preservice teacher education', in CALDERHEAD, J. and GATES, P. (eds) *Conceptualizing Reflection in Teacher Development*, London, Falmer Press.

LAKATOS, I. (1970) 'Falsification and the methodology of scientific research programmes', in LAKTOS, I. and MUSGRAVE, A. (eds) *Criticism and the Growth of Knowledge*, Cambridge, Cambridge University Press.

LOUGHRAN, J.J. (1995, April) 'Practicing what I preach: Modelling reflective practice to student-teachers'. A paper presented at the annual meeting of the American Educational Research Association, San Francisco.

MACKINNON, A.M. (1989a) 'Conceptualizing a "reflective practicum" in constructivist science teaching'. Unpublished Doctoral thesis, University of British Columbia.

MACKINNON, A.M. (1989b, March) 'Reflection in a science teaching practicum'. A paper presented at the annual conference of the American Educational Research Association, San Francisco.

MAIN, A. (1985) 'Reflection and the development of learning skills', in BOUD, D., KEOGH, R. and WALKER, D. (eds) *Reflection: Turning Experience into Learning*, London, Kogan Page Ltd.

MALCOLM, C. (1994) 'Structures, force and stability: Design a playground (year 6)', in FENSHAM, P.J., GUNSTONE, R.F. and WHITE, R.T. (eds) *The Content of Science*, London, Falmer Press.

McIntyre, D. (1993) 'Theory, theorizing and reflection in teacher education', in Calderhead, J. and Gates, P. (eds) *Conceptualizing Reflection in Teacher Development*, London, Falmer Press.

Mikkelsen, N. (1985) 'Teaching teachers: What I learn', *Language Arts*, **62**, 7, pp. 742–53.

Munby, H. and Russell, T. (1989) 'Educating the reflective teachers: An essay review of two books by Donald Schön', *Journal of Curriculum Studies*, **21**, 1, pp. 71–80.

Noddings, N. (1986) 'Fidelity in teaching, teacher education, and research for teaching', *Harvard Educational Review*, **56**, 4, pp. 496–510.

Oberg, A. (1990) 'Methods and meaning in action research: The action research journal', *Theory Into Practice*, **29**, 3, pp. 214–21.

Polanyi, M. (1962) *Personal Knowledge: Towards A Post-Critical Philosophy*, London, Routlege and Kegan Paul.

Richardson, V. (1992) 'The evolution of reflective teaching and teacher education', in Clift, R.T., Houston, R.W., and Pugach, M.C. (eds) *Encouraging Reflective Practice in Education: An Analysis of Issues and Programs*, New York, Teachers College Press.

Richert, A.E. (1987) 'Reflex to reflection: Facilitating reflection in novice teachers'. Unpublished doctoral dissertation, Stanford University.

Richert, A.E. (1990) 'Teaching teachers to reflect: A consideration of programme structure', *Journal of Curriculum Studies*, **22**, 6, pp. 509–27.

Rodderick, J.A. (1986) 'Dialogue writing: Context for reflecting on self as teacher and researcher', *Journal of Curriculum and Supervision*, **1**, 4, pp. 305–15.

Ross, W.E. and Hannay, L.M. (1986) 'Towards a critical theory of reflective inquiry', *Journal of Teacher Education*, **37**, 4, pp. 9–15.

Russell, T. (1989) 'Documenting reflection-in-action in the classroom: Searching for appropriate methods', *Qualitative Studies in Education*, **2**, 4, pp. 275–84.

Russell, T. and Munby, H. (1992) *Teachers and Teaching: From Classroom to Reflection*, London, Falmer Press.

Schön, D.A. (1983) *The Reflective Practitioner: How Professionals Think in Action*, New York, Basic Books.

Schön, D.A. (1987) *Educating the Reflective Practitioner: Toward a New Design for Teaching and Learning in the Professions*, San Francisco, Jossey-Bass.

Shor, I. and Freire, P. (1987) *A Pedagogy for Liberation: Dialogues on Transforming Education*, South Hadley, MA, Bergin and Garvey.

Shulman, L.S. (1986) 'Those who understand: Knowledge growth in teaching', *Educational Researcher*, **15**, 2, pp. 4–14.

Shulman, L.S. (1988) 'The dangers of dichotomous thinking in education', in Grimmett, P.P. and Erickson, G.L. (eds) *Reflection in Teacher Education*, New York, Teachers College Press.

Shulman, L.S. (1993, November) 'Appraisal: Ways of seeing teacher thinking'. Seminar presentation, Monash University, Melbourne, Australia.

Staton, J. (1988) 'Contributions of the dialogue journal research to communicating, thinking and learning', in Farr, M. (ed.) *Interactive Writing in Dialogue*

Journals: Practitioner, Linguistic, Social, and Cognitive Views, Norwood, NJ, Ablex.

TOM, A.R. (1985) 'Inquiry into inquiry-oriented teacher education', *Journal of Teacher Education*, **36**, 5, pp. 35–44.

VALLI, L. (1989) 'Collaboration for transfer of learning: Preparing preservice teachers', *Teacher Education Quarterly*, **16**, 1, pp. 85–95.

VALLI, L. (1993) 'Reflective teacher education programs: An analysis of case studies', in CALDERHEAD, J. and GATES, P. (eds) *Conceptualizing Reflection in Teacher Development*, London, Falmer Press.

VAN MANEN, M. (1977) 'Linking ways of knowing with ways of being practical', *Curriculum Inquiry*, **6**. 3, pp. 205–28.

VAN MANEN, M. (1991a) 'Reflectivity and the pedagogical moment: The normativity of pedagogical thinking and acting', *Journal of Curriculum Studies*, **23**, 6, pp. 507–36.

VAN MANEN, M. (1991b) *The Tact of Teaching: The Meaning of Pedagogical Thoughtfulness*, Albany, New York, State University of New York Press.

WALKER, J. and EVERS, C. (1984) 'Towards a materialist pragmatist philosophy of education', *Education Research and Perspectives*, **11**, 1, pp. 23–3.

WHITE, R.T. (1988) *Learning Science*, London, Blackwell.

WHITE, R.T. and GUNSTONE, R.F. (1992) *Probing Understanding*, London, Falmer Press.

YINGER, R.J. (1990) 'The conversation of practice', in CLIFT, R.T., HOUSTON, R.W. and PUGACH, M.C. (eds) *Encouraging Reflective Practice in Education: An Analysis of Issues and Programs (73–94)*, Teachers College, Columbia University, New York.

ZEICHNER, K.M. (1983) 'Alternative paradigms of teacher education', *Journal of Teacher Education*, **34**, 3, pp. 3–9.

Author Index

Baird, J.R., 4, 9, 108
Barnes, D., 26, 183
Bean, T.W., 8, 74, 77
Berliner, D., 16
Boud, D., 3
Bown, O.H., 58, 84

Clandinin, D.J., 120, 193
Clarke, C.M., 8
Connelly, M.F., 120, 193
Crews, R., 74, 75, 82

Dewey, J., 3, 4, 5, 6, 10, 13, 18, 21, 52,
    58, 61, 64, 66, 69, 71, 72, 82, 94,
    148, 156, 177, 189, 190
Dobbins, R., 8, 76

Erickson, G.L., 189
Evers, C., 4, 73

Ferro, S.C., 74
Freire, P., 77
Fuller, F.F., 58, 84, 85

Goodman, J., 7, 13
Grimmett, P.P., 6, 15
Gunstone, R.F., 9, 27, 58, 84, 158

Hannay, L.M., 13

Kemmis, S., 58
Keogh, R., 3
Kounin, J.S., 180
Krogh, S.L., 74, 75, 82

LaBoskey, V.K., 18
Lakatos, I., 73
Lenz, K.B., 74
Loughran, J.J., 29

MacKay, L.D., 58, 84
MacKinnon, A.M., 6, 8, 16

Main, A., 18
Malcolm, C., 121
McIntyre, D., 19
McTaggart, R., 58
Mikkelsen, N., 77
Mitchell, I.J., 4
Munby, H., 6, 177

Noddings, N., 121
Northfield, J.R., 4, 9

Oberg, A., 58

Polanyi, M., 74

Richardson, V., 7
Richert, A.E., 9, 74, 75
Rodderick, J.A., 8, 74, 77
Ross, W.E., 13
Russell, T., 6, 177

Schön, D.A., 6, 8, 15, 16, 21, 52, 57, 66,
    177, 181, 187, 189
Shor, I., 77
Shulman, L.S., 4, 18, 20, 83
Slattery, M.S., 9
Staton, J., 74

Tom, A.R., 189

Valli, L., 9, 17
van Manen, M., 20, 43, 103, 162,
    177

Walker, D., 3
Walker, J., 4, 73
White, R.T., 27, 32, 36, 158

Yinger, R.J., 57

Zeichner, K.M., 189
Zulich, J., 8, 74, 77

Subject Index

actions,
  conceptualising, 17
affective domain, 113, 157
Andrea,
  interviews, 41, 43, 47
  retrospective reflection, 111
  suggestions, 65
Anthony,
  in class, 35
  responsibility, 61
  suggestions, 64
anticipatory reflection, 20, 108, 123, 137,
  144, 152, 175, 192
artifactual tools, 9, 10, 21, 192
attitudes, 4, 18, 57–58, 64, 82, 103
  also see open-mindedness,
    responsibility, whole-heartedness

case-studies,
  introduction to, 121
  Jack, 136
  Pearl, 142
  Perry, 122
  Sarah, 129
classroom,
  critical incidents, 69
  management, 62, 69, 70, 130, 153, 154,
    165
  reflection, 20
Cleo, 35, 36
co-operative group work, 26
concept maps, 124
conceptual framework, 18, 21, 22, 192
concerns,
  also see issues
  influences on, 191
  of student-teachers, 81, 85, 97, 159,
    192
  changes/shifts, 51
contemporaneous reflection, 21, 114, 125,
  127, 138, 175, 180
  (*also see* Jack, Pearl, Perry and Sarah)

content knowledge, 115, 128, 141, 153,
  156
context/contextual,
  factors influencing reflection, 20
  issues, 15
  of teaching and learning, 14, 18, 21, 33,
    37, 97, 125, 152, 190, 192

Dick, 35–37
Diploma in Education (Dip. Ed.), 10, 37,
  38, 81
Dorothy, 35

elements,
  of memory, 32
  of reflection, 5, 57
experience, 48, 51
  (*also see* learning, school and
    teaching)

Filipa,
  in class, 34
  open-mindedness, 59
  imaginative testing, 71
Follow Me, 8, 16
fruitful, 70

group work, 65

Hall of Mirrors, 8, 16
hypothesis,
  definition, 5
  element/phase of reflection, 19, 34, 68
  Perry's testing, 123
  with reasoning, 27

interpretive discussion, 26, 183
interview-observation-interview cycle, 120,
  152
interviewed group, 40, 94, 96
interviews, 12, 84, 97, 99, 101, 102, 104,
  107

issues, 58, 96, 103, 153
  (*also see* concerns)

Jack,
  anticipating/responding to problem, 154,
    179, 186
  attitude of responsibility, 60
  contemporaneous reflection, 114, 178
  content-knowledge, 158
  in class, 35, 36
  in interview, 44, 90
  open-mindedness, 167
  retrospective reflection, 111, 116, 163
  valuing modelling, 48
jigsaw groupwork, 33
John, 35–36
Joint Experimentation, 8, 16
Joshua, 69
journal,
  and interviews, 193
  and thinking aloud, 38
  in TAL, 32, 36, 74
  John's, 29, 40, 75
  per student per phase of the reflective
    cycle, 89–90
  proportion of writing, 90–91
  purpose, 12
  writing, 8, 11, 17, 29, 35, 57, 74, 101

learning,
  about learning about teaching, 17, 186,
    193
  about reflection through modelling, 14
  from experience, 19, 27, 192
  from reflection, 14
  student-teachers thinking about, 96, 139
  styles, 26, 33
lesson planning, 19, 108, 132, 151, 159
levels,
  of reflectivity, 43, 103, 162
  of use of the reflective cycle, 95

Marg,
  attitude of responsibility, 60
  in class, 36
  journal writing, 81
Meno paradox, 15, 187
Miranda,
  interview, 43, 49, 90, 99, 101, 102
  journal writing, 78
  times of reflection, 107
  retrospective reflection, 112
  understanding & valuing reflection,
    118

Mitchell,
  in class, 36
  reasoning, 70
modelling,
  Perry's view, 45
  pre-lesson planning, 33
  purpose, 43
  reflection, 9, 10, 15–17, 18, 21, 28, 34,
    40, 44, 118, 187, 189
  through journal writing, 77, 191

Nadine,
  course issues, 96
  in class, 36
  journal writing, 78
  reasoning, 69
narrative inquiry, 120, 193
Nick, 35
Nigel, 35, 36, 51, 59, 102
non-interviewed group, 92, 94, 96

open-mindedness,
  attitude, 18, 58, 59, 82, 95, 128, 143,
    190
  definition, 4

paradox, 15
Pearl,
  anticipatory reflection, 109, 157
  attitude of responsibility, 61–62
  contemporaneous reflection, 116, 176,
    178
  in class, 35, 37
  interview, 90
  journal writing, 77
  reflective cycle over time, 170
  reframing, 184
  overt testing, 72
  view of modelling, 44, 50
pedagogical,
  action, 94
  approach, 34
  moment, 177, 182
  problem, 147
  reasoning, 8, 28, 83
  thinking and development, 96
pedagogy, 11, 21, 27, 113
Project for the Enhancement of Effective
    Learning (PEEL), 4
Peggy,
  attitude, 67
  in class, 35, 37
  journal writing, 81
  problem recognition, 66

Perry,
  anticipatory reflection, 110, 158
  attitude of whole-heartedness, 61, 62
  contemporaneous reflection over time, 184
  contemporaneous reflection, 117
  hypothesis formation, 169
  in class, 35, 37
  in transition, 173
  interview, 52, 90
  problem recognition, 67
  retrospective reflection, 113
  valuing of modelling, 53
personal knowledge, 74
Prediction, Observation, Explanation (P.O.E.), 26, 27, 62
pre-service education, 8, 85, 117, 189
problem,
  anticipated, 178
  definition, 5
  element/phase of reflection, 66–68
  leading to suggestions and hypotheses, 190
  situation, 18, 33–34, 51, 94, 122
  unanticipated, 180

questionnaire, 37–38

Ralph,
  hypothesis by, 68
  journal writing, 78
reasoning,
  definition, 5
  element/phase of reflection, 20, 34, 69, 91, 110, 190
reflection,
  as a learning about teaching tool, 49, 51
  conceptualising, 6, 13
  content, 18
  conversation, 57, 58
  cycle over time, 94
  cycle/sequence, 14, 21, 45, 64, 66, 72, 91, 94, 95, 101, 103, 110, 152, 190
  for action, 20
  guided, 8
  impediment to, 135
  in action, 6, 58, 177, 187, 192
  in pre-service programs, 13
  initiating, 95
  learning from, 14
  levels of, 91
  modelling of (*see* modelling)
  on action, 6, 20, 21, 192
  on practice, 21, 27, 34, 38, 44

phases, 5, 21, 89, 91
practice/practitioner, 47, 82, 94, 95, 101, 152
readiness, 81, 84
recognition, 4, 6, 21, 35, 41, 64
relationship to attitudes, 172
stimuli for reflection, 17
the 'when'/time of, 19, 57
reframing, 6, 20, 21, 66, 181, 182, 186
research, 12, 53, 175, 188, 193
responsibility,
  attitude, 60, 83, 95, 139, 190
  definition, 5
retrospective reflection, 20, 111, 125, 136, 162, 168
  (*also see* Jack, Miranda, Pearl, Perry, Sabina and Sarah)
rhetoric, 25
risk(s), 75, 135, 138
role-play, 26, 65
role-model, 8
  (*also see* modelling)

Sabina,
  contemporaneous reflection, 115
  in class, 36, 37
  journal writing, 79, 80
  recognition of modelling, 45
  retrospective reflection, 113
  value of reflection, 51–52
Sarah,
  anticipatory reflection, 155
  contemporaneous reflection, 114, 178
  journal writing, 78
  problem anticipation, 179
  retrospective reflection, 112, 163
  view of modelling, 44, 50
school,
  students' learning, 191
  teaching experience, 41, 53, 68, 93, 104
seminar group discussions, 7
Sharon,
  attitude of open-mindedness, 59
  journal writing, 81
  suggestions, 65
silent discussion, 34, 71
Social Foundations of Schooling (SFS), 11
social tools, 9, 10, 21, 192
student(s),
  ascertaining their views, 34
  learning, 22, 33, 35, 149, 159, 160
  teacher planning, 19
  teachers' concerns, 58, 84, 86–87

teachers' learning about reflection, 15, 22, 93–94
teachers' perceptions of modelling, 34, 40
teachers' reflection over time, 97
teachers' views of journal writing, 77
teachers' voice, 193
Stephen,
anticipatory reflection, 110
in class, 36
journal writing, 79
view of reflection, 46
suggestions,
definition, 5
element/phase of reflection, 14, 19, 40, 110, 122, 131

Teaching and Learning (TAL), 10, 11, 29, 38, 46, 51, 80, 191
teacher/teaching,
(*also see* Diploma in Education)
as learner, 27
education programs, 25–26, 193
educators, 95
experience, 51, 101, 190
for understanding, 15
learner relationship, 25

learning about teaching, 25, 27, 49, 56, 191
technical aspects, 15, 43
thinking, 9, 14–15, 25
technical rationality, 6
test/testing,
definition, 5
imaginative, 71, 125, 148
overt, 72
element/phase of reflection, 20–21, 50, 70–72, 91, 102, 190
responses to, 168
thinking aloud, 17, 28, 32–34, 41, 139, 189
thinking time, 170
time frames, 91
touchstone, 4, 73
trust, 25, 41

valuing reflection, 47, 51
video observation, 8, 65, 140, 146, 181
vignette, 34

wait-time, 33
whole-heartedness,
definition, 5
attitude, 18, 61, 83, 95, 143, 190
withitness, 180, 182